INDUSTRIAL RELATIONS RESEARCH
ASSOCIATION SERIES

ORGANIZATIONAL BEHAVIOR

Research and Issues

Edited by

GEORGE STRAUSS
University of California, Berkeley

RAYMOND E. MILES
University of California, Berkeley

CHARLES C. SNOW
Pennsylvania State University

and

ARNOLD S. TANNENBAUM
University of Michigan

i

Organizational Behavior Research and Issues

First Edition

Library of Congress Catalog Card Number: 74-15899

PRICE $6.00

INDUSTRIAL RELATIONS RESEARCH ASSOCIATION SERIES

Published seven times yearly: PROCEEDINGS OF ANNUAL WINTER MEET-
ING (May); PROCEEDINGS OF ANNUAL SPRING MEETING (August);
Annual Research Volume, or MEMBERSHIP DIRECTORY every sixth year
in lieu of the research volume (October); IRRA NEWSLETTER (issued
quarterly). Gerald G. Somers, Editor; Richard U. Miller, Secretary-Treasurer;
Mrs. Elizabeth S. Gulesserian, Executive Assistant.

Inquiries and other communications regarding membership, meetings, publications and the general affairs of the Association, as well as orders for publications, copyright requests, and notice of address changes, should be addressed
to the IRRA publication office:

INDUSTRIAL RELATIONS RESEARCH ASSOCIATION
7114 Social Science Building, University of Wisconsin
Madison, WI 53706 U.S.A. Telephone 608 262-2762

CONTENTS

iii

PREFACE

The question of whether to publish a book devoted to Organizational Behavior (OB) caused strenuous debate within the IRRA Executive Board. There was one group which felt that OB did not really belong with Industrial Relations. The other group was willing to provide an opportunity to test OB's relevance. We share some of the doubts expressed by the first group, though in our concluding chapter we hope to show the links between Organizational Behavior and Industrial Relations. As for the responsibilities thrust upon us by the second group, we are somewhat abashed. We will do our best.

From the entire field of OB, we have picked a sample of six subject matter areas to deal with here. Each of these is of great current interest to OB scholars and seems to have practical relevance to the larger concerns of society generally. There are other areas of perhaps equal concern—small group behavior, role theory, career paths, and reward systems, to provide a few examples—but space does not permit us to be exhaustive.

The editors wish to thank Barbara Porter for her typing and editorial assistance and for ensuring the smooth flow of the manuscripts through the editorial process. We are also grateful to Natalie Lun for preparing the bibliography.

CHAPTER 1

An Overview of the Field

The purpose of this introductory chapter is to lay the foundation for the material which follows by attempting to define our field and then to present a brief, nonchronological picture of how the field has developed. In so doing, we hope to provide a framework to pull together the chapters which follow.

WHAT IS ORGANIZATIONAL BEHAVIOR?

Defining any academic field is difficult, but Organizational Behavior (OB) may be more difficult to define than most. As a new field, it has yet to stake out its jurisdiction definitively; further, as an applied field, it draws very heavily on more basic fields, making it difficult to distinguish between what is rightfully OB's and what belongs to the parent disciplines.

OB represents a combination of at least parts of two older fields in business schools, Human Relations and Management (the derivation of which will be discussed below), but, as just mentioned, it also includes liberal elements of other disciplines, especially of psychology and sociology. Political science, economics (at least those elements dealing with decision making and information economics), anthropology, and psychiatry have also had some (probably too little) influence on the development of OB. In addition, an increasingly substantial contribution is being made by a younger generation of scholars who have received their training in business schools under the rubric of Organizational Behavior itself (or some related term).

As an academic discipline, most of what is called OB is taught in business schools and thus is focused primarily on profit-making organizations. But OB people are also interested in government, schools, hospitals, social agencies, and the like. In fact, much of the most interesting research has been done in these areas, and OB courses (though not necessarily under the title OB) are increasingly being taught in schools of education, public administration, public health, hospital administration, social work, and even forestry. It seems increasingly clear that OB principles apply (or do not apply) equally well in the nonprofit as well as in the profit sector, under socialism as well as capitalism. And—as we discuss in Chapter 9—they most certainly apply to unions.

OB is an applied area, but some of the best OB research is not directly applicable. Seventeen years ago, in the Industrial Relations Research Association's last review of this subject, Wilensky (1957) argued that "not everything done by the social scientist can or should help the practitioner . . . the social scientist's job is basically different from the executive's job . . . much of what he comes up with is of only limited use to the practitioner" (pp. 27, 35). Some progress has been made since 1957 in developing management applications; nevertheless Wilensky's warning still has much validity: in general, OB research is not designed to provide solutions for specific management problems.

True, much of what passes as OB "research" is mere description of management practices and sometimes consists of normative prescriptions not based on empirical data. However, the best research goes beyond this and is designed to develop theories or models which in turn can help scholars and practitioners understand behavior in organizations and therefore predict and even modify behavior.

Let us be a bit more specific as to OB's value to the practitioner. Untutored, the typical person draws inferences from his own immediate experience, and, on the basis of this experience, he develops "models" which consciously or unconsciously affect his perceptions of events and how he reacts to them. To take an example: if, on the basis of early experience (or folk wisdom picked up from others), a manager concludes that workers are generally lazy and seek to shun responsibility, he is likely to supervise his own subordinates closely, thereby to alienate many of them, and thus to induce them in fact to evade responsibilities. Under these circumstances, the manager's original hypothesis is confirmed.

For the practitioner who is a victim of this (and related) counterproductive cycles, OB may possibly offer three kinds of services:

1. Like any other science, OB is concerned with the relationships among organizational phenomena. On the basis of these observed relationships, theories (or models) can be developed and tested. Tested theories may, in turn, help the practitioner to

understand the impact of his own current behaviors by telling him, "If you do X, there is considerable likelihood that Y will occur." As Kurt Lewin, one of the most influential of the early contributors to this field, was fond of saying, "There is nothing so practical as a good theory."

2. From the systematic study of behavior (in both real organizations and laboratory-based, simulated organizations), OB research can suggest a broader range of possible behaviors to the practitioner than he had previously considered—as well as the implications of each. Combined with good theory, an expanded repertoire of managerial behaviors can significantly extend the action alternatives most practitioners possess.

3. Finally, by expanding the practitioner's range of alternative behaviors and by placing these within frameworks which provide some basis for estimating the possible impact of each form of behavior, OB research may help the practitioner make informed evaluations of his future behaviors and their likely outcomes.

The Development of the Field

A brief history of OB's development may be helpful to place the above comments and the following chapters in context. At least two main trends have occurred. First, two earlier fields, Human Relations (which stressed individual factors) and Management (which emphasized nonhuman elements of the organization, such as goals, technology, structure, policies, procedures, etc.), merged into Organizational Behavior, a field which (still inadequately) attempts to integrate concern with both people and organizations. Secondly, there has been a move away from the search for the "one best way"—universalistic prescriptions for supervisory behavior, the design of jobs and organizational structures, conflict resolution, and the like—to a *contingency* approach which takes into account the particular personality and situational variables associated with specific organizational problems.

While healthy for the field and necessary to its long-run development, these trends were not without their costs. Key among these was the broadening gap between researchers and practitioners. The simpler models of earlier years were inadequate, but their implications were clear and their impacts on managerial practice were sizeable. Contingency concepts, on the other hand, may be more descriptive of reality but at the same time more difficult to interpret and apply. A quick survey of developments over the past seventy or so years will illustrate these trends and their benefits and costs.

TRADITIONAL APPROACHES

Scientific management. The systematic study of management dates back to the latter part of the 19th century and perhaps even earlier, with primary attention being focused on the task of analyzing and rationalizing the modern complex organization. F. W. Taylor (1911), for example, believed that tools, methods, and procedures could be "scientifically" designed to produce order, efficiency, and machine-like synchronization of work flows and that scientific methods could be used to select and train employees to fill these standardized slots. Similarly, he argued, scientific methods could be used to determine both a fair day's work and a fair day's pay and thus would remove the basis for most industrial disputes.

Bureaucracy. While Taylor was promoting science as the cornerstone of industrial governance at the shop level, the German sociologist Max Weber was describing the benefits (and some of the shortcomings) of organizations built around clearly defined positions (offices) to which people were promoted on the basis of merit and in which subordinate officeholders were governed by defined policies, procedures, and rules. Weber argued that rule by office—bureaucracy—was impersonal, efficient, and equitable and was the only basis of organizational authority and administration compatible with the values of democracy.

Following this pattern, other management theorists (e.g., Mooney, 1947; Urwick, 1943; Graicunas, 1937; Brown, 1947) attempted to develop rational principles which could be used to design organizations and to guide managers toward the most effective use of their resources. Graicunas, for example, argued that no man could effectively supervise more than seven subordinates, while Brown concluded that "organizations should determine the selection of personnel rather than personnel determine the nature of organization" (p. 101).

There is little question that the teachings of these early management authorities have greatly influenced organizational practice and performance. The field of industrial engineering has continued the search for standardization and workflow efficiency, the civil service systems which pervade government still seek to provide the orderly progression of the meritorious through a hierarchy of offices as described by Weber, and a contemporary version of the early efficiency expert—the computer scientist—has done much to simplify and expedite organizational communications and to improve the quality of information used in decision making.

Nevertheless, it became increasingly clear that the traditional Management approach was somewhat one-sided in that it was primarily concerned with what Leavitt calls "organizations without people," since it paid relatively little attention to questions of human needs or motivation other than those which were purely economic. Traditional organizational designs were highly dependent on the compliance of organization members with the organization's demands. Taylor, for example, dealt with this issue simply by arguing that compliance could be expected if employees were provided adequate compensation and if the most demeaning effects of particularism (e.g., favoritism) were removed. Furthermore, the rigidity of the traditional Management approach made no provision for rapid adjustment to changing organizational environments.

Human relations. By the early twenties, managers and scholars were pointing to what they believed were signs of work rebellion against excessive standardization and impersonalization (e.g., the growth of unions) and argued that organizations had lost sight of the human needs for belonging, social interaction, and the feeling of importance (e.g., Tead and Metcalf, 1920; Douglas and Kornhauser, 1922). These early criticisms of the rationalized, bureaucratized organization were soon augmented by the interpreters of the famous Hawthorne experiments (conducted in the late twenties and early thirties). These developments gave birth to the Human Relations movement which dominated the field of Organizational Behavior during the forties and fifties.

Human Relations dethroned *Economic Man* and installed *Social Man* in his place. In so doing, it stressed what were then called "irrational" (as opposed to "rational" or economic) needs— needs for approval, belonging, and group membership. Its solutions to organizational problems included strong, cohesive work groups, the training of supervisors and consultants to listen to workers' problems, and generally the introduction of management policies which would treat workers with greater fairness and dignity—as people rather than machines.

A host of specific managerial practices flowed out of the Human Relations movement, such as suggestion systems, safety and cafeteria committees, and fringe benefits designed to reward organizational loyalty. Most importantly, this movement stimulated a focus on effective leadership (see Chapter Three) which it defined primarily in terms of such slogans as, "Take care of your employees and they will take care of you," and "A happy worker is a productive worker." Unquestionably, the Human Relations movement contributed to the reduction of harsh, autocratic, dehumanizing leadership behavior.

The Human Relations approach to organization behavior, while hailed by its proponents as a revolt against existing organizational practices, was in fact much more an accommodation than a revolution. It challenged none of the basic tenets of traditional management thought dealing with standardization, rationalization, or specialization. Instead, it accepted existing technology, organization structure, and job design as given and sought merely to "humanize" these as best as possible through concerned, supportive supervision and some degree of member participation in routine (basically non-workflow related) decision making. (By emphasizing the social needs of organization members, the human relationists assumed that workers would respond cooperatively to managerial edicts.)

Thus, Human Relations humanized the work context but left the nature of work itself unchanged. Quite aptly, Leavitt has called this movement "people without organizations." The essential hypothesis of human relations was that sound personnel policies would lead to happy workers and that happy workers would work harder, or at least be more cooperative. And yet it was clear by the late fifties (Brayfield and Crockett, 1955; Herzberg, *et al.*, 1957) that there was little direct relationship between morale and productivity or between considerate supervision and most measures of performance. Happy and considerately supervised workers did not necessarily work harder. At best, Human Relations made work more tolerable and so reduced employee dissatisfaction; it did little to provide motivation or to satisfy what psychologists had begun to call higher order needs, such as those for challenge and self-actualization on the job.

More Recent Approaches

Human Resources. By the late fifties, the term Human Relations had fallen into some disrepute, as did many of the oversimplified concepts accompanying it. To adopt a Hegelian analogy, if traditional management theories can be called the thesis, then Human Relations, the reaction against traditional theories, can be called the antithesis, and the new Organizational Behavior was the synthesis.

Organizational Behavior, a term which began to emerge in the early sixties, differed from Human Relations in two important respects. In the first place, it was concerned with both organization (the nature of tasks, structure, reporting relationships, and the like) *and* people. Secondly, at least some of its early advocates hypothesized that people wanted more from their work than merely financial rewards, job security, humane treatment, and a rich social life.

Those who placed primary emphasis on this second factor (e.g., Argyris, 1957; McGregor, 1960; Likert, 1961, 1967) might appropriately be called Human Resources theorists. Human Resources theorists argued that beyond physical and social needs, man has the desire to gain recognition and fulfillment from his job—to realize his potential through doing meaningful work. Managers, therefore, should consider not only how they supervise people but should also rethink how they use them—they should redesign jobs, decision processes, and control systems so as to provide greater opportunities for gaining a sense of accomplishment from work.

While participation and involvement in routine areas had been advocated by the Human Relationists to enhance feelings of importance and cooperation, Human Resources theorists advocated participative practices as a means of bringing more talent (and more commitment) to bear on important organizational decisions— and thus to make better use of the pool of human resources untapped by traditional organizational procedures. Such practices as job enrichment, management by objectives, self-controlled work teams, etc. have flowed out of this movement, as have some of the formal participative schemes discussed in Chapter Four. Most importantly, this concept of human needs restored performance as a legitimate concern of management—managers and their subordinates were expected to jointly set high performance goals and to exercise responsible self-control in their achievement.

Human Resources theorists resolved some of the outstanding dilemmas in the field of Organizational Behavior. They acknowledged that structure and responsibility were crucial but argued that these could be jointly achieved by superiors and subordinates working together, rather than unilaterally by superiors alone. Similarly, they acknowledged man's needs to belong and to feel important but argued that these could be designed into jobs and processes, rather than appended to them. Change, they argued, was important but should be introduced participatively by such processes as Organizational Development (see Chapter Seven).

Although the Human Resources approach represented a considerable advance over simple Human Relations, for many scholars this was not enough. In the first place, early Human Resources seemed wedded to finding a "one best way" appropriate to all situations. Secondly, it appeared to focus primarily on the work team—the manager and his immediate subordinates; it did not directly address itself to the growing concern for coordination across departmental and hierarchical levels. In part to answer these two objectives, there arose two new lines of research, one of which has become known as the *contingency approach* and the other as *organizational sociology*.

The contingency approach. The Human Resources approach seemed to argue, at least in its most oversimplified versions, that all workers were desirous of self-actualization on the job and that participative management was uniformly appropriate in every organizational context. Surely, its critics argued, not all employees are equally responsive to enriched jobs or opportunities for joint goal setting, and certainly one cannot advocate the same degree of self-direction and self-control across all types of technological and structural characteristics. Furthermore, others argued, not all organizational objectives require the same level of commitment and utilization of human resources. Routine, repetitive work may still be best accomplished through well planned, directive procedures which require only that subordinates make a minimal emotional commitment to organizational objectives. Conversely, jobs whose nature is difficult to specify in advance may require a high degree of employee motivation and even radically new organizational structures.

As early as the mid-fifties, laboratory research with simulated organizations revealed "quite dramatically what type of organization is best suited for which kinds of environment. Specifically, for simple tasks under static conditions, an autocratic, centralized structure, such as has characterized most industrial organizations in the past, is quicker, neater, and more efficient. But for adaptability to changing conditions, for rapid acceptance of new ideas, for flexibility in dealing with novel problems, generally high morale and loyalty, the more equalitarian and decentralized type seems to work better" (Bennis and Slater, 1968, p. 5). And there were other studies (e.g., Blauner, 1964; Whyte, *et al.*, 1955; Dubin, 1959) which suggested that workers differed greatly in their expectations about their jobs and that these expectations were in large part determined by variations in individual personality and cultural background.

Leading out of this early research, there has been a stream of studies which seek to specify which forms of motivation, supervisory practice, etc., work best with what sorts of people and with what sorts of jobs. As a consequence of this research, a host of complicated, multi-variate models of motivation (Porter and Lawler, 1968), job design (Hackman and Lawler, 1971), leadership (Fiedler, 1967), and departmentalization and coordination (Lawrence and Lorsch, 1967) have emerged within the last ten years, along with a massive body of theory and research which examines the linkages between environmental demands, technology, and organizational structure and processes.

Some impacts on managerial practice can be associated with this movement. New approaches to interdepartmental coordination and conflict resolution appear to be emerging in many organizations; NASA, for example, has experimented with a variety of novel organizational forms (Sayles and Chandler, 1971). Perhaps most importantly, the recognition of variability among individuals and situations has helped (perhaps forced) managers to search for and consider a wider range of alternatives in solving their human and organizational problems.

Organizational sociology. The Human Relations and the Human Resources approaches shared a common focus on the individual and his needs and motivations. Though the Human Resources approach led to important insights regarding leadership behavior and the design of reward systems, the emphasis was still on personal and interpersonal factors. Indeed, it can be argued that early Human Resources theorists viewed the ideal organization as a series of cohesive and committed interlocking work groups.

An increasing number of scholars (e.g., Selznick, 1953; Chandler, 1962; Woodward, 1965; Thompson, 1967) during the mid-sixties became concerned with questions relating to the structure of the organization as a whole and, in a sense, returned to issues of primary interest to traditional theorists. For the most part, these scholars were sociologists (as opposed to those in the Human Resources school, who tended to be psychologists), and their work is increasingly becoming known as *organizational sociology*. (Another name for this field is "complex organization," to distinguish it from the simple or face-to-face organization of primary interest to psychologists.)

Organizational sociology is concerned chiefly with what are sometimes called the formal aspects of organization—written rules, channels of communications, reporting relationships, control and reward systems, and the like. Included within its domain are such issues as staff-line relationships, centralization and decentralization, product vs. functional organization, and spans of control. And, as we shall see in Chapter Five, the subject of greatest interest today relates to how the organization adjusts to the demands of its technology and external environment. The approach of organizational sociologists is heavily contingency oriented, but by contrast with some psychologists, the former focus on impersonal rather than personal determinants of structure.

A systems approach. As will be mentioned below, some OB scholars stress the individual orientation of the Human Resources approach more than the structural approach of the organizational sociologist, and vice versa. Similarly, there are some who look primarily for generalizations applicable to all organizations while others carry the contingency approaches to the point where they insist that no generalizations are possible. More and more, however, there has been argument on the need for systems models which take all of these factors into account—which explicitly acknowledge the great variability among people, tasks, and environments—and that these factors are constantly changing.

TENSIONS WITHIN OB

As a recognized academic field, OB is little more than ten years old (in 1958, Harold Leavitt had great difficulty finding a publisher for his now highly respected book, *Managerial Psychology;* most publishers felt that there would be no market in this area). OB is still "an orphan among fields. It has no professional society, no leading journal, no annual convention, and one of the most imperfect, disorganized labor markets in all academia" (Strauss, 1970, p. 146). Nevertheless, the subject is taught in almost every major business school, and there is now surprising agreement among OB scholars as to the subject matter and limits of their field.

Despite this basic agreement as to domain, there are some important differences as to emphasis, research methodology, and values. To these we now turn.

People vs. organizations. As mentioned above, OB represents something of a merger of the older fields of Management, with its emphasis on the impersonal factors of organization, and Human Relations, which stressed people problems. Though there has been a considerable resolution of the issues, the synthesis is far from complete, and the field is still marked by considerable disagreement in emphasis. For some, these differences are merely matters of research emphasis or training (psychology as against sociology), but for others they take on moral connotations. There is considerable agreement among OB scholars that organizational pressures sometimes inhibit the full development of the individual personality. Some see this as inevitable; others feel a strong ethical imperative to help make the organization more participative and thus expand the area of individual freedom.

Harmony vs. conflict. A related question concerns the role of conflict between the individual and the organization, or among individuals or even subdivisions of the organization. On one side are those who see conflict as inevitable and even desirable, at least within limits. On the other side are those who believe that the ideal organization should enjoy substantial harmony. Likert (1961) suggests that in such an organization, "Every member of the organization would see the accomplishment of (organizational goals) as the best way to meet his own needs and personal goals" (p. 269). Again, something of a contingency approach is developing which seeks to identify the situations under which conflict may be helpful and to channel it so that it does greatest good and least harm.

Research vs. application. Probably more serious is the split between those who are research oriented and those who are practice oriented. The Traditional and Human Relations approaches were primarily prescriptive—they had a message for management. Their research methodology (if any) was fairly naive. It usually consisted of case methods and anecdotal material, and its meaning to management was obvious and direct. Over the years, both research and theory have become more complex. The simple case method has given way to survey research methodology, controlled laboratory experiments, and the like (for a brief survey, see Chapter Three). Research results are frequently reported not as easy-to-understand stories but in terms of sophisticated conceptual and statistical analyses. Even when these findings are comprehensible to the practitioner (or the student), they seem to add up to "it all depends." No wonder there are many OB research-oriented professors who enjoy high status within academia but are virtually unknown among practitioners—and vice versa.

Other scholars have gone the applied route, and even among these there are some substantial differences in value orientation. There are those who see their role simply as helping to make the organization more efficient, but there are others who, as Bennis (1966) put it, are working "ambitiously to transform the basic value system of the enterprise so that humanistic and democratic values are infused and related to policy" (p. 192). This second group insists that OB cannot and should not be value-free, and it sees its mission primarily as helping the individual operate more effectively and creatively in the organizational context—with the expectation that greater individual creativity will also redound to the benefit of both organizations and society generally.

Obviously, there is considerable overlap among these positions. At one end of a possible continuum, we find humanistically and application oriented scholars who tend to engage in research which focuses on individuals rather than the organization as a whole and who tend to value organizational harmony relatively highly. At the other pole are more sociologically oriented individuals who use sophisticated methodologies to study impersonal, structural organizational characteristics and who make few claims as to the applicability of their work to real life (often insisting that their work is value free). Between these two extremes lie the majority of the profession—individuals who mix research and practice, make use of a variety of research techniques, and hope eventually to arrive at the kind of systems approach previously discussed. (For an interesting statement of the issues, see Argyris's *The Applicability of Organizational Sociology,* 1972, and the various reviews discussing this book which appeared in the March 1973 issue of the *Administrative Science Quarterly.*)

OB OVERVIEW

Our discussion to this point has emphasized the development of OB and the divisions still existing within the field. And, yet, as mentioned earlier, there is substantial agreement among OB scholars as to the general area covered by the field. One way of illustrating this consensus is the chart below (adopted from Miles, in press), which may also help us to understand the interrelationships among the chapters which follow.

Although, as noted earlier, OB scholars vary in their interests, all recognize the fact that organizations are made up of both organizational and people variables. Because no organization could perform effectively and still maintain a high level of job satisfaction among its members with these two sets of variables operating independently, it becomes management's task to successfully integrate people and organizational variables by manipulating the integrating mechanisms—that is, by designing jobs and organization structures in appropriate ways, by planning for the use of and controlling resources, by creating motivating reward systems, and so on.

In addition, as indicated by the arrows in the chart, there is a synergistic relationship among the people and organizational variables and the integrating mechanisms employed to bring them together. Managerial action taken in any one area is quite often likely to affect processes in another. Thus, a management which designs jobs so as to allow a great deal of employee discretion and responsibility is also likely to use participative leadership methods and nonpunitive approaches to control. The overriding factor

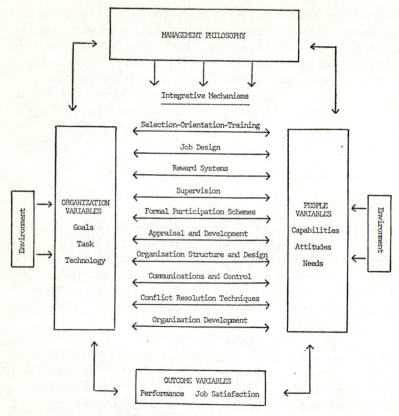

here is management philosophy. For instance, managements which
make the assumption that their employees are responsible and
capable of self-control are likely to approach the use of the integrating mechanisms in a manner which is consistently different
than that employed by managements which believe their employees
are lazy and seek to avoid work.

Finally, the chart shows that the organization does not exist in
a vacuum. Environmental factors affect both organization members and the task and structural characteristics of the organization.
On the individual side, environmental factors such as societal and
family practices have an impact on the beliefs and behaviors individuals bring to the organization. Conversely, the goals and tasks
of the organization are influenced by environmental factors such
as the nature of the product market, governmental pressures,

changes in technology, and the like—and all of these may be changing rapidly.

SUMMARY OF THE BOOK

The chapters below illustrate the breadth of OB's subject matter
but have been selected primarily because they (1) deal with
various pieces of the model presented above, (2) treat questions
of considerable research interest, and (3) have important implications for practitioners. Together these chapters attempt to describe
and criticize a variety of attempts to resolve major organizational
problems through raising both individual satisfaction and organizational effectiveness.

Chapter 2, by Strauss, is primarily concerned with the current
debate as to whether workers are becoming increasingly alienated
from their jobs—and whether job enrichment may be the answer
to this problem. In considering these issues, the chapter includes
a preliminary discussion of individual needs and motivation and
then examines these in the context of current widespread efforts to
redesign jobs. Strauss concludes, among other things, that job
redesign cannot be considered apart from questions relating to
supervision and organization structure generally. Furthermore, he
suggests that job redesign might work best when accompanied by
some mechanism for formal participation, such as the Scanlon Plan.

Turning to the issue of supervision, Ritchie, in Chapter 3,
reviews both the historical development of supervision and current
issues associated with this topic. Although noting that the behavior of the supervisor may only account for a small portion of
the productivity of his subordinates, Ritchie nevertheless suggests
that supervisory behavior may make the difference between organizational success and failure. He also concludes that the supervisor's freedom to adopt a particular supervisory style, participative
or otherwise, is heavily constrained by his own attitudes and such
situational factors as the nature of the work task, organizational
level, the location of information, skills and expectations of subordinates, and a host of other factors. The supervisor's attitudes
(e.g., how much trust he places in his subordinates) are an important determinant of subordinate satisfaction, but both attitudes
and behaviors are important to subordinate performance. Finally,
Ritchie considers several policy issues in the area of supervision,

most notably the degree to which supervision is keeping pace with changes in societal values and the extent to which supervisors can be trained to adopt attitudes and behaviors which will have a long-term impact on their subordinates.

To the extent that Ritchie's review discusses participation, it is "informal" participation—that is, the amount of influence allowed subordinates due to the attitudes and behaviors of supervisors. In Chapter 4, Tannenbaum discusses, from a behavioral point of view, formal schemes which permit workers to participate in management. Tannenbaum's definition of formal participation includes not only legally defined participation (e.g., German co-determination, Yugoslav Workers' Self-management, and methods used in Israeli kibbutzim) but also suggestion (or consultative) schemes (e.g., the Scanlon Plan), collective bargaining, and several participative approaches which have emerged from the behavioral sciences. Tannenbaum concludes not that formal participation *will* work in all organizational situations but that it *can* work, and he outlines the conditions where participation is most likely to be effective.

Although they do not use the specific term, the first three authors appear to argue for a *systems* point of view: if new approaches to job design, supervision, or workers' participation are to be effective, all parts of the organizational system must work in concert. The systems view is well illustrated in Chapter 5, in which Ouchi and Harris discuss organizational environments, technology, and structure. Whereas the first three chapters deal with human behavior in organizational settings, Ouchi and Harris describe the setting itself. In particular, they discuss three crucial systemic linkages in organizational behavior—relationships between (1) the external environment and organizational technologies, (2) the environment and organization structure, and (3) technology and structure. Their review of research in this area indicates that OB scholars are only just beginning to develop generalizations about these issues, but research findings appear to promise a convergence between these macro-organizational problems and the micro-organizational issues discussed in the first three chapters.

Having reviewed research in the areas of both people and organizational variables, the final two chapters deal with integrating mechanisms which are available to managers. In Chapter 6, Nightingale discusses the vitally important subject of conflict and conflict resolution. Using a framework which approaches organizational conflict from two different perspectives, conflict is first treated as an essentially "bad" phenomenon, something which signifies a breakdown in the system and is to be avoided (the human relations approach). Then, conversely, conflict is treated as a phenomenon which, if not allowed to become excessive and when properly channeled, becomes a force which may be functional to the organization (the pluralist approach). After developing each of these perspectives, Nightingale examines three theories of conflict resolution which take into account both the human relations and pluralist approaches, and he argues that managers should be familiar with the conditions where each theory is most appropriate.

The issue of how the concepts presented in Chapters 2 through 6 might be implemented in ongoing organizations is the subject of Chapter 7, in which Miles deals with the topic of Organization Development (OD). As the applied edge of the field of Organizational Behavior, OD has captured major attention over the past few years, particularly among practitioners, and its terminology and tools are now commonplace in many organizations. Miles points out that while its advocates promote OD as a highly participative, systematic program of planned change across the entire organizational system, OD in practice frequently falls far short of this claim. More often than not, Miles notes, OD focuses on interpersonal barriers to organizational performance and ignores technological, structural, and procedural constraints. Only most recently, and in a limited set of organizations, has OD been expanded to include the full set of issues and variables described in the model presented earlier. Miles provides a cautious interpretation of OD's efficacy at this point—noting that the evidence is limited and definitive research is difficult if not impossible to design—but adding that on balance some important gains are apparent.

This appraisal may well be applied to the entire field of Organizational Behavior at this point.

Finally, let us note again that the six chapters which follow provide only a partial introduction to the issues covered by Organizational Behavior. There are numerous other issues—reward systems, small group behavior, career patterns, role theory, and communications, to mention only a few examples—which also provide significant theoretical and practical insights but which, for reasons of space, are not discussed in this volume.

Job Satisfaction, Motivation, and Job Redesign

GEORGE STRAUSS
University of California, Berkeley

Recent years have seen the resurrection of the issues of work satisfaction (especially of blue-collar workers) and of job design—issues which were of great concern during Organizational Behavior's infancy, but which were largely ignored during the late 1950's and the 1960's. Today we are in the midst of a considerable national (and even international) debate over questions relating to worker alienation and job enrichment.

Ranged on one side of this debate is an unusual alliance of social critics and Establishment representatives who are agreed that worker discontent is rapidly rising and that work reforms are urgently needed. "People are growing balky on the job," as Yankelovich (1974) puts it. "They seem less willing than in the past to endure hardships for the sake of a living" (p. 19). Representatives of this position point to a ten-point drop in job satisfaction, as registered by the Gallup Poll from 1969 to 1973, and to data suggesting lowered productivity and higher quit, accident, and absentee rates. This widespread unrest is blamed for a variety of ills, including the Lordstown strike, our unsatisfactory balance of trade, our galloping inflation, as well as mental and physical illness and political extremism. Some proponents of this point of view, which is eloquently expressed in *Work in America* (1973), suggest the need for job enrichment and participatory democracy, and they point to experiments in companies such as Volvo and General Foods, as bellweathers for the future.

The arguments for the other side have been repeatedly stated in the *American Federationist* (but there are representatives from unions and management on both sides of the question). According to these arguments, the extent of worker job dissatisfaction has been overstated, and workers' primary demands are still for higher pay and greater job security. Thus, workers can best be satisfied through traditional means such as enriching the paycheck (rather than the job), providing shorter hours or early retirement (on the argument that if the job is bad, one should spend less time on it), and showing greater concern for occupational safety and health. Proponents of this view naturally pooh-pooh experiments on job enrichment, arguing (possibly inconsistently) that job enrichment is a speedup in disguise and that it will be undesired by workers and excessively expensive to management.

As in most debates, the arguments have been overstated and in the process some perfectly decent concepts, such as "alienation," have assumed value-oriented meanings which substantially reduce their utility for scientific analysis. Furthermore, the debate has lumped together some issues which are at least partly separable. One can be unconvinced that work satisfaction has decreased and still be concerned with work problems in America. Similarly, one can be pessimistic as to these two issues and still believe that job enrichment is not a promising solution.

The purpose of this chapter is to first provide a broad perspective in which the issues of work satisfaction and job redesign can be analyzed. In so doing, I will review three important OB topics— job satisfaction, motivation, and job design—placing special emphasis on research developments since my 1970 IRRA article (Strauss, 1970). Against this framework, I will discuss the specific issues associated with the work satisfaction-job enrichment debate. This discussion will be heavily focused on blue-collar workers, even though they constitute a continually declining minority of the work force, because this group is the target for most of the writers engaged in this debate. In so doing, I will largely ignore the rich stream of research dealing with managers, professionals, and other white-collar workers.

Very briefly, my thesis is as follows: most workers report satisfaction with their work, and there is no evidence of rising dissatisfaction. Although the typical worker reacts positively to having more challenging work, he has learned to cope with a lack of challenge (sometimes at a considerable psychic cost); blue-collar workers at least tend to focus their lives away from their jobs and to give higher priority to economic benefits and adequate working conditions than to intrinsic job challenge. As a consequence, they are motivated to produce only a "fair day's work" (whatever this may be in local context). Job design schemes, such as job enrichment, offer hope of increasing satisfaction and productivity in some cases, though perhaps their main advantage lies in providing a more flexible work force, in improving communications among workers, and in increasing the supply of "amenities" on the job.

One other caveat: this is a controversial area. It is difficult to be dispassionate, and I will make little attempt to be so.

Job Satisfaction

As a useful beginning, let me start with what might be called the "personality vs. organization hypothesis." This hypothesis, which is implicit in the early work of social scientists such as Allport (1937), Argyris (1957), Maslow (1954), and McGregor (1960), suggests that employees will be almost inevitably frustrated with traditionally structured jobs, especially in mass production industry.

Oversimplified, the argument runs as follows: workers seek social belonging, independence, and social growth. In other words, they aspire to ascend what Maslow has called the "needs hierarchy" ladder, from satisfaction of physical, through safety, social, and egoistic, to self-actualization needs. Thus, once basic *extrinsic* needs are satisfied, *intrinsic* needs assume greater importance. Furthermore—and this is a critical point—such satisfactions are desired *on the job*. Organizations, according to the hypothesis, fail to recognize these aspirations and follow instead what McGregor called Theory X assumptions that workers dislike work and wish to avoid responsibility. In so doing, they structure work in such a fashion that the individual is condemned to isolation, passivity, dependence, and the use of minimal abilities. Consequently, workers become alienated from their work.

It is suggested that, for a variety of reasons, this problem has become more serious in recent years. Allegedly we are seeing a massive change in our cultural values (Yankelovich, 1974), particularly among young workers (a group which increased dramatically as a consequence of the post-World War II baby boom). Younger workers have always been less satisfied than older ones, and this particular generation has been raised according to permissive standards, affected by the campus revolts of the 1960's, and is thus particularly resistant to authority. Arguably, these younger workers are less afraid of economic insecurity than their elders and less willing to postpone gratification; success among them is measured less in monetary and physical terms and more in terms of self-fulfillment, living an agreeable life style, and doing meaningful work.

Associated with these cultural changes have been shifts in the relations among races and sexes. Blacks have reasons for dissatisfaction of their own, but for the most part seek traditional economic goals. The women newly entering the work force seek more than these, however; they look upon their jobs not just as a means of earning a living but also as a source of self-expression. Both minorities and women show decreased willingness to accept second-class jobs.

All this occurred during a period when confrontation and overt expressions of dissatisfaction became the mode. Civil rights agitation, campus revolts, Women's Lib, consumerism, and ecological action groups have all lead to heightened expectations on the part of various sectors of our population and a greater willingness to protest when these expectations are denied.

It is claimed that all these developments have contributed to a greater dissatisfaction with work, especially with work which is boring and meaningless. Is there any concrete evidence to support these allegations? Has dissatisfaction increased? How great is worker demand for challenging work? How do workers adapt to nonchallenging work—and at what cost? Let us consider these questions before turning to the question of motivation and job redesign.

STUDIES OF JOB SATISFACTION

The concept of job satisfaction is an elusive one. Job satisfaction is, obviously, related to the meaning of work, but the meaning of work is clearly also related to one's view of life. Therefore, it may be misleading to try to measure something so inherently qualitative in a purely quantitative manner. Satisfaction, after all, depends on expectations and goals. Reported satisfaction may mean merely resignation; that is, it may mean acceptance of one's lot or merely face-saving.

Considerable efforts have been made to refine job satisfaction measures (e.g., Wanous and Lawler, 1972). Nevertheless, the various measures are poorly correlated with each other, in part because they approach job satisfaction from different angles. Single-question measures, such as "On the whole, would you say you are satisfied or dissatisfied with the work you do?" may be useful for some purposes. For other purposes, it may be better to ask a battery of questions which seek to probe attitudes toward specific aspects of work and then aggregate the results. Despite these problems, we can summarize the job satisfaction literature as follows.

Overall satisfaction. One uniformity stands out in almost all studies: most workers report themselves to be satisfied with their work. With the exception of certain groups, such as black workers under 30, more than 75 per cent of the work force reports itself satisfied. Reporting oneself satisfied may mean, as indicated above, that self-respect forces oneself not to admit that one cannot find a better job. Nevertheless, roughly half of all workers report themselves *very* satisfied, and more than half would recommend "a job like" theirs to a "good friend," would decide to take their present job if they "had to decide all over again," and feel that their current job very much measures up to the kind of job they wanted (Gallup Poll Index, 1973; Survey Research Center, 1971).

Changes in satisfaction. Despite much controversy, the best evidence from psychological surveys suggests that average levels of job satisfaction in this country have remained fairly stable since the early 1960's and that satisfaction today is higher than it was during the 1940's and 1950's. True, the Gallup Poll did indicate a ten-point drop from 1969 to 1973, but there is reason to discount these findings and the more careful Michigan studies indicate no significant change in job satisfaction during the period (Quinn and Mangione, 1973).

Economic (behavioral) evidence is also consistent with these psychological (attitudinal) findings. Recent unfavorable changes in productivity and quit rates, absenteeism, strikes, and accidents can be largely explained by standard economic variables, such as changes in hours of work, unemployment, and the occupational and demographic composition of the work force (Henle, 1974; Flanagan, Strauss, and Ulman, 1974). Once the impact of these variables is filtered out through regression analysis, there is no consistent, significant trend over time which suggests an attitudinal variable at work.

Neither the attitudinal or behavioral measures proves that worker attitudes have remained unchanged or that quality of work life has not gotten worse. At best, they suggest that whatever changes may have occurred have not been great enough to affect the rather insensitive measuring devices presently available. Perhaps there is latent dissatisfaction which has not yet broken through, something qualitative which has not shown up on quantitative measures. Anecdotal reports by many managers and union leaders to this effect should not be completely discounted.

Demographic and occupational variables. There are important demographic and occupational differences in job satisfaction which emerge, especially when multi-question measures are used. Age, sex, race, education, and occupation seem to be the most important. Once appropriate allowances are made for the fact that women, blacks, and poorly educated persons tend to hold less challenging and less well paid jobs, the differences based on race, education, and sex decline substantially—and on education are reversed (Tannenbaum, 1974). There is one important exception, however: workers with "some college" but no college degree seem less satisfied than one might expect from their age and occupational distribution; these workers feel considerably overeducated for their jobs (Survey Research Center, 1971).

Economic vs. noneconomic rewards. Occupation is related to satisfaction, but is this because higher status jobs offer greater economic rewards or because they offer greater challenge, autonomy, and meaning? This question has divided industrial relations people since the founding of the field, with economists and psychologists typically taking opposite points of view.

In a sense, both positions are correct. People want jobs which are both economically and psychologically rewarding. Further, there is considerable room for convergence in economic and psychological theory. Economic theory would lead us to predict that as jobs become better rewarded and more secure, the marginal utility of additional income declines and the relative marginal utility of noneconomic benefits (such as job challenge) would increase (Flanagan, Strauss, and Ulman, 1974). This hypothesis is, of course, consistent with Maslow's psychological theory that as lower level (primarily economic) needs are satisfied, higher level needs become more important.

There is already some evidence supporting this hypothesis. To illustrate: all during the 1940's and 1950's, employees generally ranked *job security* as the most important thing they wanted from their jobs (Herzberg, *et al.*, 1957, p. 46). By contrast, in a 1969 survey (Survey Research Center, 1971), the average of *all* workers placed *interesting work* first, with job security coming eighth and pay fourth. However, these shifts in rank order may exaggerate the extent to which real change has occurred, and there are some important differences among demographic and occupational groups. For blue-collar workers good pay and job security—as well as having sufficient information and help to get the job done—receive roughly equal top rank. For white-collar workers all this is subsidiary to having work that is interesting and being able to develop their own special abilities (U.S. Manpower Administration, 1974). Yet even among blue-collar workers, there is important research which suggests that discretion is a more important determinant of job satisfaction than is pay (Sheppard, 1974; Shepard, 1973)—and that with increasing education the relative importance of financial rewards goes down, while that of challenge goes up (Quinn, 1973, p. 204).

By and large, these studies indicate that those who hold higher status jobs (which are also better paid) tend to place relatively greater stress on noneconomic rewards than do those further down the occupational hierarchy.

Hygienes and motivators. The foregoing discussion between economic and noneconomic rewards is far too simple. A variety of noneconomic rewards are available, as is suggested by the highly controversial but ingenious research by Herzberg (1966) and his collaborators, who conclude that job satisfaction and dissatisfaction are not opposite points on a continuum but in fact two separate dimensions. "Context" factors, such as unfair company policies, incompetent supervision, or unsatisfactory working conditions, may lead to dissatisfaction. Such dissatisfaction may be reduced by "hygienic" measures such as fringe benefits, human relations training for foremen, or better company policies, but such measures will not make workers satisfied, only apathetic. For true satisfaction to be obtained, "content" factors must be provided such as achievement, accomplishment, responsibility, and challenging work. Only content factors motivate people to work harder. For this reason, Herzberg calls context factors hygienes, while content ones are motivators.

The usefulness of distinguishing among various sources of non-economic rewards is supported by the landmark Michigan study (Survey Research Center, 1971) which identified five separate facets of satisfaction: Pay (including fringes and job security), Challenge (variety, opportunity to learn, skill required, etc.), Comfort (physical conditions of work, job speed, difficulties commuting to work, and the like), Resources (having adequate machinery, supplies, assistance from one's boss, etc.), and Coworker Relations. Of the lot, only Challenge is clearly what Herzberg calls a motivator.

The relative importance of these facets depends on the measure of importance used and also on demographic (and probably personality and cultural) factors. For a large per cent of the work force, Resources and Comfort were clearly more important than either Pay or Challenge (Barnowe, Mangione, and Quinn, 1973). Of the various specific aspects of the job, "having a 'nurturant' supervisor" and "receiving help, assistance, etc." were more closely correlated with overall job satisfaction than a "job with 'enriching' demands," which itself ranked higher than pay and security. But note that these factors are clearly related. Workers on challenging jobs tend to be more satisfied with their pay than are workers on nonchallenging jobs, even though the two groups may in fact be paid the same (Tannenbaum, *et al.*, 1974), thus suggesting that hygienes and motivators complement rather than substitute for each other.

PERSONALITY AND CULTURE

According to Maslow's theory, the fact that some individuals seek hygienes may only mean that their "lower level needs" are still unsatisfied. Once these become satisfied—and as individuals mature—they will seek increasing opportunities for self-actualization, including the freedom to be creative, to develop their skills to the maximum, to exercise autonomy, and the like. The Maslow scheme is highly flattering to professors and managers, two occupations which place a high value on self-actualization. Nevertheless, in its oversimplified form it can be criticized on a number of grounds (Strauss, 1963), and Maslow himself never claimed that all people would wish to ascend his needs hierarchy, and certainly not in the same way. In fact, as his later writings make clear, his "mature, normal" individual is a rather special breed.

Personality and cultural factors help determine whether people desire self-actualization. The work of McClelland (1961) and his associates suggests that people vary substantially in the relative importance they attach to various needs and, further, that there is no necessary hierarchy (i.e., that people do not inevitably emphasize self-actualization after lesser needs are met). McClelland posits three basic needs (besides physical needs) : *need achievement, need affiliation,* and *need power.* Persons high in need achievement react well to challenge; those who are low in this dimension are concerned primarily with playing it safe and avoiding failure. Presumably this latter group (particularly those high in need affiliation) prefer direction to autonomy. Though McClelland's work is subject to debate, it does seem reasonable that because of personality differences people vary considerably in their need for challenge and autonomy (Vroom, 1960). Personality differences, in turn, may be caused by variations in culture and family upbringing, and even in genetic factors (a question not to be considered here is whether child raising practices may be changing sufficiently to cause substantial alterations in attitudes toward work).

One cultural variable which has lead to considerable recent debate relates to possible differences between rural and urban backgrounds in terms of what employees want from their jobs. Both Turner and Lawrence (1965) and Hulin and Blood (1968) found that urban workers reacted less positively to more complex tasks than did rural workers. Hackman and Lawler (1971) report that urban workers are relatively more concerned with satisfying physical and social (as opposed to egoistic) needs than are their country cousins. Susman (1973) suggests that rural workers react to job discretion with greater pride in job accomplishments, while for urban workers greater discretion is related only to involvement and to time seeming "to drag" less often.

These findings have been subject to considerable debate, and other studies report inconsistent findings (Shepard, 1970; Korn-hauser and Reid, 1965; Wild and Kampner, 1972). Furthermore, they can be interpreted in a wide variety of ways (Strauss, 1974). Nevertheless, they raise the possibility that work may be more central to workers' lives in rural areas. And this in turn raises the question of the role of work in life—a matter which is largely culturally determined.

THE ROLE OF WORK IN LIFE

How important is work in human life? Dubin (1959) distinguishes between those individuals whose life is job centered and those who are community and home centered. A similar framework characterizes work as *instrumental,* a means to another end, or *expressive,* a valued end in itself. It seems well established that the orientation of many factory workers is instrumental, that their main goal is to earn more money, to obtain greater job security, and to enjoy more leisure (Goldthorpe, *et al.,* 1968). For some women, commitment to work is secondary to commitment to family and home; this is especially true when the work is routine and poorly paid. Turnover for such women tends to be high, and they seek pay and social satisfaction more than intrinsic rewards (Beynon and Blackman, 1972).

That a worker adopts an instrumental orientation toward his work does not mean that he is totally unconcerned as to whether his job provides intrinsic interest or challenge. However, instrumentally oriented workers prefer jobs which are high paid to those which are interesting (Goldthorpe, *et al.,* 1968; Cotgrove, 1972).

Neither does an instrumental orientation mean that the worker prefers not to work at all. An important clue to the role of work is provided in the research of Morse and Weiss (1956) which asked a sample of white male workers, "If by chance you inherited enough money to live comfortably without working, do you think you would work anyway?" The vast majority of all respondents answered affirmatively even though the percentages were slightly higher for middle-class (86 per cent) than working-class workers (76 per cent). Why would they work? Here a surprising phenomenon occurs. As expected, the main reason middle-class workers would continue working was for "interest and accomplishment," but for blue-collar workers (many instrumentally oriented) the main reason for continuing to work was "to keep occupied." This latter group would rather work than not work, even though working involves just filling in time.

This may be a depressing commentary on the meaningfulness of life off the job, but it suggests the centrality of having a job—any job—to the average male (women answer differently) as a source of identity, status, self-respect, and as an opportunity for social interaction. As Form (1973) puts it, "Most auto workers would rather stay on the job, not out of a sense of duty (to satisfy the moralists) or to get their quota of sociability (to satisfy the social scientists), but rather because working provides organizational cement to their lives" (p. 13). All this suggests that workers do adjust to boring work, though perhaps at a cost.

ALTERNATIVE FORMS OF ADJUSTMENT

Perhaps the above discussion will make greater sense if we think in terms of the scheme below (which is analogous to an approach suggested in Argyris, 1973).

| | | Type of work | |
		Nonchallenging	Challenging
Employee orientation	Expressive	3	1
	Instrumental	4	2

We can divide work into that which is challenging and that which is not (using the term "challenge" in an oversimplified fashion to cover such factors as autonomy, variety, opportunity to participate, and the like—factors which are far from perfectly correlated with each other). In a similar oversimplified fashion, we can distinguish between expectations toward work in terms of expressive and instrumental orientations. Those with instrumental orientations look upon the job merely as a means toward another end; those with expressive orientations tend to rank high in terms of need achievement and desire for self-actualization on the job (though they obviously may also have strong economic needs).

By middle-class standards, those who fall in Cell 1 are the lucky ones. They are the professors, managers, etc., who seek self-fulfillment on the job and are fortunate enough to find jobs on which this is possible.

Those who fall in Cell 2 are less happy. They are faced with greater challenge than they want—possibly because the job is beyond their abilities, because they are low in need achievement, have a low tolerance for ambiguity, or because they center their lives away from the job. Of course, through proper training such individuals may possibly learn to enjoy greater responsibility and to change their orientation. Alternatively, they may reject their responsibilities outright or perform them in the most routine, bureaucratic fashion possible. However approached, Cell 2 represents an unstable situation. People placed within it tend either to change their own orientation (and move to Cell 1) or change the nature of the job (and move to the safety of Cell 4). Those who can do neither may well report themselves dissatisfied.

Cell 3 is also unstable. It consists of those who seek self-actualization on the job and are unable to obtain it. Faced with this predicament, some people simply quit. Others, through sabotage, fantasy, or empire building transfer routine work into something challenging (i.e., move to Cell 1), but the most common solution is to withdraw psychologically from the job, to lower one's expectations, and to change one's orientation from expressive to instrumental (and move to Cell 4). Some individuals develop a rich social life on the job; others transfer their attention to family or recreational activities. And still others become alienated from society generally and may well suffer from mental illness. The few who fight fate and refuse to change their orientation are among those likely to report their jobs as "dissatisfying."

Cell 4 is stable. It consists of those who have withdrawn from an expressive orientation and those who never developed it. They work to earn a living or even for self-respect but not for the challenge of the job. These people are apathetic and unmotivated to do much more than a "fair day's work." However, as long as management provides hygienes such as adequate pay, fair supervision, good working conditions, opportunities for social interaction, and the like, they will not be actively dissatisfied (and will report themselves satisfied to a pollster). Unable to see other alternatives to work, they may well respond that they would continue to work in order to "keep occupied" even if they had the money to do otherwise.

THE ADJUSTMENT PROCESS

People adjust to nonchallenging work (i.e., move to Cell 4) in a variety of ways and with various degrees of success—through daydreaming, fantasies of getting better jobs elsewhere (Chinoy, 1955), moonlighting, and increased consumption. Three other "escape routes" deserve special mention.

Social life on the job. For many workers, the social life around the job can provide substitutes for those lacking in the job itself. In a context of humdrum routine, human ingenuity is able to extract surprisingly rich meanings from seemingly trivial events. Horseplay, lunch-time card games, gossip around the watercooler, football pools, and the like do provide satisfaction, particularly for those with high need affiliation. As the job becomes less rewarding, the social group may become more so.

But this is not always the case. Cohesive work groups do not arise automatically whenever the work is boring. Jobs differ substantially in the opportunity they provide for social interaction. The automobile assembly line, for example, permits the typical worker to communicate only with the men directly ahead of and behind him in the flow of work and so provides relatively less opportunity for interaction than do most other lines of work.

Union participation. Unions also help to provide solidarity, at least for the small core of active members. However, participation in union activity is not likely to be high in groups which are not already socially cohesive, and considerable evidence suggests that workers who are dissatisfied with their jobs tend also to be dissatisfied with their union (e.g., Purcell, 1953).

Recreation off the job. Do workers on unchallenging jobs make up for this with challenging recreation and the creative use of leisure time, either at home or in the community? Of course, value judgments are involved here. What the professor-researcher might think creative (e.g., chess, bird watching, and reading this paper), the blue-collar worker might find totally boring.

Kerr *et al.*, (1964) predicted that work in the future would become increasingly routine and provide fewer opportunities for challenge or discretion; on the other hand, there would be a new "bohemianism" off the job, and "Leisure will be the happy hunting ground of the independent spirit" (p. 237). Certainly there is some evidence of "bohemianism" (now called the "counter culture") among professionals. But is this bohemianism likely to counteract the boredom of blue-collar workers? And will it take the form of active recreation or of passive escapism?

In other words, can instrumentally oriented workers make up for the limited satisfaction from their jobs through creative activities off the job? Here more research is required. Certainly some workers do (e.g., the working mother with a large family), but there are many others who relax from boring, discretionless jobs by watching TV or engaging in similar forms of passive recreation. And, according to Meissner (1971), the second group is larger than the first.

HEALTH, PERSONALITY, AND THE JOB

Most people can adjust to boring work in one way or another, through social activity on or off the job, through daydreams, etc. But what is the cost in doing so? And how about those who achieve neither ego or social satisfaction on the job or creative leisure off it? Argyris (1964) argues that unchallenging jobs constitute a major cause of physical and mental illness. They may also contribute to alienation from society and therefore to political extremism. And, possibly, if work force education expands faster than that demanded by jobs, this problem will become increasingly serious.

It is well established that work stress can lead to physical illness, especially heart disease and ulcers and a host of psychosomatic and mental ailments. But a significant proportion of these conditions can be attributed to "overload"—too much variety, uncertainty, and responsibility—rather than routine work and boredom.

The impact of objectively challengeless work (that is, work

which most observers—especially professors—classify as challengeless) is less clear and somewhat difficult to measure. Two studies of auto workers (Kornhauser and Reid, 1965; Siassi, *et al.*, 1974) come to almost diametrically opposed conclusions as to whether assembly-line work has a deleterious effect on mental health. Other studies suggest that reported satisfaction with work is generally correlated with reported satisfaction with life (though the direction of causation is not always clear). Finally, some research (e.g., Smith, 1955) indicates that people on challenging, complex, varied jobs which permit self-direction tend to show relatively high self-esteem, to be less authoritarian, more intellectually flexible, and more willing to accept change.

How is this congruence between personality and job achieved? In part, it is a matter of organizational and self-selection: people gravitate toward jobs consistent with their need patterns. But the reverse also occurs: jobs mold people and sometimes induce fundamental changes in attitudes and values. Obviously, both factors are at work, but Kohn and Schooler (1973) conclude that jobs tend to determine personalities somewhat more than personalities determine jobs. At the very least, we can conclude that jobs can alter personalities, and sometimes (but how often?) the psychic cost is great. What remains to be answered is, What makes the critical difference? Challengeless work may lead to poor mental health, but is lack of challenge the critical element or is it other factors associated with such work, as for example, low pay, irregular employment, and low social status? For those at the bottom of the occupational totem pole, these around-the-job factors may swamp the effects of the job itself.

EVALUATION OF JOB SATISFACTION ISSUES AND RESEARCH

Job satisfaction is clearly an adaptive social process of adjusting to reality. It is not enough to know that a person says that he is satisfied. We have to know the kinds of psychic adjustments he went through to make that response. As we have seen, there are a variety of adjustments to "objectively" challengeless work. For example, the worker may develop a rich social life on or off his job, he may become active in his union, he may "enlarge" his job through sabotage or output restriction, or he may lower his aspirations and delude himself that he is truly happy—and thus become resigned and apathetic (and even classified as low in mental health). Adjustments can be made, though often at a psychic cost, and the cost may become so great that some observers fear an explosion.

Note, too, that much dissatisfaction is caused by low income, job insecurity, inadequate fringe benefits, or tyrannical supervision. Indeed, to me, the evidence suggests that for many workers at all levels—even many managers and professionals—lack of challenge may be less oppressive than lack of income. Instrumental orientation is quite widespread. Of course, there is some evidence that this orientation may be changing. In 1948, the average education of the employed labor force was 10.6 years; in 1972, it was 12.4. Education is positively correlated with the desire for challenging work. Further, the present generation of younger workers is the first not to be born in the shadow of the Great Depression; for them the specter of job insecurity may have been licked. With their lower level needs largely satisfied, younger workers may be in a position to demand satisfaction of their self-actualization needs. If so, such workers will be less likely to settle for jobs which offer high income and a rich social life but no intrinsic satisfaction. Possibly—but today's luxuries may become tomorrow's necessities. Wants grow as fast as paychecks, and economic motivation may not atrophy as fast as some psychologists suggest.

Even so, there are numerous workers today—and probably an increasing number tomorrow—who would react positively to more challenging jobs. Many of these fail to aspire for challenging work now because they know that for them it is not available. Such workers may not be actively dissatisfied, but they are poorly motivated, resulting in not only lack of fulfillment for themselves but the loss of their energies for the economy as a whole.

Motivation

My discussion so far has been concerned with job satisfaction. But managers (and perhaps the economy as a whole) are more concerned with motivation and productivity, and one thing which recent research has made clear is that there is no simple relationship between satisfaction and productivity. Happy workers do not necessarily work harder, and, in some cases, the most dissatisfied ones are the ones most motivated.

Space permits discussion only of a few of the recent developments in motivation research, especially those which help us test the value of job redesign. For the most part during the late 1950's and early 1960's, instructors in Organizational Behavior distinguished simplistically between two forms of motivation: Theory X, based on economic rewards and fear of discharge, and Theory Y, which emphasized provisions for self-actualization at work so that employees "will willingly and voluntarily work for organizational objectives" (McGregor, 1960). Theory X, it was assumed, would lead to alienation, sabotage, and the like, while Theory Y would provide high motivation and productivity.

MIDDLE-GROUND APPROACHES

By the mid-1960's, many authors (e.g., Argyris, 1964) began postulating a middle ground somewhere between the harsh autocracy of Theory X and the full participation of Theory Y. Under these conditions (consistent with my Cell 4), reported employee morale might be high and a "fair day's work" done, despite the absence of job enrichment or similar forms of self-actualizing motivation. This middle-ground theory was, of course, consistent with that of Herzberg who, as previously discussed, postulated conditions under which the worker would be neither dissatisfied nor satisfied or motivated. Herzberg's approach has been subject to considerable controversy and research, with probably a majority of the profession rejecting his methodology. Still, his distinction between extrinsic and intrinsic job factors is a helpful one, even though there may be numerous occasions when extrinsic factors operate as motivators and intrinsic ones merely reduce dissatisfaction.

EXCHANGE THEORY

The middle-ground approach is also consistent with what has been variously called "transaction," "exchange," or "reciprocity" theory. This kind of theory views social behavior as a series of transactions involving exchange and at least some form of reciprocity. As far as motivation for work goes, it assumes that the employer enters into an "implicit bargain" or "psychological contract" with his employees, the terms of which call for the employer to provide fair pay, fair supervision, decent working conditions, and other hygienic conditions for his employees, in return for which the employee will provide a fair day's work. What is defined as a fair day's work may well depend on local tradition and expectations, nevertheless it is well understood by the parties involved. Under these conditions, workers do not feel alienated and, indeed, have considerable control over their lives.

One version of exchange theory, "equity theory," has received the greatest research attention. Equity theory postulates that each person feels that his rewards from the exchange process should bear the same relationship to his investments (efforts) as it does for the "significant other" with whom he compares himself. If it does not, he is dissatisfied. Equity theory predicts, for example, that not only will those who feel underpaid feel unhappy, but also those who feel overpaid—with "feel overpaid" being the critical term (Adams, 1963). Stated in these terms, the theory has been difficult to prove experimentally except in special situations (see Goldman and Friedman, 1971). More generally, however, it suggests that when workers accept a job they also accept a moral contract to do a "fair day's work" in return for "fair" rewards (both pecuniary and nonpecuniary). Presumably, as long as management is perceived as adhering to this contract, no further motivation is required.

PATH-GOAL ANALYSIS

Transaction theory—primarily a sociological theory—has received far less recent attention than path-goal analysis, which is primarily a psychologist's contribution (see especially Porter and Lawler, 1968, and Schwab and Cummings, 1970). Early human relationists seemed to argue that high satisfaction would lead to harder work. Path-goal analysis reverses the direction of causation. It suggests that employees will be motivated to work only if they perceive that productivity is a *path* toward a goal that they value, or more explicitly, that increased effort will lead to increased productivity (performance), that increased performance in turn will lead to rewards that will satisfy needs important to them—and that the satisfaction from this effort is sufficiently great (equitable) to make the effort worthwhile.

Note that this chain of causation can break down at any point. There may be little perceived relationship between effort and performance (perhaps because the employee is untrained, or, as on the assembly line, his influence on the production rate is small); higher performance may not be perceived as being rewarded (promotion may be based on seniority rather than performance or performance may be difficult to measure); the reward may not satisfy an important need (it might be praise when the worker wants pay); finally, any of these relationships may exist but not be perceived as existing (i.e., there must be feedback).

Path-goal analysis has the advantage of permitting the integration of a large number of variables and of specifying the conditions under which various motivational approaches (such as job enrichment) might be successful. For example, if sense of achievement is to operate as a successful motivator, then the following conditions (among others) may have to be attained: (1) the employee in question must have an active or latent high need achievement motive (McClelland, 1961): (2) the task in question must be viewed as a meaningful challenge (it must not be too easy, too hard, or irrelevant to his interests); and (3) the employee must have some feedback as to whether, in fact, he completed his task. Obviously, numerous personality and cultural dimensions can be plugged into this model. Those caught in the "culture of poverty," for example, have learned through sad experience that their efforts are not rewarded; middle-class children, on the other hand, are taught and usually find that hard work brings success.

A complex relationship of this sort is difficult to prove (Heneman and Schwab, 1972), although there have been many efforts. The relatively "objective" elements, such as effort, performance, and rewards, are extremely difficult to measure—even more so are the kinds of psychological relationships specified, for example, the perceived relationship between effort and performance or between performance and satisfaction. Nevertheless, path-goal analysis has a number of important administrative implications. The key to improved motivation is to increase the *perceived* relationship between effort and need satisfaction. This may require doing a better job in selecting rewards or changing the perceived relationship; for example, it may be helpful among managers to tie salaries more closely to performance and then to publicize salary scales so that managers see that effort does in fact pay off (Lawler, 1966; Schuster and Colletti, 1973).

EVALUATION OF MOTIVATION THEORY

Both exchange theory and path-goal analysis carry us beyond the simplistic views of the early 1960's and permit us to frame questions relating to work motivation in new and realistic fashions. More important, for our immediate purposes, they provide a framework we can use to evaluate the effectiveness of various forms of job redesign.

Job Redesign

The last few years have seen a growing interest in job redesign, a generic term covering efforts to restructure jobs so as to reduce dissatisfaction and increase productivity, especially in mass production industry. These efforts have been most widespread in Europe, where job redesign experiments at Saab, Volvo, Fiat, and Philipps have been widely publicized, and there have been attempts to develop "autonomous work" groups in Norway (Emery and Thorsrud, 1969) and Yugoslavia. In the United States, the best known work has been done at General Foods (Walton, 1972), AT&T (Ford, 1969), Texas Instruments (Roche and MacKinnon, 1970; Myers, 1970), Donnelly Mirrors, Prudential Insurance (Morse and Reimer, 1956), and Non-Linear Systems (Kuriloff, 1963; Business Week, 1973; Maslow, 1965). Among the best general discussions of these programs are in Dowling (1973), Walton (1974), and Davis and Taylor (1972).

Job redesign experiments have been generally confined to small plants (such as General Foods' Topeka, Kansas dog food plant with 100 employees) or single departments of larger organizations (e.g., a motor homes assembly line at General Motors). Even at Volvo, only a few work groups are involved. Luthans and Reif (1973) estimate that from 3 to 10 per cent of the workers in

Fortune 500 companies enjoy job enrichment, but these figures may be misleading. On the basis of Census data, Brown (in press) concludes that as of 1970 67 per cent of the work force was in occupations which already permitted significant discretion.

Before discussing job redesign programs in greater detail, let me stress two points: (1) despite Herzberg (1968), who argues that job enrichment should be restricted to providing motivators, most programs in practice combine both hygienes and motivators, and (2) most of the changes being adopted were prescribed by personnel books as early as the 1950's (Sayles, 1974). What is new is the better coordinated systems approach in *some* companies, the greater public interest, and perhaps a more adequate theoretical scheme for predicting what happens.

Most of the discussion has been focused on blue-collar work, although opportunities for job enrichment in clerical and professional work would seem to be greater. Changes in such jobs tend to be less costly; furthermore, managers, professionals, and white-collar workers generally are more expressive in their orientations and more likely to react favorably to the kinds of challenges job redesign provides.

THE NATURE OF JOB CHANGES

Terminology in the area is rather imprecise. Some authors refer to "job enrichment," others to "autonomous work groups" or "quality of work experiments." I have used the term "job redesign" with the hope that it is broad enough to cover them all. Whatever the terminology, the main experiments in this area have involved at least one (and usually a number) of the job changes listed below.

Job rotation permits workers to switch jobs (either in terms of a fixed schedule or on an ad hoc basis to cope with absenteeism or emergencies) without necessarily changing the character of these jobs. This most simple of reforms provides the worker more variety, both in his work and perhaps in his social relations. On the other hand, Herzberg (1968) has argued that two boring jobs are little better than one. Further, making frequent changes may interrupt the peace and quiet of the instrumentally oriented worker who has adjusted to daydreaming on the job.

Job enlargement adds elements to the job "horizontally," typically lengthening the work cycle, requiring additional skills, and providing a greater sense of accomplishment and task identity. At times, for example, a worker may be permitted to follow a job from beginning to end. Often this is accomplished by shortening the assembly line. Though there is evidence that lengthening a job cycle will raise job satisfaction and lower absenteeism for some workers (Walker and Guest, 1952), it is obvious that everyone has his own optimum job cycle (even professors wish to spend no more than two or three years per book). *Integrated work teams* permit the application of job enlargement principles at the group level, particularly where individual job enlargement is not feasible. Here, instead of work moving from A to B to C, as it might prior to job redesign, A, B, and C handle the job together from beginning to end.

Job enrichment (narrowly defined) adds "vertical," quasi-managerial job elements, especially those of planning, supply, and inspection, and thus adds to workers' control over their work and to their sense of autonomy. *Self-managing work teams* (sometimes called "autonomous work groups") involve a group form of job enrichment. Typically, such groups meet periodically to determine job assignments, schedule work breaks, and decide the rate, quality, and quantity of output. As Dowling (1973) has observed at Volvo, "the production team, a group of 5 to 12 men with a common work assignment, elects its own chargehand, schedules its own output within standards set by higher management, distributes work among its members, and is responsible for its own quality control" (p. 59), while at Saab-Scania, "the jobs of all members of the production group were enlarged by making them jointly responsible for simple service and maintenance activities, housekeeping, and quality control in their work area, duties formerly performed by staff personnel" (p. 56). At General Foods' Topeka dog food plant, production groups participate in hiring and firing employees. Other work groups have been given the responsibilities of developing relations with vendors, determining which operations can be handled individually and which by the group as a whole, training new employees, and at Non-Linear Systems, even keeping financial records. Indeed, job redesign may lead to some of the forms of formal participation discussed in Chapter Four.

Feedback mechanisms for providing more information are often introduced to individuals and work groups, both so that they can make the decisions that their new responsibilities require and to enhance their sense of accomplishment.

PSYCHOLOGICAL MECHANISMS AT WORK

In terms of path-goal analysis, job redesign should raise motivation in a number of ways, at least for some workers. First, by giving the employee greater freedom to determine how he will do his work, the relationship between effort and performance is strengthened. Secondly, by involving him in decision making, the value of effective performance is increased (because effective performance is viewed as a test of his decision-making abilities, at least to the extent he values these abilities). Third, by permitting him to set his own goals and by allowing him greater control over whether the goal is reached, his sense of accomplishment in reaching *his* goal is increased—and, therefore, his need for achievement (which may or may not be strong) is better met. In this way, in a Rube Goldberg fashion, his perceived relationship between performance and satisfaction is raised. Finally, because of more effective feedback, all of these relationships will be strengthened.

Hackman and Lawler (1969) describe the conditions required for effective job restructuring as follows:

> Individuals *who desire higher order need* satisfactions should be most likely to obtain them when they work effectively on meaningful jobs which provide feedback on the effectiveness of their personal work activities. To establish conditions for internal work motivation, then, it appears that a job must: (1) allow workers to feel personally responsible for an identifiable and meaningful portion of the work, (b) provide work outcomes which are intrinsically meaningful and otherwise perceived as worthwhile, and (c) provide feedback about performance effectiveness (pp. 262–263, emphasis added).

And, according to these authors, if the job is to meet the above requirements, it should rank high on four characteristics—variety, autonomy, task identity, and feedback— characteristics which most job redesign experiments attempt to provide. Note, however, the underlined words in the Hackman and Lawler quotation. The motivational forces listed above operate primarily when workers desire higher order needs and their orientation toward work is expressive.

Socio-technical change. Job redesign may satisfy more than egoistic or self-actualization needs, however (Sayles, 1974). New and more effective social and workflow relations are introduced (hence the term "socio-technical systems," applied to this area by Emery and Trist, 1960, and Davis, 1971). (1) Small, highly cohesive work groups are established; these work groups typically are considerably smaller (only 4–18 members) than the large departments they partially replace. Not only do members participate in group production decisions, but group pressures force individuals to adhere to these decisions. (2) Groups are given "whole tasks," workflow relations and communications are improved, and the number of friction-causing interfaces reduced. (3) There are substantial changes in worker-management relations. The work group assumes many of the responsibilities of foremen and staff; strawbosses (this role is sometimes rotated among group members) take on new importance. In any case, such participation permits informal leaders to reinforce their position: they enhance their status both by taking a leading part in making decisions and through inducing group members to abide by them.

Hygienes. The best publicized job restructuring experiments have also been accompanied by important hygienes. Indeed, some might argue that these hygienes have a more significant impact on job attitudes than any changes in job design themselves. These hygienes have begun to reduce what UAW Vice-President Bluestone (1974) calls "the double standard that exists between workers and management. . . . Workers challenge the symbols of elitism traditionally taken for granted, such as salary payment versus hourly payment; time clocks for blue-collar workers; well-decorated dining rooms for white-collar workers versus plain, Spartan-like cafeterias for blue-collar workers; privileged parking for the elite, but catch-as-you-can parking for workers" (p. 47).

At General Foods' Topeka dog food plant, for instance, there are no reserved parking lots, no time clocks, and no differentiation in decor between management offices and worker lounges. Most important perhaps, workers in at least one department are free to make phone calls on company time (Schrank, 1974). Such reductions in status differentials not only tend to reduce dissatisfaction, they also help an atmosphere of trust and confidence to develop between workers and management, and, to some extent, they lead to a covert renegotiation of the previously discussed "implicit bargain." Thus, a "fair day's work" may mean much more than it previously did.

All of the above suggests that successful job redesign involves more than changes in individual jobs. Socio-technical systems are altered and important hygienes introduced. Further, as we shall see below, system-wide changes in organizational structure and processes are required.

WIDER ORGANIZATIONAL CHANGES

Job redesign is unlikely to be effective unless accompanied by congruent changes in other aspects of organizational life (Walton, 1974). It is especially important that the method by which the plan is introduced be consistent with the plan's general philosophy (see Chapter Seven). In some companies, the job redesign plan is drawn up by higher management or a special staff group, with the newly improved jobs being imposed on workers whether they (or their unions) like it or not. In a sense, this involves using Theory X techniques to reach Theory Y objectives. The limited evidence suggests that job restructuring will be more successful if those involved help plan it and retain the freedom to opt out, either individually or as a group. (Indeed, the suggestion has been made that the conventional assembly line should be continued alongside autonomous work groups, with workers permitted to choose between the two kinds of work.)

Changes in supervisory behavior are also required. Fewer first-line supervisors will be needed, and those who remain must learn to let subordinates make decisions for themselves. Equivalent adjustments are required in higher management and in the organizational climate generally. The locus of decision making must be lowered; even budget and control systems need revamping (Argyris, 1972). Continued top management support is required, especially during periods of crisis when the temptation to withdraw subordinate discretion is particularly strong. Pressures for short-term savings (e.g., through layoffs) should be avoided as much as possible. Many managers find changes of this magnitude difficult to make, and some must be replaced (Walton, 1974); a full-scale Organization Development program may be required (see Chapter Seven).

It is difficult to introduce a radically new job redesign program in one department without affecting others. A self-managing work team in a toy factory worked so hard that it disrupted the work flow of the factory as a whole and obtained incentive earnings so high as to disrupt the entire plant's social structure (Whyte, 1956). Cohesive, highly motivated work groups may make demands on management which it may not be prepared to grant, especially with regard to compensation.

The literature says little about whether workers get paid more for their special efforts; most companies apparently feel that increased satisfaction and more interesting work should be reward enough. This has been a sore point in a few cases (e.g., Hill, 1971) with workers, not surprisingly, arguing that their harder work and higher productivity should be reflected in their paychecks—and management being very hesitant to upset sensitive interdepartmental pay relationships. Effective resolution of this problem may require something like the Scanlon Plan (see Chapter Four), but such a plan is difficult to introduce on a single-department basis.

All of the above problems may explain why some of the most successful job redesign programs have been introduced in small new plants which are removed from the contaminating influences of the larger and more traditional parent organization. The problems involved in introducing major work structure changes in large organizations are immense—as are those of extending successful experiments from the small departments in which they started (where conditions for experimental success may have been greatest) to the larger organization.

THE ROLE OF THE UNION

No consideration of job redesign should ignore the role of the union. Unions in the United States find the issue of job redesign fuzzy and hard to deal with, and management has generally taken the lead in this area. The labor movement has been accused of being so single-mindedly concerned with satisfying physical and security needs that it has been insufficiently responsive to workers' egoistic and self-actualization needs. Management, it is alleged, has kept more up to date.

The quasi-official AFL-CIO position (as presented in the *Federationist*) is quite suspicious of the entire job enrichment movement, viewing it as a form of manipulation and speedup and an attempt to divert attention from more important problems such as wages, job security, and safety. The *Federationist,* however, may portray labor as having a more closed mind than it actually has. To be sure, the problem of worker dissatisfaction is difficult to handle through traditional adversary techniques. As Nat Goldfinger of the AFL-CIO has been quoted, "A union demand is a negotiable demand which, if not satisfied, can be met by a strike. How can we talk about these other questions in terms of a negotiable demand and a possible strike?" (Jenkins, 1974, p. 317). Yet, privately, many labor leaders agree that work alienation does present a problem which their union has an obligation to help solve. The recent UAW agreements have established joint union-management committees to sponsor research in this area and "commits both sides to seek joint answers to the difficult questions of job enrichment" (United Automobile Workers, 1973). The chief objection of many unions is to changes being unilaterally introduced.

European unions have been far more willing to take the initiative in job restructuring than have those in the U.S., in many cases because of strong ideological commitments to increased power sharing. In any case, it can be argued that job redesign programs will never be successful without greater worker participation generally and that this, in turn, is impossible without increased openness and trust between workers and management (which can be obtained best when workers have the security of a union contract). Finally, I agree with Bok and Dunlop (1970) that unions have a moral obligation to be concerned with the psychological meaning of work to their members.

EVALUATION OF JOB REDESIGN EXPERIMENTS

How successful have job redesign projects been to date? Aside from the work of Lawler (1969), Dowling (1973), Walton (1974),

Morse and Reimer (1956), and Hulin and Blood (1968), most of the writing in this field has been devoted to describing and often extolling individual experiments rather than carefully evaluating their results. Successes are more widely publicized than failures, and, frequently, reports are written by the very consultants who introduced job restructuring—hardly unbiased observers.

Rigorous research in this field is difficult. Companies are loath to admit independent outside observers, particularly if their reports are not subject to editorial control. Outside observers often complicate already complicated situations. Adequate control groups (to be compared with the experimental groups) are difficult to find. Perhaps action research (see Chapter Three) is especially appropriate here, but the results of action research are difficult to evaluate or compare.

The U.S. studies have involved chiefly small, nonunion plants. Workers in some situations have been carefully selected (at the Topeka dog food plant, 70 applicants were accepted out of 600; at Shell in England, 156 out of 3,000). Furthermore, the success at some of the plants was undoubtedly influenced by widespread favorable publicity and an influx of distinguished visitors. And even if one can demonstrate success in one situation, comparisons between situations are difficult to make since "experimental sites" differ greatly in terms of their technologies, the nature of the work force, and the kinds of changes introduced. Thus, the most the research can tell us is that job restructuring worked in a given situation, not that it will necessarily work well elsewhere.

Ignoring these problems, what do the available reports tell us? Turnover and absenteeism have generally gone down. Quality has improved, sometimes dramatically, and satisfaction, to the extent that it has been measured, has increased. As for production, there is more question. Ford (1969) and Herzberg (1968) report positive results. Only six of ten early U.S. studies report higher productivity, though all report higher quality (Lawler, 1969). Productivity at the automated and job-restructured Topeka dog food plant is much higher than at its traditional counterpart in Kankakee, but Topeka has a much higher capital investment per man. On the basis of his European studies, Dowling (1973) concludes that the greatest productivity gains from job restructuring seem to accrue chiefly from reducing the rigidity of the assembly line. Since the work force is more flexible (and work flow relations are less complex), a single bottleneck is less likely to disrupt the entire production process and line balancing is simpler. Technological change is easier to introduce, and cost savings result because fewer first-line supervisors and staff personnel are required. On the other hand, less effective use can be made of special purpose equipment.

Ironically, although job restructuring has been presented as a motivator, in practice it may work more like a hygiene. Turnover, absenteeism, and satisfaction have improved. But as far as production is concerned, the clearest gain seems to be that the work force is more flexible, not that it is more highly motivated.

One limitation of most of the published reports is a failure to take into account cultural and personality variables. Hackman and Lawler's (1971) study of individual workers concludes that job enrichment factors (variety, autonomy, task identity, and feedback) are satisfying and motivating chiefly to those who are desirous of higher order need satisfaction. Yet, as we have seen earlier, a large proportion of the work force seems to be instrumental in its orientation. Indeed, I suspect that for many workers control over work time may be more attractive than control over the work itself.

Control over work time. Unions and managements are acting as if they believed that workers' primary demands are not for improvements in the nature of their work, but for greater freedom to leave it. Some inroads have been made in the traditional concept of a 8 a.m.–4 p.m. workday, a five-day week, and retirement at age 65.

The four-day week (with ten hours of work a day) was the first to catch public attention, but this seems to have been less widely adopted than other forms of "flex-time." A number of companies have given their employees the freedom to decide when they want to come to work, the length of their lunch hours, whether to take other breaks (e.g., to see a dentist), and even how long their total work week should be—of course, all within specified limits. Women's Lib groups have gone even further: they have demanded that employees be permitted to decide how many weeks they want to work each year and that doubling arrangements be permitted, for example, so that two employees could hold the same job, with each working six months a year or four hours a day. For the most part, these changes have occurred in clerical, professional, and quasi-managerial jobs, where the number of women (with their special family needs) are greatest and where work flow can be relatively easily adjusted to special schedules. (However, the extent of any of these changes to date should not be exaggerated. See Hedges, 1973.)

Blue-collar workers seemingly have shown less interest in such changes (and indeed some unions have insisted that any deviations from the standard work week be compensated by overtime or other penalty payments). Nevertheless, the demand for voluntary overtime played a major role in recent UAW negotiations, many unions have won voluntary retirement rights at ages considerably below 65, and the proposed pension reform bill would provide vested pension rights under some circumstances, thus making it easier for workers to change jobs altogether.

The demand for flex-time has been largely associated with the growing number of women in the work force. It certainly helps eliminate Bluestone's "double standard" between workers and management. It gives workers considerably more control over their work life (it is nice to know that one *can* change his work hours or refuse overtime, even when one does not take advantage of this right). Further, it may represent a changing life style which downgrades work as a source of job satisfaction. Most important—for the purpose of this paper—it should be viewed as a major (and possibly more fruitful) alternative to job redesign as a form of work place reform.

Conclusions

Widespread public attention has been given recently to allegedly mounting job dissatisfaction and to the possible means of alleviating it. In turn, this has lead to increasing concern with questions relating to the determinants of job satisfaction and motivation, as well as to job design. To date, there is relatively little attitudinal or behavioral evidence that worker dissatisfaction has increased in this country. (The situation may be different in Europe where there have been great difficulties in keeping mass production factories fully manned.) At the most, we see some slight upward shift in preferences for more challenging work.

By and large, it is fair to conclude that most blue-collar workers—and perhaps many white-collar workers as well— (1) would prefer some increase in challenge and autonomy in their jobs, or would learn to like these if they had them, but (2) are not prepared to give up much in the way of material benefits, at least at the moment, to obtain challenge and autonomy, nor (3) would they give higher priority to challenge and autonomy than to various hygienes such as higher pay, safety, flex-time, voluntary overtime, and the like. Instrumental orientation is quite widespread and most workers have adjusted to the nature of their jobs in one way or another (through recreation and social life on or off the job, through union activity, through heightened concern for their family, etc.).

Argyris (1964) argues that adjustment of this sort is essentially unstable. Workers' ability to tolerate "meaningless" work is not unlimited, and such adjustments will be increasingly difficult to maintain, especially as our educational levels and standards of living go up and our national values change. Eventually there may be a breaking point, and some observers (myself excluded) see signs of this already.

Can we ever expect workers to find self-actualization on an assembly line or in a dog food factory (Schrank, 1974)? I doubt it. But most people would like a little more control over their lives, and job redesign may help provide this—but so does flex-time. Job redesign may make the job a little more easy to take. Further, the forms of redesign we have discussed represent a more efficient use of manpower in many cases (apart and beyond any questions of satisfaction or motivation). For these reasons, I would encourage job redesign experiments, hopefully with union participation.

Job satisfaction, motivation, and job redesign—none of these can be meaningfully discussed apart from supervision. One of worker's primary demands is for fair supervision; supervision itself can be both a motivator and a hygiene; and job design, as we have seen, is directly related to supervisory style. All these issues—and more—are discussed in the next chapter.

CHAPTER 3

Supervision

J. B. RITCHIE
Brigham Young University

At a recent management development program, I was talking with an individual who really supervises in contrast to those of us who mainly talk and write about it. This middle-level executive said he had recently enjoyed reading *The Peter Prescription* (Peter, 1972) because it was straightforward and understandable compared with the confusing material he usually encountered in the area of leadership and supervision. My experience suggests that this critical viewpoint is shared by a substantial number of managers, administrators, union leaders, and students, in addition to many academicians. In fact, supervision may be the "most researched and least understood" of all organizational concepts (Filley and House, 1969, p. 391). Nevertheless, there are many who claim that they do have a successful philosophy of supervision for which they cite supporting evidence in speeches, writings, and financial reports (e.g., see Ford, 1969; Meyer, 1972; Marrow, 1972; Chaney and Teel, 1972; and Goble, 1972).

From the volume and variety of writings on supervision, the large number of supervisory training programs, and the persisting interest of academicians and practitioners, it is clear that supervision is both an important and complex phenomenon—important because of the presumed impact of supervision on organizational performance and complex because of its continued resistance to clear-cut prescriptions.

Thus there is plenty of incentive for managers and administrators to search for better ways to supervise. Obviously, there will be a high payoff for anyone who establishes a convincing relationship between supervisory behavior and certain dimensions of organizational effectiveness.

This chapter is organized into seven major sections. First, there is a brief consideration of some conceptual and methodological issues associated with the study of supervision. Next, in succeeding sections, the topics of supervisory style, attitudes, and context are discussed. After this, a comment on a related aspect of supervision—the notion of organization climate—is followed by a discussion of some policy questions which subsume supervisory issues. Finally, the implications and conclusions of this review are presented. In order not to lead the reader astray, however, let me note at the outset that my intent is not to be exhaustive in the discussion, but rather to highlight major trends and issues.

CONCEPTS, METHODS, AND ISSUES IN SUPERVISION RESEARCH

In the most fundamental sense, the supervisory role is to mobilize human and material resources in the accomplishment of a task. The human aspect of this activity is usually considered under the topic of leadership, an issue about which most people hold strong assumptions. Based on these normative leadership assumptions, individuals feel that they know how a supervisor *ought* to think and behave as he interacts with his subordinates. This means that we must recognize the presence of many subjective biases as we look at attempts to define and measure supervision.

Historical perspectives. Over time, the study of supervision has steadily shifted its emphasis, from an early focus on individual traits, to the analysis of superior-subordinate relationships (supervisory "style"), and, finally, to a "systems" approach where the supervisor is viewed as only one part of a larger organizational process.

Early leadership studies focused on traits of the leader, the dominant theme being an attempt to identify personality characteristics of a "good" supervisor. Napoleon's argument that "there are no bad regiments, only bad colonels" had its counterpart in the logic that "there are no bad work groups, only bad supervisors." Stogdill's (1948) review of the personality trait studies indicated that while some demographic, cognitive, and behavioral characteristics might be related to supervisory effectiveness, the findings were so general and inconsistent that their usefulness was limited. More recent studies (see Campbell, *et al.,* 1970; Ghiselli, 1971) confirm the view that successful managers are likely to possess certain personality characteristics, but these characteristics are individual rather than organizational (i.e., personality criteria may predict who will be promoted, but they fail to adequately predict whether a manager will be effective in leading subordinates).

Realizing the limitations of predicting performance solely in terms of supervisory personality, researchers switched their emphasis to finding an optimal supervisory "style." It was reasoned that although individual supervisors differ from one another, they could learn all the "principles" of supervision—the *one best way* to behave so as to achieve maximum output and subordinate satisfaction. The "human relations" programs of the 1940's and 1950's are monuments to this crusade.

As confusing and sometimes contradictory results were observed with the "optimal" supervisory style, it became apparent that one style of supervision might be effective with a given set of subordinates while the same style in different circumstances might lead to low performance. This realization has culminated in the situational or contingency approach to supervision, which argues that appropriate supervisory strategies are a function of many different factors: (a) characteristics of the supervisor, (b) characteristics of subordinates, (c) the nature of the task, (d) organization structure and climate, and (e) even the external environment of the organization.

While the object of supervisory studies was taking on a broader perspective, so also was the content. Although investigators moved beyond the early attempts to measure the personality traits of supervisors, the newer research was still dominated by a constricting reliance on such dichotomous characterizations of supervisory behavior as autocratic-democratic, authoritarian-participative, etc. Part of this logic assumed that the supervisor was interested in either people *or* productivity. Subsequent work suggested that he might be interested in neither, or both, and that attention to the quality of relationships among his subordinates and between them and the technical and coordinative demands of their job might be important aspects of supervisory style. Moreover, there is now a growing sophistication in identifying the multivariate components of the context of the supervisor-subordinate relationship which are essential to understanding performance and satisfaction. In fact, in many respects the development of the concept of organization climate (the surrounding complex of reporting relationships, policies, rules, procedures, etc.) has evolved from the failure of a simple model of supervision to predict subordinate behavior or organizational effectiveness.

As the input variables have changed, however, so has the concept of appropriate output measures. At first, the test of supervisory effectiveness was the short-term satisfaction or performance of his subordinates. It then became obvious that most organizations must have the potential to function in subsequent time periods. It is not enough to conclude that a certain strategy leads to good results today; an equally significant question is, what is the supervisor doing to the work group's ability to change or adapt in a manner to be productive tomorrow? This belief contributed to the "systems" emphasis which increasingly characterizes supervision research today—the idea that superior-subordinate relations represent only a single aspect of the dynamic organizational system.

Alternative research methods. The study of supervision has been characterized by at least five primary research methods, each having made important contributions: (1) field studies, (2) laboratory experiments, (3) field experiments, (4) survey research, and (5) action research. *Field studies* (e.g., Lawrence, 1958; Whyte, 1948) involve observing the behavior of supervisors in action. Here the researcher can identify numerous dimensions of supervisory behavior, thus enabling him to learn a great deal about the specific situations being studied. From such studies, many hypotheses have been generated for further research. However, obtaining meaningful access to on-going operations is difficult. Moreover, the complexity of real organizational relationships, the lack of controls, and observer bias make it extremely difficult to establish cause-effect relationships. Field studies, therefore, tend to be an important but limited step in an overall research program.

The popularity of *laboratory experiments,* of course, flows from the ease of controlling variables in a contrived or simulated setting (Litwin and Stringer, 1968; Lowin, Hrapchak, and Kavanagh, 1969). The researcher does not have to wait for things to happen as he does in the field, but, on the other hand, he misses the richness of on-going superior-subordinate behavior. While a great deal of information can be collected in a short time period, the significance of long-term effects, so crucial in organization, is lacking in lab studies. However, the laboratory is an excellent place to further test and elaborate on questions and hypotheses developed in field studies.

Most research strategies would suggest the potential value of *field experimentation* (e.g., Morse and Reimer, 1956), where a limited number of changes (usually one or two, such as a change in reporting relationships, increased skill resulting from training, modification of work design, a new supervisor, etc.) are introduced in order to study their effects in a natural setting. The intent, of course, is to limit the changes to those variables which are to be studied, but seldom does one know what else is changing. There is a greater possibility of identifying cause-effect relationships than in field studies but still not the precision of a laboratory experiment. The long-term studies at Harwood Manufacturing (Marrow, Bowers, and Seashore, 1967; Marrow, 1972) have provided rich research insights, but the cost in terms of time and effort has been high, and many important questions remain unanswered and unanswerable.

Survey research uses questionnaires or interviews to collect a large amount of data for comparative purposes (e.g., Bowers and Seashore, 1966). This approach is one of the most commonly used because data can be collected quickly and the form of the information lends itself to a multitude of statistical analyses. Furthermore, this approach can be employed in a variety of field and laboratory situations along with other means of data collection. It should be noted, however, that one of the strengths of this approach can also become a weakness. The ability to collect, store, and perform complex analysis on large amounts of data means that we can identify relationships previously beyond our computational ability. However, simply improving the mechanics of data analysis does not insure good research, and I see an increasing need to guard against the pitfall of substituting elegant data manipulation for careful and innovative conceptualization and measurement. The precision and finality of average satisfaction or output measures or correlation coefficients mask the very subjective nature of the concepts and measurements which form the basis of the analysis. The question of what to measure is much more complex than many of our questionnaires imply.

The last research approach, *action research,* is the most recent in terms of its application and use. Action research (e.g., Argyris, 1971) is a form of field experimentation where the purpose is to improve the organization by using the data that are collected; the organization being studied participates in determining the nature of the experiment as well as the kinds of data that will be employed to measure the experiment's success. A positive aspect of this emphasis is the inherent design of before-after measurement over a period of organization change. However, with the explicit emphasis of action over research, long-term research findings may give way to short-term exigencies. On balance, though, I believe we stand to benefit considerably from the increased use of action research where both researcher and organization members have an interest in measuring and understanding changes in supervisory, climate, and organizational variables.

Research difficulties. Research on supervision is beset with difficulties and unresolved dilemmas. Consider the following:

1. Likert (1967) has suggested that one variable which should receive increased research attention is that of *time*. He argues that cross-sectional measurements of organizational variables (i.e., measurements taken at a single point in time) neglect the lag between the change in supervisory behavior, subsequent changes in organizational climate, and, finally, subordinate reactions to these changes. In the absence of measurements over time, we must assume that measures of supervisory behavior or climate taken at one point in time were either representative of these influences over an extended period or that their effects were instantaneous. While cross-sectional methods may be relatively economical and convenient compared to longitudinal studies, we should realize that variables which imply one kind of relationship in the short run may imply quite another kind of relationship when a longer time framework is employed (Marrow, 1972). To take one example: authoritarian supervision may lead to production increases in the short run but not necessarily in the long run (Morse and Reimer, 1956).

2. Especially in survey research it is difficult to discriminate between "real" attitudes, socially desirable answers (usually assumed desirable to the boss), climate, and supervisory behavior. Dimensions of the problem are reflected in the limited evidence which establishes a simple or direct link between attitudes and behavior (Michaelson, 1972), the inconsistent perceptions of superiors and subordinates (Miles, 1964), and conflicting reports of a supervisor's behavior from his superior and subordinates (Nealey and Owen, 1970). While these situations provide interesting an-

alytical possibilities of their own, they also suggest limitations when using data generated from one research method.

3. A third issue is the criterion problem: what do we measure in determining effectiveness? The following example illustrates this problem: according to French *et al.* (1960), "the pioneering study by Lewin, Lippitt, and White (1939) revealed that children showed better interpersonal relations, higher morale, and greater productivity under a democratic style of leadership than in an autocratic atmosphere" (p. 3). In contrast, Vroom (1964) comments on the same study by saying that "the highest level of productivity occurred under autocratic leadership" (p. 221). These conflicting conclusions come about because of the different criteria used to evaluate productivity, including the time unit employed.

4. When a study demonstrates a relationship between supervisory behavior and subordinate performance, what is the direction of causality? For example, does democratic supervision cause high performance, or is democratic behavior a luxury permitted only supervisors whose subordinates are already highly productive? Consistent with the latter direction of causality, Goodstadt (1970) presents evidence which indicates that work groups which are effective (for whatever reason) will elicit general supportive behavior by superiors while a less effective unit will generate close supervision. On the other hand, Livingston (1969) suggests that a superior's behavior and expectations will condition the attitudes and behavior of subordinates and thereby lead to performance consistent with these expectations. (It should be recognized, of course, that this "pygmalion" argument can go both ways—subordinates' expectations might also condition supervisory behavior.)

5. In recent years, a new problem has surfaced: resistance to being researched. A high percentage of American managers has been associated with research either as subjects or in management development programs where research data were discussed. Some managers report incidents where they felt research data were used against them, and clearly there are many who do not believe that "all responses will remain completely confidential." There are organizations (and some whole communities) where the standard response is, "We've been researched to death" (with an implied, if not stated, feeling that little was accomplished). While I think

that much of this suspicion is unjustified, and the majority of managers are very cooperative in paticipating in research projects, there is an increasing need for researchers and executives to insure that false expectations are not created and that confidences are carefully maintained.

With these introductory remarks and caveats, let me now turn to some of the main research findings on supervision.

SUPERVISORY STYLE

The pivotal research that reflected the evolution from an emphasis on supervisory traits to a concern with overall organization climate began in the 1940's at the University of Michigan and at Ohio State University. For many years, the primary focus was on supervisory attitudes and behaviors with respect to *people* and *productivity*. But this raised the question of whether supervision should be measured along a *single* continuum with employee-centered (people) style at one end and task centered (production) on the other—or should each be considered a separate dimension? And are these two variables the only ones of importance? If not, what other dimensions should be considered?

The emphasis on people-productivity dimensions derives in part from the Lewin, Lippitt, and White (1939) leadership studies, which may have gotten the field off to a false start. While an important contribution, their classification scheme (an authoritarian-democratic-laissez faire continuum based on the degree of subordinate participation in decision making) provided the rationale for an oversimplified model of the complex supervisory role. This classification suggested that the authoritarian supervisor was interested primarily in production, and the democratic supervisor primarily in people. In retrospect, of course, it is easy to question why a democratic supervisor could not be interested in both production *and* people, but the scheme was nevertheless very compelling.

The Michigan studies. As part of the early Michigan research on supervisory effectiveness, Likert (1961) compared employee-centered against job centered supervisory styles, finding that supervisors who were employee-centered generally led work groups that had both higher production and greater employee satisfaction than did work groups under job-centered supervisors. (This employee emphasis was part of the human relations orientation discussed in Chapter One.) Mann's (1965) revised formulation included a mixture of technical and administrative skills in addition to the human relations skills. An optimum mix of skills in Mann's theory depended on the particular situation; for example, moving from higher to lower organizational levels, administrative skills may become less important and human relations skills more important. Or, in periods of organizational transition, technical skills seem to be valued more by subordinates, while in more stable periods human relations skills are more appropriate.

In 1966, Bowers and Seashore introduced a four-factor theory which implied that the effective supervisor not only provided psychological support, but also stressed the achievement of work group goals, facilitated interaction among group members, and provided members with the resources necessary to do an effective job. This notion is consistent with Likert's (1967) well known System I-IV conceptualization—exploitive authoritative (I), benevolent authoritative (II), consultative (III), and participative group (IV)—which classified the supervisory context *and* style along a number of dimensions which are presumed to affect performance (see Chapter Four).

The Likert framework has clearly gone beyond any simple classification of supervisory style. His emphasis on causal-intermediate-end result variables introduced a time sequence where effects are not presumed to occur immediately but influence other intermediate variables (effective group functioning) which in turn affect end results (performance). Likert's concept of the linking-pin function of supervisors—whereby the supervisor provides the key link between his own work group and the other groups with which he interacts—implied that it was important to consider not just the superior-subordinate relationship but also the integration of organizational parts. Also, his human asset accounting approach indicated a broader definition of organizational resources, including a computation of the financial investment in human assets. Even though the Michigan models may be incomplete (Mott, 1972), they represent an important theoretical contribution with an evolving explanation of the complex role of supervisory behavior.

The Ohio State studies. Developments in the Ohio State Leadership Studies (Fleishman, Harris, and Burtt, 1955; Stogdill and Coons, 1957) did not move through the same stages as those at Michigan. The attempt to develop a theory based on many observations of leadership functions resulted in a broader view than the authoritarian-democratic classification. The extensive Ohio State investigations ultimately identified two primary components of the supervisory role: *Consideration* (a genuine feeling of warmth and trust with subordinates) and *Initiating Structure* (an emphasis on goals and production).

The many attempts at replication of the Ohio State model have produced enough supporting evidence to indicate that important dimensions have been identified, but there is reason to believe that these two factors alone fail to explain performance. Also, Kavanagh (1972) has questioned the independence of the constructs (see Korman, 1966, for an early review of this research). Lesage (1973) has modified the Ohio State framework, arguing that both Consideration and Initiating Structure need to be broken down into two separate components, one relating to attitude and the other to supervisory style.

Fiedler. Fiedler (1967; Fiedler and Chemers, 1974) has made a major theoretical and empirical contribution with his "contingency model" which states that the appropriate leadership style in a given situation is a function of (a) leader-member relations, (b) task structure, and (c) position power. The combination of these variables (which are listed in order of importance) determine the "favorableness of the situation" in which the supervisor must lead. When the situation is relatively favorable, the supervisor will be more effective if he exerts a leadership style which is high on interpersonal emphasis; if the situation is unfavorable, he will be better off if his style emphasizes task considerations. Leadership style in turn is based on a measure—LPC—which is derived from the supervisor's evaluation of his "Least Preferred Coworker." If he evaluates the Least Preferred Coworker relatively high, the supervisor is presumed to have a personality which emphasizes interpersonal relations; if his LPC evaluation is low the supervisor is presumably task oriented. The underlying logic for this concept remains a mystery, but Fiedler stands on his evidence.

For Fiedler, then, the people-productivity classification is not a characterization of style, but in his argument it does become a personality trait which interacts with other variables. As with other theories, limitations of the "contingency model" have been argued (Graen, *et al.*, 1970), and there is some inconsistent evidence regarding the use of the LPC questionnaire instrument (Reilly, 1968; Sashkin, 1972).

The Managerial Grid. Still another effort to reconcile the people-productivity issue was the Managerial Grid developed by Blake and Mouton (1964). They argued that the two styles (concern for people and concern for production) are not mutually exclusive and, in fact, are both important in determining performance. On their Grid, concern for people *and* production scores are plotted separately on two independent scales from one to nine. This logic reflects a model where concern with either dimension can be high or low in various combinations.

Limitations of the concept of supervisory style. In spite of the contributions noted above, the primary overall classification scheme employed by many individuals is still some version of the people *vs.* productivity continuum. Clearly, some theories die hard, and in a sense I think we have created a straw man. While I am sure that good supervisors were never really unconcerned with productivity, the human relations emphasis did provide a rationale for the dichotomy.

A precise assessment of this area is difficult because of the changing models and mixed results. However, it does seem to me that more has been expected of the models than is reasonable. Though many useful dimensions of supervisory behavior have been identified, they do not constitute the total framework. None of the models has consistently predicted performance or satisfaction, although satisfaction has a much better record (Yukl, 1971). But I would ask: Why should these models be expected to be so all encompassing? The question is not whether the model *always* predicts an outcome but rather the conditions under which it does. Most constructs are only partial descriptions of the supervisory role, more predictive in one situation than another, but not universal. Fiedler (1973) makes a most cogent observation: "We must stop searching for a direct link between human relations skills or job skills and leadership performance" (p. 92).

A good deal of the confusion which arises out of the use of the supervisory style concept has to do with the failure to make a distinction between *attitudes* (what the supervisor believes, or says he believes) and *strategy* (how he interacts with subordinates to accomplish the task). There is evidence that what the supervisor *really believes* is crucial in the explanation of superior-subordinate interaction and is more important than what he says or how he behaves.

Attitudes toward participation. Nowhere is this confusion between attitudes and strategy more obvious and significant than in the area of participation. As Leavitt (1973) suggests, participation is one of two concepts (the other being the group) providing the major focus for the field of organization behavior. "The idea of participation as a principle of organization has produced exciting and spectacular results," Schultz (1951, p. 201) puts it, and his optimistic approach is typical. In many respects, the history of the field can be traced in terms of testing and refinement of the concept of participation, as more and more qualifications were placed on the hypothesis that participative supervisory leadership is the single determinant of work group effectiveness. (A more cynical description might be that this process involves "a sequence of defensive retreats.")

The criticism of democratic supervision has often centered around what was assumed to be an implied recommendation for a "quantity theory"—the more the better—of participation (Miles and Ritchie, 1971). Often, the argument is linked to the assumption that McGregor's (1960) Theory Y provided a justification for participative management under every circumstance. This belief in a linear relationship between participation and effectiveness or satisfaction was most unfortunate and, I might add, a misrepresentation of McGregor.

McGregor (1967, p. 79) tried to qualify what many were claiming to be his advocacy of a universal supervisory style:

Theory X and Theory Y are *not* managerial strategies. They are underlying beliefs about the nature of man that *influence* managers to adopt one strategy rather than another. In fact, depending upon other characteristics of the manager's view of reality and upon the particular situation in which he finds himself, a manager who holds beliefs that I called Theory X could adopt a considerable array of strategies, some of which would be typically called "hard" and some of which would be called "soft." The same is true with respect to Theory Y.

Attitudes and strategies. Extending McGregor's point, I would suggest two dimensions of the supervisory role which need to be differentiated. (1) Supervisory *attitudes* include a set of assumptions about the nature of individual behavior, a self-image, and components of interpersonal relationships. This variable may be influenced by demographic considerations, experience, and to some extent the current organizational environment. (2) *Strategy* concerns the means employed by the supervisor in making decisions and directing his subordinates. While the first variable is basically a property of the individual, strategy is more a function of the situation. Attitudes are (a) important in determining the supervisor-subordinate relationship and (b) an input to the strategy which a supervisor might follow in a given situation. Strategy will vary depending on such factors as technology, organizational level, location of information, time constraints, interdependence with other groups, skills and expectations of subordinates, union contracts, etc. Attitudes tend to remain constant, at least over the short run.

There is evidence that supervisory attitudes and strategies, while not completely independent, must be recognized as separate inputs to the supervisory process. For example, attitude may be more important than strategy in subordinate satisfaction (Ritchie and Miles, 1970), but both need to be accounted for in performance (Wofford, 1971). It should be expected (and, in fact, it is the case) that attitudinal or objective measures of participation would be more consistently correlated with subordinate satisfaction than with subordinate performance (Yukl, 1971; French and Caplin, 1972). Predicting performance involves a much more complex set of situational variables, and, therefore, participation would be expected to explain a smaller part of the variance (Lowin, 1968). Vroom (1973) has suggested that, "It makes more sense to talk about participative and autocratic situations than it does to talk about participative and autocratic managers" (p. 77).

These criticisms of the "quality theory" of participation have led to a broadening of the definition of participation. Rather than the number of decisions where subordinates are consulted or have final choice, participation now usually refers to an overall degree of individual *influence* in organizational processes. An important contribution to this expanded definition was Tannenbaum's (1968) treatment of control. The logic and evidence that control (or influence, or participation) is not a zero-sum game means that everyone can exert more. In other words, each member can have more impact on the direction of the organization by increasing the total control of the system. However, while participation may increase everybody's discretion, it may also increase the amount of control or influence to which they are subjected. (See Chapter Four for further discussion of formal participation.)

While it appears that current trends are toward a more careful formulation of participation theories, I find the message reaching few managers. Many are still hearing and responding to the oversimplified recommendation of "soft management" as the solution to all of their problems. Understandably, there is a strong urge to resist this recommendation.

One explanation of the situation seems to lie in the "human relations" barrage which hit students and managers for so many years. Miles (1965) claimed that we were sold the form without the substance of effective supervision. Human relations was too often preached and perceived as a means to squeeze more work out of subordinates by engaging in a form of "industrial courtesy." The essence of the problem is that supervisors advocate a democratic supervisory style while at the same time doubting their subordinates' ability to make effective contributions. Pseudo-democracy of this sort may subvert attempts to develop a productive superior-subordinate relationship (Marrow, 1972). This contradiction is found not only in samples of American managers, where participative management has been so widely preached, but also in international studies (Haire, Ghiselli, and Porter, 1966; Clark and McCabe, 1970). Cummings and Schmidt (1972), in a study of Greek managers, conclude that their results "confirm the cross-country generality of managers subscribing to participative management practices, even though they are doubtful of the capacities of their subordinates to participate meaningfully" (p. 271).

In an earlier review of this topic, Strauss (1970) attempted to place the issue in historical perspective by suggesting that in the 1950's there was substantial agreement among academicians regarding the existence of a model of effective supervision: general rather than close, people-centered rather than production-centered, considerate rather than arbitrary, and participative rather than authoritarian. Even though empirical evidence was limited, there was a firm belief that future research would validate the model. This may have resulted in the model being oversold. In retrospect, I would argue that although the model as then described was a bit oversimplified, it was primarily its interpretation and the extensive demands placed on it that caused problems.

While participation is not a panacea, there is good evidence that when attitudes and conditions are appropriate, it can have a substantial impact on both satisfaction and performance. Some of the variable conditions which contribute to greater effectiveness of participation are as follows:

1. The degree to which subordinates have relevant skills and information (Marrow, 1972; Maier, 1965; Coch and French, 1948; Fleishman, 1958; Vroom and Yetton, 1973).
2. The degree to which subordinates perceive that their involvement will affect outcomes (Pelz, 1952; Lammers, 1967; Patchen, 1970; Kavcic, 1971; Yukl, 1971).
3. The degree to which subordinates are motivated to participate and thereby achieve outcomes (Alutto and Belasco, 1972; Maier, 1965; Vroom, 1959; Baumgartel, 1956; Fleishman, 1958; McClelland, 1961).
4. The greater the feeling of legitimacy regarding participation (French, Israel, and As, 1960; Patchen, 1970; Scontrino, 1972).
5. The less the status difference or expertise between participants (Mulder, 1971; Haythorn, 1956; Lammers, 1967).
6. The greater the degree of trust and support exhibited by the supervisor (Miles, 1965; Ritchie and Miles, 1970; Zand, 1972; Likert, 1967).

THE SUPERVISORY CONTEXT

In looking at the supervisory context, the primary need is to identify situations which allow the superior to assist his subordinates in task goal achievement. Path-goal analysis (see Chapter Two) is useful in considering when the supervisor can contribute (or when he detracts) from the process (House, 1971; Evans, 1970). The degree to which the supervisor defines his role as assuming responsibility for such facilitating behavior (Meyer, 1972), and the degree to which he can mobilize the resources to accomplish it, determine his effectiveness.

There are many problems in trying to apply the findings from studies of leadership *generally* to the problem of supervisors in specific situations. These problems are especially acute when we attempt to carry over findings relating to informal leadership. And among these problems is the fact that it is difficult to compare studies or to aggregate findings. I agree with Yukl (1971) that, "Much of the apparent inconsistency in the leadership literature may be due to semantic confusion about leader behavior and to the absence of a conceptual framework which includes intermediate and situational variables" (p. 414).

One of the situational variables needed in the study of leadership concerns the specific resources and constraints which exist in the various task situations in which supervisors find themselves. In attempting to generalize from studies concerning national leadership, emergent leadership in informal groups, or general business leadership, we often missed the unique features of such leadership situations. And, conversely, studies of first-line supervision often developed specific "principles of supervision" which were inappropriate in the larger context of leadership in general or even for different supervisory positions or levels.

Because of the interactive and multiplicative relationships between the following organizational and individual variables, it must be remembered that although they are discussed separately, they do not have an independent effect.

Nature of work task. Beginning with organizational variables, probably the most discussed is the nature of the task, factors such as technology, complexity of process, and routinization (discussed in Chapter Five). Woodward (1965) identified technology as a determinant of structure (size of work groups) and supervisory behavior (style), and, of course, task structure is one of the variables in Fiedler's Contingency Model. One finding which is supported by many different studies has to do with the complexity of the task, the associated dimension of subordinate skill level, and style of supervision (House, Filley, and Kerr, 1971; Meyer, 1972; Wofford, 1971; Andrews and Farris, 1967; Mohr, 1971). In simple, highly structured tasks, where conventional wisdom would suggest the necessity of authoritarian task-oriented behavior, evidence indicates that a supportive style may be related to both high satisfaction *and* productivity. On such unrewarding jobs, particularly where superior-subordinate contact is frequent and where the work may be machine-paced, workers need much personal interest, and authoritarian, task structuring behavior may be seen as harassing. Meyer (1972) puts it, "Perhaps in the highly simplified jobs that characterize most factory operations, the employees really do not need much supervision and therefore prefer a boss who is not continually looking over their shoulders and giving them orders" (p. 195).

By contrast, in less structured, more flexible situations, subordinates actually seem to appreciate a more directive structured role by their superior. It has been suggested that where the job is intrinsically rewarding, less personal interest is usually needed by subordinates, and structuring behavior by superiors is seen as supportive and helpful. In each case, the issue seems to be the potential opportunity for the supervisor to contribute to the subordinates' effective and satisfying work experience.

I would suggest, however, that we are probably dealing with a difference in definition when we classify a first-line production foreman and a team leader of an R & D group along the same dimensions of structure or participativeness. The nature of different jobs makes certain behaviors more legitimate or appropriate in one context than another. For example, in the Vroom and Mann (1960) study, it was desired and effective for truck drivers, who were seldom in contact with their supervisors, to receive precise and definitive instructions. The drivers would then be on their own in completing their task. The technology of their jobs gave them much freedom, even though their supervisor acted in what many would term an authoritarian style. By contrast, warehouse workers preferred a more democratic supervisor in order to compensate for the routine working conditions and frequent interaction.

Organizational level. This dimension is similar to task in some respects because the typical tasks performed by employees at high levels are usually different from those at lower organizational levels. There has been some evidence that different styles of supervisory behavior are appropriate at different organizational levels (Georgopoulos and Mann, 1962; Nealey and Blood, 1968). But in addition to the differential style appropriate at different levels is the effect across levels or the impact of style congruence between levels. The need for congruence was argued by Kahn and Katz (1960) in terms of the support a supervisor needed from his superior in order to follow a certain leadership style. This finding was supported in a study by Wood and Sobel (1970). In contrast, however, Nealey and Fiedler (1968) found higher subordinate satisfaction where supervisory styles were noncongruent across levels.

In a laboratory study by Hunt (1971), there was a greater relationship between subordinate performance and satisfaction when these were correlated with characteristics of higher level superiors than with immediate supervisors. It seems that higher level superiors may augment or compensate for lower level supervisory behavior. However, Hunt, Hill, and Reaser (1973) obtained only slight evidence for second-level supervisory influence on workgroup effectiveness. A study by Mott (1972) may shed some light on this issue. He analyzed subordinate perceptions of supervisory impact on work group performance. At lower levels, about one-third of the employees agreed that their supervisor had very little effect on their performance, while at higher levels no one admitted such a limited supervisory role. This finding supports the notion that the effects of supervision depend on level, technology, subordinate skills, and other climate variables.

Supervisors' upward influence. The degree to which subordinates perceive their supervisor as a means to winning benefits from higher management may determine the effectiveness of his style (Pelz, 1952). Time spent by superiors with organization staff or higher management as an "advocate" for subordinate interests may be more important from the subordinates' point of view than time spent by the superior with subordinates since time spent with the former may well result in higher payoffs for subordinates (Meyer, 1972). The supervisor is often limited in what he can do in the direct superior-subordinate relationship, but he may be able to make a substantial difference if he concentrates his efforts on those who have power in the organization. **Findings by Rowland and Scott (1968) support this position.** They found that a supervisor's influence with his superior related to work group performance and satisfaction in a naval ammunition depot.

Work group homogeneity. The homogeneous nature of a work group, the similarity of members and superior, is a variable which can positively affect satisfaction and performance (Haythorn, 1956). Mulder (1971) also found that when differences in expertise are great, participation is less effective.

Work group size. Meyer (1972) found that in small work groups supervisors tended to behave more like technical specialists, while those in larger groups emphasized interpersonal and administrative functions. These work groups were supposedly doing the same type of work, but the size of the group generated opportunities or demands for different behavior. Size was also identified as a significant moderating variable in a study of brokerage offices (Taylor, 1971). In large offices, where account executives were fairly autonomous, goal emphasis and conflict resolution (problem solving facilitation) by supervisors was related to effectiveness. However, in small offices, a more supportive interpersonal style seemed more effective. One explanation is that large offices deal with expanding markets where there are many opportunities to succeed; small offices are in less attractive markets, and, therefore, members can achieve success and satisfaction only by working together.

Compensation systems. The organizational compensation system is another important variable in the supervisory process. Lawler (1971) stresses the obvious point that the easiest way to get many employees to work harder is to convince them that harder work will lead to higher pay. Where organizational pay policies make it impossible for supervisors to provide such a reward, other supervisory efforts to increase motivation may be to no avail—and this would especially seem to be the case for workers whose orientation is primarily instrumental (see Chapter Two).

Technical and structural factors. According to a study of R & D groups (Andrews and Farris, 1967), the greatest innovation occurred under supervisors who were competent and aware of the technical details of their subordinates' activities. Rossell (1970, 1971) found a relationship between the technological structure of the organization and supervisory behavior at different levels. However, in a study of bank managers (Litzinger, 1965) and two laboratory experiments (Maier, 1968; Maier and Thurber, 1969), structural variables (e.g., degree of centralization) did not affect leadership style or effectiveness.

In a study of managerial decision making, Vroom and Yetton (1973) argue that differences in decision issues and the decision structure of organizations make different styles of supervisory behavior effective or ineffective. As a variable which is partly subject to management policy and partly determined by the internal and external environment, the supervisor's role is to define the decision context and then act accordingly.

Women supervisors. An issue which has generated much public debate but little research is concerned with the impact of women in supervisory positions. A natural question for management might be what difference a female supervisor would have on work group effectiveness. Day and Stogdill (1972), in a study of male and female supervisors in government service, concluded that there was no difference in patterns of behavior or effectiveness. However, in lab studies (Maier, 1970; Sashkin and Maier, 1970), female supervisors were somewhat more cautious and less likely to act on their own than their male counterparts, although they were equally effective in implementing an explicit program.

ORGANIZATION CLIMATE

The failure of the dichotomous people vs. productivity supervisory model and its extension to include a more complex set of relationships is in many ways the evolution of the concept of organization climate. As Tagiuri (1968) said, "Having tried to account for variations in performance by means of such interpersonal variables as attitudes and personality, studies of behavior are now turning to the environment for part of the explanation" (p. 11). Likert's work (1961, 1967) has played an important part in developing the concept of climate as his research has attempted to identify variables which generate an organization profile: leadership processes, motivational and reward forces, communication patterns, influence and control procedures, and the mechanisms for decision making and goal setting. While the conceptualization of climate is much easier than its measurement or the prediction of performance, theoretical and empirical analysis have seemed to generate a rough consensus regarding the relevant dimensions. Almost all those who attempt to develop or measure an aspect of climate (e.g., Halpin and Croft, 1963; Forehand, 1968; Litwin and Stringer, 1968; Lawrence and Lorsch, 1967; Campbell *et al.*, 1970; Schneider and Bartlett, 1968; Tagiuri, 1968) focus on variables which can be included in the following categories: (1) the degree of certainty-uncertainty or risk-taking in the organizational setting; (2) the amount of freedom or autonomy an individual has in his work; (3) the means of handling conflict; (4) the decision-making structure; (5) the reward system; (6) the degree of interpersonal support; and (7) the extent of work structuring and facilitation.

Policy Questions

As a manager or administrator attempts to develop and implement policy in the area of supervision, there are many questions he must consider. Foremost among these questions is (a) how much impact supervision really has on organizational performance, (b) the extent to which supervision is keeping pace with changes in societal values, and (c) the efficacy of supervisory training programs.

Does supervision really make a difference? How much impact does a supervisor have on productivity and organizational effectiveness? Many years ago, Argyle, *et al.* (1958) concluded that while general supervision (democratic, supportive) seemed most conducive to high employee productivity, the total impact of different supervisory styles was limited, probably affecting no more than 15 per cent of total output. Several years later, Dubin, Homans, Mann, and Miller (1965) considered the same question, and from different perspectives they each emphasized the complex situational variables which impinge on the supervisor constraining his influence. Dubin and Homans indicated that supervision may account for no more than 10–20 per cent of the variance in work group performance. In research where supervisors are transferred between work groups, Rosen (1970) found that in some units performance changed substantially while in others little effect was observed. (Of course, one must still question the time period involved in studies of this sort.)

Herzberg (1966) views supervision as a "dissatisfier" which functions primarily to eliminate the negative consequences of work and argues that it has limited value as a positive motivator to effective employee performance. He suggests that when conditions are bad, supervision may have a substantial impact in eliminating the barriers to better performance, but under more favorable conditions, so called intrinsic motivators, such as job challenge, become more relevant. Therefore, Herzberg's emphasis is on job enrichment rather than supervision. In this context, the supervisor's impact becomes a function of his ability to alter the climate or change the fundamental nature of the job. It should be noted, however, that Herzberg's work has concentrated on job attitudes (satisfaction and motivation) as the dependent variable rather than performance.

Finally, Mott (1972) attempted to correlate measures of individual supervisory effectiveness with overall organizational effectiveness in government agencies. He found the two only slightly related; the amount of variance in work group effectiveness explained by supervision only varies between 0–36 per cent, with major organizational units averaging 10–20 per cent. While these findings may be discouraging to those who believe that supervisory leadership is a single panacea, I would suggest that the 10–20 per cent figure may make the crucial difference between organizational success and failure.

Values. From a number of fronts, we are hearing calls for increased humanization of work (e.g., Kahn, 1973; *Work in America,* 1973; Sheppard and Herrick, 1972; Sexton and Sexton, 1971; *Dissent,* Winter, 1972; Westley and Westley, 1971). This is neither an utopian dream nor the human relations argument of the past, but rather the demand for a decent job. The attainment of challenging and responsible jobs has been an often repeated goal of organization members and philosophers, and *some* supervisors, but to make it a matter of individual right, supported by public commitment and by government investigation and legislation, might provide a new and different emphasis.

Along with the concern regarding the humanization of work, there is a broader interest in the impact of the work environment on the mental and physical health of individuals. Programs such as the long-term Mental Health in Industry study conducted by the

Institute for Social Research at Michigan (French and Caplan, 1972) deal with both the protection of the individual and the effective utilization of resources. If supervisory behavior has sufficient negative effects on the subordinate's health to impair his job performance, the organization may become interested independent of any legal sanctions. For example, interest in safety, alcohol, drug, and racial problems have evolved into programs with substantial impact on the role of the supervisor. In fact, *Newsweek* (August 27, 1973) claims that in an auto plant foremen must be "more pop psychologist than drill sergeant."

A related value issue concerns *manipulation*. For many, this term has an ethically undesirable connotation. Consequently, there have been efforts to idealize an organization climate or type of supervision as nonmanipulative. Litwin and Stringer (1968) suggest that we have been avoiding the real issue; that is, we should not look to democratic supervision (or another normative conceptualization) as a means to *eliminate* manipulation. Democratic management may reduce exploitive manipulation or make it more acceptable to a particular value system, but it does not eliminate the reality of supervisory control functions; these exist when you have people with different goals and skills, at different levels of the hierarchy, with different degrees and types of information. The title of a current book in the field, *The Sensitive Manipulator* (Dyer, 1972) suggests an interesting perspective on this issue. Therefore, it seems the only question is how to make supervision more consistent with a given value system.

This issue leads to a final comment on the value perspectives which relate to supervision. For many individuals, there is an ethical and aesthetic dimension to interpersonal relationships which serve as ends in and of themselves. In this context, efficient performance is neither a necessary nor sufficient justification for humanist supervisory behavioral norms. People ought to behave with decency and respect for others, and such norms should not be violated to achieve higher output. For such individuals, our empirical or theoretical evidence regarding supervision and productivity may alter some behaviors, but others are related to different criteria. I find such norms being generated from both the bottom-up and the top-down in organizations, and I would expect this emphasis to increase in the future.

Supervisory training. Even if we could identify the optimal style of supervision in a particular organizational setting, would it be possible to train supervisors to behave in this fashion? While training will be discussed in greater depth in Chapter Seven, a few comments with respect to supervisory training seem appropriate. The volume of training programs geared to teaching supervision is overwhelming. Many supervisors have participated in more programs than they can remember: team-building and decision-making exercises, supervision of minority employees, discipline, and grievance handling.

Questions regarding supervisory training programs are not new. Almost 25 years ago, Roethlisberger (1951) was reflecting on a decade of heavy emphasis on supervisory human relations training and concluded how ineffective and unrealistic so many programs were. A current persistent voice on this theme is that of Fiedler (1970, 1973), who has summarily dismissed supervisory training and experience as a reliable means to improved organizational performance. Actually, Fiedler says that certain training may well improve *one* supervisor's performance but harm another's, depending on the task (Fiedler and Chemers, 1974, Chapter 8).

In a test of the lasting impact of Management-by-Objectives training, Ivancevich (1972) found that short-term changes did not carry over in the long run (a finding supported in many different studies). The failure of higher management to reinforce the newly trained supervisors seems to be the deciding variable (also see Fleishman, 1953). It seems that in those cases where supervisory training programs are successful (Campbell, *et al.*, 1970, Chapter 13), the program is carefully designed to meet a defined need, there is follow-up training, and organizational reinforcements are provided when the supervisor returns to his job (Golembiewski and Carrigan, 1970). Still, the effects are often limited to short-run changes in attitudes; there is limited evidence related to long-term *performance* (House, 1968).

CONCLUSIONS

In reviewing the material for this chapter, I came away with the belief that the pleas for good supervisory research have not fallen on deaf ears. In recent literature, I found few of the sweeping generalizations so prevalent in early studies and much more careful qualification of research findings. The only thing that has not changed is the plea for more research—with the hope for carefully controlled, multivariate, longitudinal studies which include all relevant variables. In closing, I offer the following observations on supervision research.

1. Recent research on supervision has reflected a much more balanced research methodology with consequent improvement in the qualification and application of findings. However, still more care needs to be taken in communicating results to managers. To a large extent, they still hear academicians advocating a one-best-way to supervise. One of the reasons, however, for this condition is that so many managers are still demanding simple answers to complex supervisory problems. Although a situational, contingency logic is much more difficult to present, more creative efforts are needed in this regard.

2. More has been promised from research than has been delivered. Often expectations have not been realistic, or they have not been shared by researchers and managers. Supervisors and subordinates may be asked for information, promised feedback or change, and then nothing happens. The disenchantment of blue-collar workers with their treatment by behavioral scientists is evidence of this problem. I see the need for maintaining the integrity of participants in research an increasing and significant problem.

3. Progress has been made—but more needs to be done—in understanding the differences and implications of supervisory attitudes vs. supervisory strategies. Attitudes do not depend on contingencies, but strategies do! An attitude of trust and confidence does not necessarily mean that the supervisor will always employ a participative strategy or that subordinates will always want it.

4. Identification of the many situational and climate variables has provided increasing evidence for a more tentative approach to theorizing about supervision. But while we know "it all depends," we are just beginning to identify what it depends on and to what extent.

5. As many authors have pointed out, the ultimate forces which affect organizations are those beyond easy control. The changing values in society, such as racial and sexual equality,

changing attitudes regarding rewarding and safe work, national and international economic conditions, are not easily subject to supervisory or academic edict. However, such realizations should not provide a rationalization for inaction. While these changes will clearly impose demands on supervisory behavior, it may well be that supervisory attitudes and style will determine how such changes are received in organizations. The ability to create an organization climate which facilitates creative adjustments to such conditions may indeed be within our control. If so, future efforts regarding supervision (for both practitioners and academicians) will be of even greater importance.

One of the main topics in this chapter has been participation. Here we have viewed it largely as a supervisor-subordinate relationship. In the next chapter, we look at broader, frequently organization-wide systems facilitating participation.

CHAPTER 4

Systems of Formal Participation

ARNOLD S. TANNENBAUM
University of Michigan

The demand for workers' participation in industry is being expressed widely throughout the industrial world. In many socialist countries, workers' participation is a matter of political doctrine. In Western Europe, participation is endorsed by groups which span a broad range of the political spectrum. DeGaulle advocated participation, as do Christian Democrats and left-wing Socialists; even industrial managers support the idea if not the actual practice of participation (Haire, *et al.,* 1966).

Participation means different things to different people. As we see it, participation implies a system of management in which all members influence organizational decisions. Participation, therefore, means that employees at lower ranks exercise some legitimate control over decisions, along with managerial personnel. Participation is a matter of degree, and it may vary widely in form. It may be *direct,* all members entering into the decision-making process, or *indirect* through elected representatives. It may be highly formalized as in workers' councils, boards, and committees, or it may express itself more informally in the responsiveness of managerial personnel to the ideas and suggestions of those below them. Participation may be extensive in its implications and may concern decisions about organizational policy and profit, or it may be limited to the administration of plant welfare programs, or to specific decisions about work assignments or work methods on the shop floor. However it expresses itself, participation represents a modification of the traditional system of hierarchical control in which power resides at the top of the organization and flows unilaterally downward.

Industrial societies have seen a proliferation of participative schemes since World War II, and there is reason to believe that the demand for participation will continue to grow. For its advocates, participation is an answer to some of the most nagging problems of industrial society: worker alienation, industrial conflict, and political unrest. It is also a response to the need for effective management and productive efficiency within a "democratic" framework. Indeed, the rising level of education of the work force and the increasing complexity and technological sophistication of industry require at least some modification of the traditional system of authoritarian hierarchical relations in organizations (Blauner, 1964; Katz and Georgopoulos, 1971; Mechanic, 1962).

We begin the chapter with a brief discussion of the relationship between participation and control. Following this, we discuss four major groups of formal workers' participation: legal systems, collective bargaining, suggestion (consultative) schemes, and behavioral science approaches. Finally, in the concluding section, we consider some of the conditions under which participation is most likely to be effective.

Participation and Control

To talk about participation is to talk about control. To *control* means to create desired effects, or, conversely, to prevent undesired ones. The participative system differs from the nonparticipative in the way control is exercised and distributed. Workers exercise more control in the participative than in the nonparticipative system, and control is, presumably, less coercive in the participative system.

Participation is often thought to imply taking power from managers and giving it to subordinates, but in fact managers need not exercise less control where there is participation. A reduction in managerial power *may* occur but it need not, and there is evidence to suggest that participation may be a means through which managers actually increase their own control along with that of workers. Thus, contrary to stereotypes that assume participation to be a vaguely permissive or laissez-faire system, the participative organization may be one in which the *total amount of control* is higher than in the nonparticipative organization. There is no escaping the need for some system of control in organizations, participative organizations included, and the success of participative approaches hinges not on reducing control, but on achieving a system of control that is more effective than that of other systems (Tannenbaum, 1968, pp. 22–23). In fact, many participative schemes are really designed implicitly, if not explicitly, to legitimize if not to enhance the control exercised by managers. The "chief value" of participation, according to Strauss and Rosenstein (1970), "may be that of providing another forum for the resolution of conflict as well as another means by which management can induce compliance with its directives" (p. 198; see also Jacques, 1968; March and Simon, 1958; and Pateman, 1970).

Systems of Participation

We shall consider four groups of participative schemes, although the categories we employ are not mutually exclusive; they are simply a way of helping us present some of the variety of participative schemes now being employed in industry. First are those we refer to as *legal systems* since they have a type of legislative or governmental structure, including councils or governing boards where elected representatives sit and where decisions are taken through votes. Most legal systems are defined and required by law in their respective societies (and they are, therefore, legal in this sense, too). Being the product of a legal or governmental structure, they have some of the characteristics of such structures. And, being the product of a political system, their rationale is usually political. Legal systems are found in the industrial plants of kibbutzim in Israel which illustrate an extreme but eminently workable form of participation. The Yugoslav system of workers' self-management and the system of codetermination in a number of European countries can also be referred to as legal systems.

A second form of participation is *collective bargaining*. Bargaining today is not often thought of as participation, yet through unions workers can exercise some control over wages, working conditions, and aspects of personnel policy, and, in some cases, a collaborative relationship may exist between a union and a company such that the union is in effect part of the system of management in a plant.

Third is a variety of *suggestion* or *consultative schemes*. Some schemes, such as the conventional suggestion box, illustrate the limiting case of little or no participation. Others, such as the Scanlon Plan, incorporate procedures for involving members in decisions about work processes and other matters.

Finally, there are a number of formalized schemes proposed by behavioral scientists. These *behavioral science schemes* have grown out of the "human relations" movement, and they have been formulated in part on the basis of results of social research in industry. They, therefore, have a more elaborate science-based rationale than the three other types of participation schemes. Like the others, however, they define explicit, formally established procedures through which rank-and-file members contribute to the decisions of the organization along with supervisors and managers.

These are the types of formal schemes we shall describe. Not all manifestations of participation, however, are part of a formal plan. Participation can occur spontaneously and informally. Superiors who are responsive to the ideas and suggestions of their subordinates, and managers who listen to and are influenced by those below them, are fostering participation whether or not that is their intent. Such informal participation is limited to issues that fall within the jurisdiction of a superior and his subordinates, and, in most cases, this jurisdiction is relatvely narrow. But, nonetheless, it may be important to those involved because of its relevance to their daily work life. This informal aspect of participation should, in principle, be related to the formal; the implicit assumption of many formal schemes being that their effects pervade the total organization, including the interpersonal relationships within it. But, in fact, some organizations which are highly participative formally are not very participative in the informal sense, and some organizations enjoy substantial informal participation even though they do not have a formal plan (Tannenbaum, *et al.,* 1974, Chap. 3).

Legal Systems

Legal systems of participation employ procedures that resemble those of government, including decision-making councils and the election of officers and/or representatives. Many of these schemes are inspired by socialist ideology and are required by law in their respective societies. There is, nonetheless, much variety among them. Some, like the Israeli kibbutz and Yugoslav systems, place a great deal of authorithy in the hands of members; others, like systems of "joint consultation," offer no more than the opportunity for representatives to communicate a point of view which then may or may not be taken into account by the decision makers.

THE KIBBUTZ MODEL

Kibbutzim originated 60 years ago as agricultural communities, but they now include close to 200 industrial plants that in 1972 produced 6.6 per cent of the industrial output of Israel. Kibbutz plants contain, on the average, about 50 persons and are concentrated largely in six industries: plastics, electronics, metal works, food processing, furniture and wood products, and textiles. (Although kibbutz plants are small, they do not differ in size from the average American plant which contains about 56 persons; see U.S. Department of the Census, *Annual Survey of Manufactures*, 1971).

Kibbutz factories are organized according to several ideological principles. One is the Marxist injunction against private ownership; the factory is owned by the kibbutz members as a group. A second is the ideological commitment to "democracy" and the premium placed on equality in the distribution of rewards and power. All members receive the same nominal monetary allowance and all live in similar apartments and share their meals in a common dining room. Unlike the typical industrial bureaucracy, the material reward provided a member need not correspond to his ability or his contribution, and it is entirely possible that some workers receive greater material benefits than some managers, if the former have a need for special goods or services.

The ideal of equality has obvious implications for the system of participation by which the kibbutz plants are governed:

1. The kibbutz is a voluntary society where members can leave at any time. Coercive control is inconsistent with kibbutz principles, although persuasion and social pressure in the form of approval or disapproval are employed as a means of exercising social control.

2. Officers are not appointed by superiors, as in the usual industrial organization. Rather, all officers, from the first-line super-

visor to the production manager, are elected by the workers, and their tenure is usually limited to two to three years for the supervisor and four to five years for the production manager. The manager of the plant, whose tenure is also limited to four to five years, is elected by the kibbutz as a whole, which includes all members of the plant.

3. Workers can participate directly or indirectly in important decisions through a Workers' Assembly to which all workers in the plant belong and through a set of elected committees. A Management Board, which consists of the plant manager and production manager, along with workers' representatives and several elected officers of the kibbutz as a whole, also plays a role in decision making.

The kibbutz factory is extremely participative, on paper at least. Workers, through their electoral power and through their membership in the Workers' Assembly can, in principle, exercise ultimate control over a wide range of basic issues. Research, however, has yet to discover an organization that works precisely the way it should, and the kibbutz factory is no exception. Power, in fact, is not entirely equalized; kibbutz plants show the hierarchical distribution of control that is typical of industrial organizations: managers exercise more control over what goes on in the plant than do workers. Furthermore, despite the equalization of material rewards, persons at the top are more satisfied with and interested in their jobs, feel more motivated and responsible, and have more favorable attitudes toward the system than do those at the bottom. Many rewards, such as monetary compensation and material privileges, can be and are equalized, but some rewards cannot be equalized easily. Jobs at upper levels, for example, are generally more interesting or more pleasant than those at lower levels, and the kibbutz factory is subject to some of the universal facts of industrial life that discriminate between persons in different jobs and at different ranks (Tannenbaum, *et al.*, 1974).

But such discrimination is a matter of degree, and it is generally less in the kibbutz plant than in other places (Tannenbaum, *et al.*, 1974). Furthermore, the election and the rotation of officers means that substantial numbers of members eventually become a supervisor or manager, or they sit on one or another of the committees that play a central role in the decision-making process. Thus, while, the supervisor exercises more control than the workers and is likely to be more satisfied with his job, the supervisor does not remain a supervisor throughout his career in the plant, and the worker's chances of moving into a supervisory or managerial job are greater in kibbutz plants than in comparable plants elsewhere.

According to members, at least, the kibbutz factory is highly participative in practice, although not as participative as members would like. This discrepancy between the degree of participation that members say they want, and the degree of participation that they perceive to exist in the plant, occurs in all countries where research on this question has been conducted, including the United States, Italy, Austria, and Yugoslavia, but the discrepancy is relatively small in kibbutz plants compared to elsewhere. Furthermore, participation in the kibbutz plant is not only concerned with policy issues decided in formal committees and assemblies; it also occurs at the interpersonal level where superiors are receptive to the ideas and suggestions of those under them and where superiors are friendly and supportive vis-a-vis subordinates. The character of control and the bases of power in the kibbutz plants, therefore, reflect a participative managerial style. Members accede to the influence of superiors largely because of a sense of commitment to the organization rather than for reasons of coercion. Furthermore, rewards for good work and sanctions for bad are dispensed by *coworkers* as well as superiors rather than by superiors exclusively (Tannenbaum, *et al.*, 1974).

Thus, kibbutz plants adhere reasonably well to principles of participation that, in most other contexts, would appear extreme if not utopian—and the results are positive according to most standards. Not only do kibbutz plants survive well in a larger national and international economy, but, according to a controlled study by Melman (1970), these plants are more efficient than comparable non-kibbutz plants in Israel. Psychologically, kibbutz factory workers do have problems of adjustment to work, as do workers in other places, and many kibbutzniks report dissatisfaction with their job—perhaps because they are over-qualified for the relatively routine tasks that they must perform. But compared to workers in similar plants in Italy, Austria, and Yugoslavia, the adjustment of kibbutz workers is positive, motivation is high, and attitudes toward the plant are favorable. Labor-management conflict in the kibbutz is virtually nonexistent.

Workers' Self-management—Yugoslav Style

In 1950, a system of workers' councils was introduced into Yugoslav industrial and business organizations. This legal system of workers' participation is, from a formal standpoint, the most intensive and extensive national system in Europe, if not in the world. It provides to all of the employees of an enterprise ultimate authority with regard to basic policy, personnel, and technical issues of the firm.

Yugoslavia is not unique in the existence of councils in industrial organizations. Many countries in Europe, Asia, and Africa require workers' councils or enterprise committees as a means of communication between management and employee representatives or of making decisions concerning matters of interest to workers. The Yugoslav approach is unique only in its comprehensiveness.

The Yugoslav system of self-management, like the kibbutz, has Marxist ideological underpinnings. Private ownership in industry, with minor exceptions, has been abolished. Unlike other communist economies, however, the Yugoslav economy is decentralized, and Yugoslav firms compete with one another in the national and international market. Decentralization, which came about as part of the rupture in relations with the Soviet Union in 1948, is an essential ingredient in the Yugoslav system of workers' self-management since employees can have discretion in running an enterprise only to the extent that the enterprise has some autonomy from outside control.

The Yugoslav system of self-management includes direct and indirect means for worker participation. Direct participation may occur through meetings of the entire work force held once or twice a year to evaluate the financial status of the enterprise and other important issues. More frequent meetings of work units to decide issues relevant to the unit also provide direct means of participation, and referenda in which all members of the enterprise have a vote may be held to decide on changes in products, major investments, merger, the liquidation of the enterprise, and similar items.

Three elected groups provide indirect means of participation. One is the Workers' Council, which normally consists of 10 to 50 persons, depending on the size of the enterprise. Candidates for the Council are nominated by the trade union or by the workers, but they are elected by all employees. The second is the Managing Board, consisting of 5 to 15 persons elected by the Workers' Council. The Board, which is likely to include technical experts, advises the Council and interprets and expedites on a day-to-day basis the decisions of the Council. Finally, the Director is elected from among applicants who have responded to a public advertisement. The Director sits in the Council, but he does not have a vote and he can be discharged by the Council. The Council also has final decision-making power regarding such issues as approval of annual and long-term production plans, prices of products, investments, and hiring and firing of employees, especially managerial and staff personnel.

These legally defined provisions create a highly participative formal structure. Organizational reality, however, does not correspond in detail to the prescriptions and ideological intent of the formal structure. Most if not all plants do have Councils that meet regularly, and in some plants the Councils exercise substantial control, but influence is not distributed equally among members, and the Director is likely to be the single most influential person in the Council and, therefore, in the plant. Staff and supervisory personnel are also likely to have more influence than workers (Rus, 1970; Obradović, in press).

The Yugoslav organization, like all organizations, participative or not, is hierarchical: persons at the top exercise more control than do those at the bottom. Yet the differential between the top and the bottom in Yugoslav plants is not as great as the differential in comparable plants in Italy, Austria, and the United States, according to a recent study (Tannenbaum, et al., 1974). As is typical of industrial organizations elsewhere, Yugoslav managers have more "positive" reactions, compared to workers, such as higher motivation to work, sense of responsibility, and favorable attitudes toward the plant. But in some *small* (although not necessarily in large) industrial plants studied (50 to 150 employees), the differentials between managers and workers in these reactions are less marked than those in comparable plants in Italy, Austria, and the United States (Tannenbaum, *et al.*, 1974). Thus, at least in some small plants, the system seems to have a leveling effect not only on the distribution of influence and benefits (such as pay) but also on the reactions of members to the enterprise and their adjustment to it.

Such leveling can, in principle, come about because the system enhances the reactions of lower ranking persons *or* because it depresses that of top personnel, or for a combination of these reasons. The available data suggest that it is the manager's adjustment that may be suffering, at least by comparison to that of his counterparts elsewhere. The Yugoslav manager is less satisfied, more alienated, and generally less well adjusted in his role than are managers in Italy, Austria, the United States, and kibbutzim, while the Yugoslav worker does not differ very much from his counterparts in other places. We can only speculate about how much of this outcome is attributable to the system itself and how much to other factors, including the problems faced by a country undergoing rapid development. In any event, it is clear that the system has not eliminated the frustration that many workers experience and the sense of alienation that some of them feel (Obradović, 1970). In theory, labor-management conflict should not exist but it does, and, unofficially, strikes sometimes break out (Zupanov, 1973).

Furthermore, the relationship between superior and subordinate is not as participative as the model suggests it should be; subordinates see superiors as being somewhat coercive. Available data thus indicate an inconsistency in Yugoslav plants between the formal structure and the day-to-day relationship between superior and subordinate, an inconsistency that does not exist in kibbutz plants (Tannenbaum, *et al.*, 1974). Yet the Yugoslav industrial system has proved itself workable, having carried Yugoslavia through a period of rapid if not turbulent industrialization with substantial increases in national productivity (Pateman, 1970). Perhaps this is why the Yugoslav industrial system is seen by some responsible persons in developing nations as a model worth emulating and why some social theorists in Eastern Europe have looked wistfully upon the Yugoslav system as an approach to the liberalization of political life in their own societies.

CODETERMINATION

In a number of countries, the law requires that workers have the opportunity to influence decisions in their enterprises through a council of elected representatives and/or through a Directorial Board that includes representatives of management and labor. The control that workers can exercise through such councils is not as great as that formally possible through the Councils in Yugoslavia, since the issues subject to codetermination are usually narrowly defined, and, in the case of Directorial Boards where workers' representatives join management in decisions about policy, workers' representatives are usually a minority. Such systems are found in Austria, France, Spain, The Netherlands, Norway, the United Kingdom, Ireland, the United Arab Republic, Belgium, Italy, Mexico, Switzerland, and other countries (Schregle, 1970). The West German system, which is as highly developed as any in non-Socialist countries, is often cited as a model.

Every German enterprise employing five or more persons over 18 years of age is required by law to have a workers' council elected by all employees (Furstenburg, 1969; Hartmann, 1970; West German Trade Union Federation, 1973). Furthermore, all public corporations are required to have workers' representatives on their Supervisory Boards (which are like boards of directors in American corporations). Workers' representatives are usually in a minority on these Boards.

Works Councils have some influence over matters of interest to employees such as work schedules and breaks, vacation schedules, welfare services provided by the enterprise, piece rates, and principles of remuneration. Councils are also entitled to make recommendations to management with respect to such questions as the hiring and firing of employees or the transfer of personnel within the firm, but management retains its prerogatives with respect to these latter questions.

The issues over which Councils exercise some legitimate influence are like those subject to collective bargaining in the United

States, and, since union-management bargaining does not occur at the plant level in German industries, the Works Council serves some of the functions of the local union in America. The main difference is that the Council is forbidden by law from calling strikes; differences between the Council and management are settled by mediation. Councils, therefore, do not have the same coercive base that some unions have to back up their decisions.

In addition to being represented on the Council, workers in all German public corporations are represented on the Supervisory Boards of their enterprise, but workers' representatives are in a minority on each Board except in the iron, steel, and mining industries. Here the number of labor representatives equals that of management, the Board in these industries consisting of 11 members, one of whom is a "neutral" acceptable to both sides.

Codetermination schemes are purportedly designed to introduce an element of "industrial democracy" into the work organization but they have practical objectives, too, including the resolution of conflict between labor and management and the maintenance of order and effective administration of enterprises. The available documentation suggests mixed results relative to these objectives. First, the laws of codetermination are not always carried out. In Belgium, for example, Councils are, by law, required to run company welfare programs. However, some employers have circumvented the Councils by transferring these programs to independent corporations (Myers, 1958). In France, there is "a feeling that employers have diverted the attention of the committees to social welfare matters in order to avoid having to deal with them on financial and economic problems" (Sturmthal, 1964, p. 34). In Germany, according to a 1961 survey, one-third of all undertakings employing between 100 and 200 employees did not have Works Councils. Large organizations, however, are very likely to have Councils (Furstenburg, 1969).

In German plants that do have Councils, a large majority of employees who are eligible to vote for representatives do in fact exercise their franchise, although fewer white-collar than blue-collar workers vote, and the representation in Councils of white-collar workers (and of women) is lower than that of blue-collar workers (and of men). In addition to participating through the vote, workers may contact their representatives in the plant or through occasional assemblies which may occur a couple of times a year (Furstenburg, 1969, p. 106).

The prerogatives of German Works Councils are limited by law, and they are also limited in practice not only by management, which prefers not to have its power diminished by a powerful decision-making Council, but, ironically, also by the trade unions which discourage special advantages for workers in a local plant (unions favor industry-wide progress rather than "local selfishness"; see Furstenburg, 1969). If the Works Council is successful, it is not because of any substantial power it may have to determine organizational policy but rather because it helps to reduce conflict, and it contributes, therefore, to effective administration in the plant. Thus, the *outcome* can be felicitous for management and perhaps for workers, too, but because of its indirectness the *process* of codetermination does not often touch many workers at all. This indirectness is especially apparent in the case of Supervisory Boards. The few workers' representatives on such Boards are not in all cases even drawn from the work force of the enterprise. For example, in 1960, only 40 per cent of the workers' representatives came from the enterprise; 40 per cent came from the trade union organization; and 20 per cent were nominated by the trade union but were not members of the union or of the enterprise (Furstenburg, 1969, pp. 125–126).

Because participation is so distant from and indirect for the workers in the plant, many workers are unaware of its practices and implications. Nonetheless, codetermination in the iron, steel, and coal industries comes out well in worker attitude surveys, even though codetermination in these industries is not accompanied by personnel policies which are more favorable to workers than are the policies in industries that do not have workers' representatives sitting on Supervisory Boards. Worker morale in German industry has been positive, but the iron, steel, and coal industries do not seem to enjoy a special advantage in this regard despite their special status in having legal representation on the Board. Perhaps the generally positive climate in Germany is attributable in part to the legal system of participation which operates in large segments of German industry, including workers' representatives on Supervisory Boards and/or Works Councils. This conclusion is consistent with the views of some radicals who oppose codetermination precisely because of its apparent success in rationalizing existing social relationships and thereby maintaining "capitalist power" in Germany (Schauer, 1973). In the opinion of most German workers, at any rate, codetermination is a good thing (Furstenburg, 1969).

Collective Bargaining

Participation is idealized by many of its advocates as a cooperative relationship between groups of people sharing a common interest and working to achieve a harmonious synthesis of views. A prevailing stereotype of collective bargaining, on the other hand, is that of confrontation between opposing parties, each fighting to maximize its share of a limited economic pie. Power itself may become the issue at stake, one side challenging the other in order to strengthen its own position at the expense of the other. Strikes, boycotts, slowdowns, or, in extreme cases, sabotage—the ultimate union weapon—symbolize the essential antagonism between the groups.

Defined in these terms, the union-management relationship does not fit the idealization of participation, and collective bargaining is not often thought to illustrate workers' participation in industry. Furthermore, "workers' control" is not the shibboleth for unions in the United States and Canada that it is for some unions abroad, and American unions, unlike many of their European counterparts, have opposed the idea of sharing with management control of and responsibility for the enterprise. "The United States system of industrial relations rejects in principle, and almost always in practice, all forms of workers' representation in official managerial bodies. The union wishes to be a critic rather than a partner in management, and union influence is exerted almost exclusively by negotiation and grievance handling, rather than by representation on managerial bodies" (Sturmthal, 1969, p. 184). This formal separation of the union's role from that of management distinguishes collective bargaining from the legal systems of workers' participation that we have discussed above. Yet, while the American union is not formally defined as playing a management role, it does so in fact. The result, ironically, is that the American worker, who does not seek control as an end in itself, exercises more control over matters in the plant that are important to him than does his counterpart in many European countries who is ideologically committed to the concept of workers' control.

This irony is attributable in part to the almost exclusive concern by American unions for issues of immediate interest to workers such as wages, fringe benefits, and working conditions and to the use of bargaining in the plant to achieve workers' objectives. If unions in the United States are an instrument of control for workers, they are so only as a by-product of unions' pragmatic efforts to protect and enhance the security and other interests of their members in the work place. Many unions in Europe, on the other hand, are concerned with "larger" issues, and control over events on the shop floor, therefore, receives little attention.

An observation by Stagner (1957) in an Italian plant serves to illustrate, perhaps in the extreme, the role of unions in some European countries by way of contrast with their role in the United States:

> . . . I noticed a considerable number of what seemed to be fairly serious accident hazards. In talking with workers, I discovered that one of them was a representative of CIGL [the union] . . . I commented on the accident hazards, and he agreed that they had a fairly high accident rate. When I asked him what action the union was taking with respect to this, he said, "None. We are busy organizing for the revolution."

Because of the high degree of cooperativeness with labor and management in Sweden, its system of collective bargaining conforms more closely to the participative image than does collective bargaining in Italy or in the U.S. Bargaining is highly rationalized, with a good deal of reliance on neutral mediators, and the negotiation process appears to be more that of parties jointly deciding than of fighting. (There may, in fact, be more "joint deciding" in American industrial relations than meets the eye, but many negotiators in the United States believe that it is necessary to give at least the *appearance* of a struggle in bargaining.) Unions also collaborate with management through the works council in Swedish plants, thus playing a role in the legal system of participation. Collaboration has extended into industrial safety and vocational training and into the very crucial area of time and motion study and incentive pay determination (List, 1973).

In the United States and Canada, unionized workers exercise formal control in plants through the negotiation process by which the union and management establish an "agreement" or "contract" defining the rights and obligations of the parties and specifying the conditions of employment for union members. Although unions manifestly bargain about the level of benefits such as wages, insurance, and pensions, they also bargain implicitly over what kinds of decisions may be made at the bargaining table: whether the union may have a voice in production planning, employee discipline, or production standards which heretofore might have been subject to exclusive management control. Unions seek a voice in any policies of management which have a direct effect on members' working conditions. While management resists this intrusion, as Sturmthal (1969) points out, ". . . company representatives [sometimes] invite such a challenge. Whenever, in the course of bargaining, management refers to the company's ability to pay as an argument against further concessions to union demands, management in effect provokes discussions about the factors that limit the company's ability to pay—i.e., all the business policies that may affect profits" (pp. 174–175). But for most unions, participation in company decision making is concerned with pay, discipline, output rates, and the size and administration of job territory, including distribution of overtime, transfer of employees within plants, job content, and promotion to nonsupervisory positions (Derber, Chalmers, and Edelman, 1961, p. 89; Dunlop, 1960).

The bargaining process, in so far as it implies participation by workers, is *indirect* in that representatives do the bargaining, but the demands that the union makes of management are decided more or less, depending on the union, through meetings which all workers can attend, and in many unions the agreement with management must ultimately be ratified by all workers. The proportion of members who attend meetings is usually small, and principles of democracy may not be maintained in all cases, but attendance picks up when important negotiations are taking place (Sayles and Strauss, 1953). In some cases, members' inactivity means that they see the union doing well on their behalf. Otherwise, they might intervene, and union leaders are aware of this contingency. Members, therefore, affect some decisions implicitly if not overtly.

In addition, the collective agreement defines a grievance process that gives workers some direct control over conditions which affect them in the plant. Some workers prefer to bypass the union, taking their complaints directly to the foreman without filing a formal grievance. This need not imply lack of confidence in the union, however. On the contrary, where the union is strong, foremen may be anxious to settle the grievance "out of court" before it becomes a *cause célèbre* (Sayles and Strauss, 1953; Tannenbaum and Kahn, 1958). Going to the foreman first may be the more efficient and, therefore, the preferred route for the worker. Thus, the formal grievance procedure may lead to informal ones which accomplish the intended result with less cost to the worker. Furthermore, the grievance procedure may have implications beyond the settling of specific complaints by workers since the procedure is used to interpret, administer, and extend the contract (Kennedy, 1954), and grievances may be part of the skirmishing between the union and management in creating issues for future contract negotiations. In sum, the grievance process is actually part of the collective bargaining process; it follows from one negotiation and leads into the next.

The extent to which collective bargaining represents real participation for workers depends on a number of conditions. Obviously, the union itself must be participative if it is to be an instrumentality for the participation of workers in a company. The structure of barganing, too, whether, for example, it is conducted primarily on an industry-wide basis or primarily at the local level, affects how much the worker himself may be directly involved in the process. But by and large, the evidence suggests that, directly or indirectly, American workers exercise some control through their unions, and an international survey concerning decision making and control undertaken in ten matched industrial plants in each of several countries provides some relevant data. For example, in response to questions about decision making, American respondents (including managers and workers) do not indicate that workers contribute very much to decisions in the plant. The level of *decision making* reported by workers in the American plants is about equal to that reported in comparable plants in Austria and Germany, although higher than that in Italy. However, in response to a question dealing with the amount of *influence* that workers have over what goes on in their plants, American respondents report higher scores than do respondents in Austria, Germany, or Italy (Tannenbaum, *et al.*, 1974; Bartoelke, unpublished report).

American workers do not have formal authority concerning broad policy issues, and they do not contribute formally to decisions in the usual sense of the term. But they can exercise through their union a degree of control, directly or indirectly, over the "bread and butter" issues that are important to them. "If there is any meaning to the idea of workers' control," (Bell, 1958), "it is control—*in the shop*—over the things which directly affect his work-a-day life: the rhythms, pace, and demands of work; a voice in the equitable standards of pay; a check on the demands of the hierarchy over him" (p. 33). "Productivity bargaining," which has been applied in some industries in Britain as well as in the United States, illustrates how unions may share with management control over job rules. Through such bargaining, unions agree to relax rules that limit productivity (such as rules that regulate jurisdictional lines or overtime work) in return for a wage increase.

Collective bargaining implies workers' participation in management, although bargaining does not ordinarily go under this heading. In any event, bargaining has become more rationalized over the years. Management is reconciled to the existence of unions, and, in many cases, managers have established collaborative relations with their unions. The increased use of experts and professionals on both sides in the negotiation process, and the increased reliance on neutral mediators and arbitrators, has contributed further to the rationalization of bargaining and to the sublimation if not the elimination of coercive power in the negotiation process. In this respect at least, collective bargaining is beginning more and more to *look* like participation.

Suggestion Schemes

Suggestions, to the extent that they are carried out, imply influence and therefore participation. Suggestion schemes differ from many of the legal systems that we have discussed and from collective bargaining in that formal coercion and legal sanction are not employed as a basis for insisting that suggestions be accepted. Suggestions presumably carry their own weight; they are adopted if they are "logical" in the context of management's definition of organizational purposes. Some schemes, however, may be integral with the collective bargaining arrangement between a company and union, and others may be required by law and are, therefore, like many legal systems in this respect. In fact, some legal systems of participation are really suggestion schemes more than they are systems of co-management. In Britain, for example, the emphasis placed on joint consultation by the nationalization acts gave the consultation committees a form of legal sanction. But employers have been "adamant that decisions on matters discussed [in the joint consultation committees] should rest with management, however much workers might disagree with them" (Clarke and Fatchett, 1972, p. 179). All suggestion schemes fit this injunction, although some may operate in a spirit of cooperation which does not call for a test of management's ultimate right of veto.

Suggestion schemes can be distinguished from one another by several characteristics: (a) Who makes the suggestions? (b) Who evaluates the suggestions? (c) Who implements the suggestions? (d) What are the subjects about which suggestions can be made? (e) What incentives are provided for suggestions? In the suggestion box system, for example, (a) any employee may make a suggestion which is (b) evaluated by management and, if approved, (c) implemented by management. Employees can, in principle, make a suggestion (d) concerning any topic, although management obviously will be amenable only to suggestions that are likely to be beneficial in their definition of the term. Monetary rewards (e) are provided, and the employee may get his picture in the company newspaper.

Several suggestion schemes, such as the "cooperative committee" system of the Tennessee Valley Authority, the Scanlon Plan, and the so-called system of "work simplification" are, compared to the suggestion box, steps toward a more substantial system of participation.

COOPERATIVE COMMITTEES OF THE TENNESSEE VALLEY AUTHORITY

Cooperative committees at the various TVA installations have been established through an agreement between the TVA and its Trades and Labor Council. These committees, which are composed of management and labor representatives, are responsible for *evaluating* as well as eliciting suggestions from employees. They meet monthly and are concerned with "such matters as the elimination of waste; the conservation of materials, supplies and energy; the improvement of quality of workmanship and services . . .; the prevention of hazards to life and property; and the strengthening of the morale of the service. The committees shall, however, not consider and act upon subjects or disputes the adjustment of which is provided for by [the agreement with the Tennessee Valley Trades and Labor Council]" (Tennessee Valley Authority and Tennessee Valley Trades and Labor Council, 1963).

Not all of the committees are effective, but some do accomplish genuine results in the form of improved work methods. Furthermore, industrial relations between the TVA and its unions are unusually harmonious, but this harmony may not be due to the committees. TVA follows the prevailing wage rates established in the area, and other industries do the hard bargaining.

Nonetheless, the committee system does have real impact; it is taken seriously by many persons in the TVA. Incentives, at least for members of the committees, are inherent in the process. Members engage in deliberations that are challenging and interesting to them, and they make decisions that have some significance concerning work, safety, and other matters in the shop. Furthermore, the experience of having served on a committee may be a sufficient basis for maintaining the involvement of members in the system even after their tenure is completed. Patchen (1965), for example, in a study of eight administratively separate cooperative programs, found that the sense of identification with TVA and the feeling of common purpose with management were especially high in programs where a high percentage of respondents reported having served on a co-op committee at some time in the past. He found only small and nonsignificant correlations, however, between reports of the number of suggestions submitted during the past three years and measures of organizational identification.

Scanlon Plan

The Scanlon Plan has a number of features in common with the TVA system, but a vital difference is its gain-sharing incentive—a feature completely foreign to the TVA approach. Gain-sharing, according to the philosophy of the Plan, is designed to serve ethical and pragmatic objectives. Ethically, gain-sharing implies equity;

if members of the organization contribute to increased production, they should share in the rewards. Pragmatically, gain-sharing should serve as an incentive for members to work to increase production, and the gain-sharing formula provides a monthly bonus which is tied as closely as possible to the improvement in the organization's overall efficiency. The index by which this is gauged is usually the ratio of labor costs to sales dollars (Krulee, 1955).

The participative aspect of the Plan occurs in two ways. First, the Plan is *introduced* participatively. Union and management representatives explore the implications of the Plan, make decisions about how it is to be carried out, and discuss it with their constituents throughout the organization. Once agreement is reached, departmental production committees are established, and employees participate in the committees by proposing solutions to production problems.

In many applications of the Plan, the supervisor in the departmental committees will have the authority, which he may share with the committee, to accept or reject suggestions, provided that they do not entail large expenditures and that they apply to his department alone (Krulee, 1955). Otherwise, the suggestions will be passed up to the advisory committee which, like the departmental committee, includes union and management representatives. The advisory board is also concerned with decisions about the Plan's policy, including decisions about the formula by which bonuses are calculated.

Evaluative research on the Plan is sparse (but see Lesieur and Puckett, 1969; Northrup and Young, 1968, pp. 40–42; Industrial Relations Counselors, 1962), although it is obvious that the Plan works well in a number of companies and that it has not been effective in others. In a study of 18 organizations that had attempted to implement the Scanlon Plan, Ruh, Wallace, and Frost (1972) found that managers in the 8 organizations that subsequently discontinued the Plan differed in attitude from managers in the 10 organizations that continued it. The latter had significantly more confidence than the former in employees' judgment, responsibility, dependability, alertness, initiative, and willingness to change. Managers in plants that retained the Plan also held more positive attitudes toward participative decision making in general.

In a study of 21 plant sites of six midwestern organizations, Goodman, Wakely, and Ruh (1972) found mixed, although generally positive, attitudes among employees toward the Plan in their company. A majority agreed that the Plan "encouraged hard work" and that it "has helped this company's financial position." Agreement also applied (but not by so great a majority) to statements like, ". . . it is worthwhile to offer suggestions to the committees," and the Plan is "a mechanism for improving trust and confidence in the management." But employees were slightly negative about "the extent to which the Plan allows them to really influence decisions which affect their jobs," and about the Plan "as a way for management to get more out of workers."

WORK SIMPLIFICATION

The system of work simplification suggested by Mogenson (Goodman, 1958), and practiced in a number of companies with some apparent success, is another variant of the suggestion scheme. Work simplification does not incorporate monetary incentives, but effort is made to have the process inherently rewarding. Teams are created to solve production problems, and workers on these teams are given training (e.g., in the principles of time and motion study). Furthermore, the teams follow an orderly, industrial engineering format in developing and implementing solutions to production problems.

Teams first select a job to improve. The initial tasks chosen when a work simplification team is formed might well be those which are obvious candidates for improvement: bottlenecks, jobs which entail a lot of walking, high-cost operations, and those which are otherwise noted for giving trouble. As the group becomes more practiced, it is expected to choose more challenging and presumably more rewarding opportunities for improvement. A second step is to get the facts. Participants may obtain blueprints, cost and production figures, sales records, samples, etc. They may also take motion pictures of themselves as they run through a job. This gives them a detailed view of how the task is performed. Furthermore, the movies can be personally rewarding, and participants may borrow a projector to show the films at home. If all goes well, the team then develops a solution, and, finally, the improvements are implemented. Managerial personnel whose services are required for the implementation phase will be brought in at this point (if they have not yet participated). Thus, every effort is made to involve all relevant people—engineers, accountants, supervisors, workers—who are affected by the change or who may contribute to its success (Tannenbaum, 1966).

Some applications of suggestion schemes such as work simplification, Scanlon-type plans, and cooperative committees are very successful: workers are highly motivated and involved, and valuable improvements in work methods have been achieved. But these schemes do not always work effectively. For example, Strauss and Sayles (1972, p. 646) argue that the Scanlon Plan can be successful only (a) in relatively small plants, (b) where the union is not too militant, (c) when strong rivalry and competition do not exist among groups in the plant, and (d) where market demand is elastic, being able to absorb increased output. There is also an indication that in some places where attempts to introduce such schemes were not successful, management and/or workers were not ready for them. Management may not have had the necessary commitment to the principles of participation or the necessary confidence in the work force to give the principles a chance, and workers, in the context of their suspicions about management's motives, may not have seen the advantages that these schemes presumably offer.

Behavioral Science Approaches to Participation

The participative schemes discussed here assume in general that the key to effective and satisfying organization is to be found in the interaction between the superior and his subordinates and in the relationship of the worker to his task. Because of the emphasis on interpersonal relations, many behavioral science schemes require some form of "organizational development" (see Chapter 7) which may include rearrangements of people, groups, and responsibilities to expedite appropriate interactions, and training so that members will acquire the necessary interpersonal skills. Although behavioral science schemes focus on interpersonal relations, some also prescribe procedures which have implications for the structure of the organization as a whole. We shall illustrate this variety with three schemes that have been applied with some success in industry (Tannenbaum, 1966). All of these schemes are formal in the sense that they prescribe explicit procedures to be formally established in an organization.

PARTICIPATION AND THE APPRAISAL SYSTEM

In appraisal systems, the superior ordinarily enumerates the successes and failures of his subordinate and suggests ways in which the subordinate might improve. The superior may also set goals for the subordinate, and these provide the basis for subsequent evaluation. Psychologists, however, have found appraisal of this kind problematic because of the anxiety and defensive behavior that it arouses. Because of the emotionally charged nature of the appraisal, the subordinate does not really learn much from it, and he may actually resist behavior changes that could lead to improvement (Maier, *et al.*, 1964).

Consequently, a participative approach has been employed in some companies through which the subordinate formulates *his own* goals (Ferguson, 1964; French, *et al.*, 1966). These goals, and the methods by which the subordinate hopes to achieve them, are then discussed with the superior who adopts the attitude of helper rather than critic. The superior's purpose in this approach is to stimulate the thinking of the subordinate and to foster his development. The superior thus tries to help the subordinate evaluate himself and to formulate his own plans (Maier, *et al.*, 1964). Consequently, the subordinate plays a more active participative role in the appraisal process than he does in the more conventional appraisal system.

SOCIO-TECHNICAL SYSTEMS

A common critique of modern technology is that it often breaks down jobs into their simplest components, thereby frustrating workers. Psychologists at the Tavistock Institute in London, at UCLA, and at the Work Research Institute in Oslo have placed special emphasis on the *socio-technical* implications of job design and have formulated participative solutions to the problem of frustration and the consequent hostility or apathy that workers might feel.

These researchers propose that the most productive and satisfying work systems combine social and psychological considerations. In coal mining, for example, a system of cohesive teams, in which miners can support and help one another, has proved superior to the system in which workers are relatively isolated (for further discussion, see Chapter 5). A crucial feature of the socio-technical approach is that the teams be set up so that their members share responsibility for a meaningful part of the mining task (Trist and Bamforth, 1951). The socio-technical approach is like that of job enlargement discussed in Chapter 2 in that the simple decomposed elements of a job that might have been distributed among individual workers are recombined into a larger whole. But in the socio-technical approach, these reconstituted jobs are assigned to *groups* not to individuals. The objective is to establish cohesive social units of workers and superiors which correspond to meaningful technological units, and the work groups should have reasonable autonomy and responsibility *as groups* for the total task.

System 4

Rensis Likert (1961, 1967) has gone further than any behavioral scientist in formulating a model of participation that is tied explicitly to the theory and research of behavioral science and is comprehensive in its view of the organization *as a system*. Many schemes of participation either view the organization as a structure devoid of members with complex personalities and social needs, *or* they view the organization as an agglomeration of personalities without a structure. Likert's model has the virtue of considering the individual member *and* the organization.

As discussed in Chapter 3, System 4 refers to the participative end of a continuum on which System 1, the "exploitive authoritative" organization, is at the other extreme, and Systems 2, "benevolent authoritative," and 3 "consultative," fall in between. System 4 is based on several principles. One is "the principle of supportive relationships": "The leadership and other processes of the organization must be such as to ensure a maximum probability that in all interactions and relationships within the organization each member will, in the light of his background, values, and expectations, view the experience as supportive and one which builds and maintains his sense of personal worth and importance" (Likert, 1961, p. 103). A superior, in other words, must have a sincere interest in the welfare of his subordinates, be sensitive to their needs and feelings, and be receptive to their ideas and suggestions.

A second essential feature of System 4 is that the work *group* rather than the individual member is the basic building block of the organization. To achieve this type of organization, Likert proposes that each supervisor must form his subordinates into a highly cohesive group, called an "organizational family," in which he is a member. Supervisors, in turn, are members of a second set of highly cohesive groups with their superiors, who are members of a third set, and so on, up the organizational hierarchy. Most supervisors, then, are members of two groups, one in which they act as supervisors with their subordinates and one in which they are subordinates along with their own peers. Decisions are made within these groups that apply to the work of the group. Input from the group for decisions which have implications beyond the group itself are passed on through those persons who are members of a second group at adjacent echelons. Thus, the effects of the high level of control generated within the tightly knit organizational families are coordinated by the supervisors, who act as "linking pins" between groups.

Likert's model, or aspects of it, have been applied with some success in a number of organizations, sometimes in conjunction with other procedures. For example, it can be used effectively along with the Scanlon Plan (Iman, 1972). In one failing company taken over by a new owner, a number of changes in personnel were introduced along with improvements in technology. Here, Likert's model served as a guide to the development of a new system of interpersonal relations and of decision making (Marrow, Bowers, and Seashore, 1967). The result was a substantially improved profit picture for the company as well as improvements in the managerial system. Survey measures taken immediately before the introduction of the new system and five years later, for example, indicated that employees perceived themselves *and* their management to exercise more control in the plant after the change than before (Seashore and Bowers, 1970; for a critical discussion of this case, see Chapter 7).

Conclusions

The evidence for or against formal participation schemes is not entirely clear, but one assertion at least can be made on the basis of experience with these schemes. Participation *can* work. This is not to assert (or deny) that participation *will* work under any and all circumstances or that it is inevitably a more successful social system than are nonparticipative alternatives. Nonetheless, successful examples can be cited, and these, it would seem, demonstrate a principle and a possibility.

But what do we mean by successful? Several stages in the realization of a participative scheme ought to be considered. First are the specifications of the scheme, the blueprint which defines the issues subject to participative decision making and specifies the structures and procedures through which participation is to be realized. Second is the implementation of the plan, the extent to which the appropriate structures and procedures defined in the blueprint have actually been created; for example, the extent to which the prescribed meetings are held and the required votes taken. Finally, there are the outcomes the plan is designed to achieve. These include high satisfaction and motivation on the part of organization members, high quality decisions, increased productivity, and harmonious industrial relations.

Some participative schemes do not get very much beyond the blueprint stage—and the favorable effects that might otherwise be predicted, of course, cannot be expected. For example, some plants in Germany simply do not hold elections for Works Councils, even though they are expected by law to do so. In some Workers' Councils of Yugoslavia, the manager and top staff, not workers' representatives, actually make the important decisions (Obradović, in press). In some American trade unions, only a small proportion of workers are in attendance at meetings where important decisions are taken.

An obstacle to the translation of a participative plan into action in many cases is the ambivalence, if not the unreserved opposition, of managers. An international study of three thousand managers in fourteen countries showed that managers preponderantly endorse the *idea* of participative decision making. Nonetheless, most of these managers maintain that organization members are incapable of leadership and that they prefer to be directed and avoid responsibility. These inconsistencies imply the analogy of "a Jeffersonian democracy [built] on the divine right of kings. . . . The apparent enlightened democratic beliefs of managers with respect to organizational government are merely a superficial cover to basic negative beliefs about human capabilities" (Haire, Ghiselli, and Porter, 1963).

A *Wall Street Journal* article illustrates the view of some managers, citing the "reassuring" remarks of a prominent German business leader commenting on his experience with codetermination: "There aren't any problems with this system. . . because the workers haven't any real power to force their views. When the workers' advice is good, it is listened to. Otherwise the shareholders' directors vote them down." Managers obviously prefer that participation be carefully limited, and many probably do what they can to see to it that it *is* limited.

Managers who are skeptical might be right in their doubts about participation, at least under some circumstances. A poorly educated work force may not be as well suited to participation as an educated one (Tannenbaum, *et al.*, 1974, Chapter 7). Furthermore, workers themselves may not be at all agreeable to participation (Hulin and Blood, 1967; Tannenbaum and Allport, 1956; Vroom, 1960), especially if they take an instrumental view toward their job (see Chapter 2). And, for some radical workers, participation is an unacceptable compromise—or worse, since it is designed to legitimate a system that should be replaced in its entirety. The revolutionary will, therefore, oppose participation (Schauer, 1973).

A first step in the success of a plan, then, is simply to put it into action. But it is one thing to put the plan into action and another to achieve the results predicted for it. These predictions are based on theories and ideologies which may not be valid in all aspects, although there is support for some of the "principles" that are implicit in many participative schemes. For example, although the philosophy and the language differ, all schemes assume that persons in general *want* to exercise control in their work situations and that persons who exercise (or perceive themselves to exercise) some control are likely to be more satisfied with their jobs, feel a greater sense of responsibility in their organization, and feel less alienated than those who exercise little or no control. Furthermore, participation, according to some behavioral science theories, is a way of utilizing the knowledge and skills possessed by members which typically remain unused in most organizations (Miles, 1965). There is some support from research for these assumptions; therefore, participative schemes which give workers a sense of control should, in principle, create some of the above effects.

These principles make more sense, however, with respect to *direct* than indirect participation, and the limited evidence available suggests that indirect participation does not have many positive psychological effects on the mass of workers who do not sit in Works Councils and vote on the Board (Holter, 1965; Lammers, 1967; Thorsrud and Emery, 1970). This is the point at which the behavioral scientist has entered with his own models which stress the direct interpersonel and work-related aspects of participation.

International comparisons illustrate some of the variety in participation schemes and provide some perspective on what is possible and workable in the contemporary industrial world. We have selected in this chapter schemes that have proved successful in terms of at least some of the criteria considered above. First, some of the blueprints in each of the categories of participation we have discussed have actually been put into practice. There *are* industrial plants where workers actually elect managers (as in kibbutzim), where workers vote on policy questions (as in Yugoslavia), where they elect representatives on Boards (as in Germany), where they vote on demands which are agreed to by management (as in the United States), and where they make useful suggestions through group meetings concerning how the work of the plant ought to be done (as in many countries). Secondly, the predicted effects *do* occur, in at least some cases: the system is legitimated and accepted in the eyes of many workers and managers, control is effective, morale is as high as can be expected in industrial work, and many participative organizations are efficient and profitable. Some attempts at participation have not been successful, but we know, nonetheless, that participation can work, at least under some conditions. The demand for participation is not likely to be less in the future than in the past, and the question for many, therefore, is not whether participation works but rather how to *make* it work.

Participation cannot be considered apart from broader questions relating to organizational structure, technology, and environment. And, as our next chapter discusses, such factors may inhibit or encourage the development of participation.

CHAPTER 5

Structure, Technology, and Environment

WILLIAM G. OUCHI
Stanford University

AND

REUBEN T. HARRIS
Massachusetts Institute of Technology

This chapter differs from the others in two important ways. First, it takes a sociological view of the "whole" organization, and, secondly, it deals with research which has been primarily exploratory and descriptive rather than applied. Whereas previous chapters discuss the behavior of individuals and groups in an organizational setting, the emphasis here is on the setting itself—the structure of the organization within which individual and group behavior take place.

The research to be reviewed here is primarily descriptive rather than normative. Organizational sociology is a growing field, but it cannot yet offer the kinds of applications which have come from organizational psychology. Still, the groundwork has been laid for research which should have considerable social utility. Already the evidence suggests that for organizations to be effective their structures should be designed to cope with both their technologies and their outside environments. As the last two variables change, structure should, too; organizations which fail to adapt appropriately—be they unions, companies, or even governments—are headed for trouble.

Overview

A focus for our discussion is provided by Leavitt's (1972) diagram (presented below) which suggests that organizations be viewed as complex systems consisting of five mutually interdependent classes of variables: task, technology, structure, people, and environment. This chapter focuses on three of those linkages: structure-technology, structure-environment, and technology-environment.

The research discussed below attempts to understand the

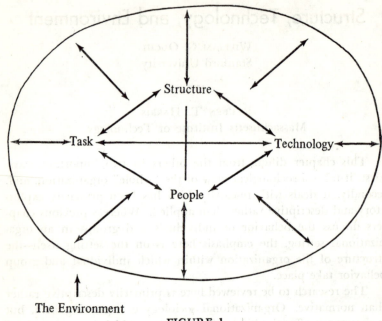

The Environment

FIGURE 1
(Leavitt, 1972, p. 264)

structure of organizations without reference to individual behavior, goals, or attitudes, Leavitt's "people" and "task" variables. It expresses the belief that organizations behave in ways above and beyond the individual actions of its members. Organizations are subject to external forces in the environment and to the demands of its technology. These forces and demands bring about modifications in structure which, in turn, affect the ways in which people work within the organization.

Definitions. To begin, let us provide some general definitions of the terms *structure, technology,* and *environment.*

Structure refers to variables which describe the organization as a whole or relationships between its subunits. Structure thus includes such things as the number of levels of hierarchy (vertical differentiation), the closeness of contact among departments (integration), and the decision-making autonomy of divisions and departments (decentralization). Defined in this manner, structure represents *organizational* rather than individual characteristics (e.g., employee motivation, job satisfaction, or level of education).

Technology is defined by Perrow (1965) as ". . . a technique or complex of techniques to alter 'materials' in an anticipated manner" (p. 915). These "materials" may consist of people, pulp, or tin plate. Thus technology refers to the ways in which the organization solves problems related to producing its final output, whether that ouput is a good or a service. As we shall see, some technologies demand highly flexible organizational structures, while other technologies fit best with more stable structures.

A simple yet complete definition of *environment* does not exist. In general, the environment consists of those individuals, organizations, and cultures which have some impact on the organization under consideration. The environment is especially difficult to identify because most organizations actively attempt to change and shape their environments in an attempt to make them less obstructive and less hostile; thus "pure" and "shaped" environment are difficult to separate.

Organization of this chapter. The study of structure, technology, and environment is in its infancy, and it is characterized by a vast proliferation of different names for similar variables and similar names for different variables. Research findings are thus difficult to compare, and theories at times appear to differ more than they do in fact. We will attempt to bring some order to this literature through reviewing the development of theories of structure, technology, and environment, with the emphasis on finding links between these areas. With the empirical findings as a foundation, we will consider the various purposes that are served by structure, particularly the ways in which structure must provide stability and regularity in the face of problems brought on by increasing size, more complex technologies, and turbulent environments.

The Structure of Organizations

The Organizational Dilemma

One individual cannot build a bridge as efficiently as can 1,000 people working together. That is why organizations exist. Alone, the single individual must be engineer, mason, quarrier, ditch-digger, surveyor, and perform a host of other jobs. With 1,000 workers, each can become master of his trade, and because of this specialization the work can be done more efficiently. But the 1,000 workers must be controlled so that their efforts mesh. The larger the organization, the greater the benefits of specialization but the greater the difficulty of control and coordination. This is a basic dilemma which has plagued organizations for years. Large size is both the goal and the bane of most organizations. The research on structure searches for both better understanding of the problems brought on by large size and identifying the structural arrangements which can best cope with these problems.

Major Dimensions of Structure

An examination of the literature yields the impression that there are dozens of "basic" components of structure. This proliferation of labels sometimes reflects subtle differences in concepts but at other times reflects vagueness or disagreement concerning the precise nature of the phenomenon. Basically, the components of structure can be subsumed by four major variables: complexity, formalization, administrative intensity, and centralization. (Although not a structural variable itself, organizational size, as will be shown, is very much interrelated with these four structural dimensions.)

Complexity refers to the degree of specialization, differentiation, or division of labor. It includes the number of levels of hierarchy (vertical differentiation), the number of divisions or departments (horizontal differentiation), and the number of different job titles (division of labor or specialization). Complexity reflects the degree to which organizational subunits are differentiated, either functionally or by products.

Formalization consists of two dimensions: (a) the degree to which the organization attempts to specify the behavior of its members through rules and procedures such as job descriptions, and (b) the extent to which the organization will tolerate deviations from prescribed rules or the degree of rule enforcement.

Administrative intensity was once a simple ratio of "all administrative" to "all other" workers but is now commonly computed as two ratios: a clerical ratio and a supervisory ratio. These ratios reflect the amount of clerical and supervisory manpower which the organization employs in order to achieve control and coordination.

Centralization most often refers to the locus of decision-making authority at high or low levels in the organization. However, it can also refer to the concentration of power over resource allocation, distribution of pay and other rewards, or other forms of centralization. It is by far the least understood of the major dimensions of structure.

The *size* of an organization usually refers to the number of organizational "members." In a nonvoluntary organization, this is typically the number of people listed on the payroll.

Relationship Between Size and Structure

As an organization increases in size, its structure becomes more differentiated in order to achieve the benefits of specialization; its procedures become more formalized in order to assure that the parts will fit together in the prescribed manner; its clerical and supervisory ratios increase to meet increased communication and coordination needs (but decrease overall due to specialization effects); and it becomes more decentralized because the knowledge necessary for control is scattered throughout its differentiated parts. That is the relationship between size and structure put simply, but there are intricate ways in which size both creates and solves problems within the organizational structure.

Size, complexity, and administrative intensity. It was Graicunas (1933) who first pointed out that in small groups, the complexity of interrelationships grows so rapidly as members are added to the group that no supervisor could effectively supervise more than five or six individuals. Caplow (1957) related this observation to formal organizations and asked how, as the organization grows, it can possibly provide a sufficient number of supervisory personnel to achieve the necessary coordination and control without overburdening itself. Caplow's thoughts were spurred by the work of Terrien and Mills (1955) who demonstrated in a study of school districts that the ratio of administrative employees to all employees was directly related to the size of the organization and speculated that this relationship would severely limit the maximum size to which an organization could grow. Building on the Terrien and Mills study, Anderson and Warkov (1961) found that large size leads to a higher administrative ratio only if the organization becomes more complex as it becomes larger. If complexity is held constant, then the pure effect of size is to decrease rather than to increase the administrative ratio (Pondy, 1969). The introduction of this new variable led to a large number of studies into the relationship between size, complexity, specialization, and the administrative ratio.

These investigations culminated in the research by Blau and Schoenherr (1971) which reported that size has a very complicated relationship with administrative intensity. According to Blau and Schoenherr, as an organization grows, it both creates and solves its own problems of coordination and control. Increasing size leads to increasing differentiation both horizontally and vertically, which adds up to greater complexity. The division of labor is greater, the organization members have time to improve their performance on particular tasks, and each supervisor can become expert in managing a particular kind of work. This growth of expertise leads to greater efficiency as well as to a decreasing administrative ratio. Because each supervisor is in charge of only one function, he can supervise a far larger number of subordinates than he could if he were in a less specialized organization where his duties would involve the supervision of a great number of different kinds of tasks and subordinates. On the other hand, the greater number of organizational subunits leads to problems of coordination. The organization, having differentiated in order to attain the advantages of specialization, must then solve the problems of coordination in order to meet the overall goals of the organization. This need for greater coordination dictates a need for more supervisory personnel, thus increasing the supervisory ratio. Consequently, the effect of size is both to increase and to decrease the administrative ratio.

Centralization and formalization. While the relationships between size, complexity, and administrative intensity have been well established, the relationships between size and formalization and centralization are not so clear. This is so largely because formalization, bureaucratization, and centralization were once considered as equivalents or at least natural accompaniments to each other (Mansfield, 1973) but now are viewed as independent dimensions.

There are many forms of centralization (Whisler, *et al.*, 1967); most studies, however, have dealt only with centralization of decision making. Although our knowledge is still limited, there appears to be some convergence in the findings. First, large size is strongly related to decentralized decision making since, as size increases, the complexity of coordinating goals and information prohibits centralized decision making, particularly when the organization has geographically separated units (Blau and Schoenherr, 1971; Hickson, *et al.*, 1969; Hinings and Lee, 1971; Child and Mansfield, 1972; Khandwalla, 1974).

Secondly, decentralization of decision making is positively related to professionalism in an organization's employees (Hage and Aiken, 1967; Blau, 1968). But note a seeming paradox. Although professionals are found in decentralized organizations, Blau, Heydebrand, and Stauffer (1966) found that among professionals there is a smaller ratio of subordinates to superiors than among nonprofessionals. In this case, the ratio (span of control) does not connote restrictive supervision but rather reflects the fact that professionals make greater demands on their superiors for information and advice.

Formalizing work procedures is a way to achieve control and coordination in large organizations. Blau and Schoenherr (1971) and Pugh, Hickson, Hinings, and Turner (1969) found large size to be positively related to formalization, while Hall, Haas, and Johnson (1967) found size and formalization to be unrelated. This disagreement is difficult to resolve because other studies of "formalization" are really studies of "bureaucratization."

THE ORGANIZATIONAL DILEMMA RESOLVED

An organization can grow and take advantage of the economies of scale inherent in specialization, but it pays a price to do so. As an organization grows, it differentiates into more levels of hierarchy and more divisions. Each of these subunits becomes specialized, thus saving administrative and labor man-hours.

These many specialized subunits become relatively autonomous in decision making since only they possess the expertise necessary for many decisions. In order to coordinate their efforts, the organization must increase its supervisory and clerical manpower; and in order to control their work, it resorts to formalization of procedures, again requiring more supervisors to see that the rules are followed. At some point, the additional burdens of control and coordination outweigh the additional benefits of further specialization, and the organization ceases to grow.

These processes occur whether the organization is authoritarian or participative, voluntary or nonvoluntary, governmental or private. The stucture of the organization, driven by size, almost has a life of its own. Whether this structure is immune to the forces of technology and of the environment, however, is a question we shall consider below.

Technology and Structure

That the structure of an organization molds itself to the demands of technology, few scholars doubt. Describing the precise nature of technology, and documenting the effect of technology on structure, however, has been extremely difficult.

Among the first to examine this question were Trist and Bamforth (1951) who investigated the effects of a change from the manual method of coal mining to the machine-assisted longwall method. This change in technology was not accompanied by any planned change in the social structure of the mine (e.g., there was greater differentiation between the organizational subunits but no coordinative mechanism; the miners could not communicate with each other easily and could not support each other's efforts). The results were high rates of absenteeism, low morale, and very low productivity. The lesson of this study, according to Trist and Bamforth, was that unless the social structure of an organization is molded to fit the demands of technology and the needs of individual workers, the socio-technical system will operate poorly. Similarly, Gouldner (1954) reported on a highly "bureaucratized" gypsum plant whose manager attempted to bring bureaucray to the mine as well. The technology of mining could not be meshed with a "bureaucratic" structure, however, and the attempt failed.

Ever since the publication of these reports, organization theorists have searched for precise ways to specify the links between technology and structure. We will proceed, first, by reviewing the development of the concept of technology as it moved from simple to complex. Then we will review the principal research reports which have dealt with this topic. With these data in mind, we will consider the theory of James D. Thompson, which effectively integrates many of the earlier efforts. Finally, we will conclude with an asssesment of the present state of knowledge concerning the relationship between technology and structure.

THE NATURE OF TECHNOLOGY

Let us begin by generally describing the development of the concept of technology as it moved from a uni-dimensional concept to a multi-dimensional concept.

The single dimension. Trist and Bamforth (1951) and Gouldner (1954) held a simple view of technology as being more or less "routine" or "specialized." In the manual mine work, there was a great deal of job rotation and teamwork, while in the machine-assisted work, jobs were more specialized and routine. This uni-dimensional approach to technology dominated for the next fifteen years. Woodward (1958, 1965) distinguished among technologies in terms of length of production run, Starbuck (1965) in terms of degree of "smoothness," and Hage and Aiken (1969) in terms of "routineness of the production process." Others to use a single dimension include Harvey (1968), who employed "technical diffuseness" as opposed to "technical simplicity," and Rushing (1968) who categorized technologies according to the "degree of hardness of the materials worked on." Stinchcombe (1959) used a simplified version of Woodward's (1958) scale, dealing with custom and mass production or continuous process technologies.

Each of thes esimple views of technology cited above revealed some relationship between technology and structure, but each differed somewhat from the others. The next logical step was to simultaneously study the effect of two or more dimensions of technology on structure. This step seemed all the more reasonable because it could be argued that each of the uni-dimensional studies had really confused two or more dimensions within its single measure. Woodward's (1958) categories, for example, were presented as a single dimension but really included the smoothness of production, the automaticity of production, the complexity of production, and other dimensions. If each of these dimensions could be identified and measured, then we would have a better understanding of technology.

Development of the multi-dimensional view. During the 1960's, the concept of technology went through a dramatic, if checkered, development. In 1967, Perrow suggested that technology be viewed as essentially a problem-solving process and proposed two dimensions along which this process could vary: (1) whether the problem could be solved in known ways (analyzable search) or required the development of new problem-solving techniques (unanalyzable search); (2) whether the problems were mostly familiar (few exceptions) or mostly unfamiliar (many exceptions).

Taking the opposite approach, Pugh, Hickson, Hinings, and Turner (1969), known also as the "Aston group," attempted to find the basic elements of technology by gathering data on many variables and subjecting them to a factor analysis. This process discovered as many as six dimensions which can be considered measures of technology (operating variability, operating diversity, work-flow integration, number of operating sites, dependence, and line control of workflow).

Keeping in mind the many distinctions made concerning technology, let us turn our attention to the relationship between technology and organizational structure.

THE EFFECT OF TECHNOLOGY ON STRUCTURE

Size and technology both determine the shape of organizational structure. We have seen how structure evolves in response to the changing demands for control and coordination which are brought on by large size. Let us now see how the various operationalizations of technology, despite their difficulties, have revealed the ways by which technology affects structure. We will consider the earlier, uni-dimensional studies first and then the findings of Woodward, Perrow, and the Aston group.

Nearly everyone agrees that technology has a significant impact on structure, but there is considerable disagreement as to how the relationship works. A common point of view has been summarized succintly by Perrow (1972):

> In its simplest form, the argument goes like this: When the tasks people perform are well understood, predictable, routine, and repetitive, the bureaucratic structure is most efficient . . . where tasks are not well-understood, . . . the tasks are non-routine, such organizations are difficult to bureaucratize" (p. 166).

Perrow's statement summarizes the conclusions reached by Emery and Trist (1965), by Gouldner (1954), and Hage and Aiken (1969). In each case, the evidence suggested that routine, repetitive technologies lead to formalized procedures, task specialization, and vertical differentiation. In such cases, the demands of routine technology lead to the same sort of structure as do the pressures of large size.

When the technology is nonroutine, however, it demands few formalized procedures, a lower degree of specialization, and less differentiation—or more integration (Lawrence and Lorsch, 1967) in the structure. Thus, nonroutine technologies force a change in the structure of large organizations away from the arrangements that earlier authors suggested are dictated by size alone. For example, though Pondy (1968) noted that the overall effect of size is to reduce the administrative ratio, it now appears that this ratio is greatly affected by the basic production technology. Stinchcombe (1959) found that while clerical workers constituted 53 per cent of all administrative workers in three manufacturing industries (automobiles, iron and steel, and chemicals), they comprised only 20 per cent of the administrative workers in the construction industry. He reasoned that the technology of construction, with its great instability of volume, mix, and location of work made bureaucratization difficult and impractical. Instead, the construction industry relies on professionalization of its work force for self-control and direction. In mass production industries, according to Stinchcombe, traditional bureaucratic methods of administration are more effective.

Harvey (1968), in a study of 43 industrial organizations, ranged technologies from "technically specific" (few product changes in the past ten years) to "technically diffuse" (many product changes). He found that as technical specificity increases, the following structural characteristics also increase: the number of specialized subunits, the number of levels of authority, the ratio of managers and

supervisors to total personnel, and the amount of program spec-
ification (formally prescribed rules for doing things). In our conceptualization of organization structure, Harvey's results show that
as technical specificity increases, complexity, formalization, and
centralization also increase. But in contrast to our previous discussion, Harvey found no relationship between organization structure and organization size.

Although the above studies seem to comprise a disorganized
melange, their findings are, in fact, in agreement on one major
point. In every case, routine, more specific technology was found
to produce structural effects similar to those of large organizational size. That is, while size leads to high complexity, a low
administrative ratio, and high formalization, routineness of technology also produces these effects. Only in the case of centralization do the forces of size and technology conflict. When the technology is nonroutine and size large, then the organization must
rely on different means of achieving control and coordination (to
be discussed below).

Let us now consider in some detail the work of Woodward
(1965) and of Perrow (1970), with a brief consideration of the
findings of the Aston group (1969). Each of these authors has
attempted, in some detail, to draw the relationships between technology and structure. Their successes and their failures provide
the groundwork for future research in this area.

Woodward. The first major study to explicitly introduce technology as an analytical variable was that of Woodward (1958, 1965).
Woodward was primarily interested in determining the extent to
which typical management "principles" (e.g., the necessity of a
limited span of control, the one man-one boss rule, etc.) were
actually used in British industry. After gathering structural data
on 100 British industrial firms, Woodward was unable to find any
consistent patterns in the structural measures when she analyzed
these in terms of classical management principles. Only when she
separated the firms into three categories according to the size of
their production runs (her measure of technology) did some iden-
tifiable relationships between technology and structure emerge.
The three types of technology which Woodward proposed were:

1. *unit or small-batch production,* those organizations
   which produced custom-made products to customers'

    specifications, small batches of products, or large units
in stages;

2. *large-batch or mass production,* those organizations
which produced goods in large batches to be subsequently assembled into units, or which produced complete units by means of assembly-line techniques;

3. *continuous process production,* such as chemicals, liq-
uids, and gases.

After classifying the firms according to their technology, Woodward found a number of relationships between technology and
structure, for example, that the number of levels of authority increases and the need for frequent coordination decreases as one
moves from the simpler unit production technology to the more
complex continuous process technology. Moving from a simple to
a complex technology, the ease of evaluating performance also
increases, and the amount of intraorganizational conflict decreases.

Woodward also discovered that those organizations whose
structure most closely paralleled the median structure of all the
organizations in their particular type of technology were more
productive than firms which had vastly different structures. To
take a single example, in continuous process production, the technology of work specifies to a high degree the tasks to be done, so
that supervisors can and should devote their time to maintaining
healthy social relationships between workers. In unit production,
on the other hand, a supervisor must both supervise the work flow
and maintain interpersonal relationships, both of which he can
do because the nature of work is highly flexible and the feedback
quick, so supervisors can make changes to satisfy both technological
and social demands. In mass production technologies, the work is
not sufficiently flexible to give the supervisor the ability to adjust
it to meet social needs, nor is it sufficiently self-controlling to free
the supervisor to look after interpersonal relationships. In this
situation, coordination and control are poor, and conflict is max-
imal. Firms which deviated greatly from these "pure" types of
supervisory behavior tended to be unproductive.

    In her later book, Woodward (1970) reviewed her earlier work,
including criticisms of it, and presented some new thoughts on
the technology-structure nexus. Reeves and Woodward (1970)
concluded that it was actually methods of organizational control,

rather than technology per se, that affect organization structure:

> This suggests that the control system may be the underlying variable linking organizational behaviour with technology. If so, an alternative solution . . . suggests itself. If control processes proved to be easier to measure and classify than technology, there would be little to be gained in persevering with what is, as has already been shown, a complex exercise (p. 55).

Reeves and Woodward argue that control systems can vary along two dimensions. First, they can reflect the direct control of one person over another (personal), or they rely on a relatively impersonal (Blau and Scott, 1962) and automatic process such as a profit center or an automated production line (mechanical). Secondly, a control system may be universally applied within an organization (unitary), or local standards may apply within each of its differentiated subunits (fragmented). Creating a four-fold typology (Figure 2), Reeves and Woodward then assert that each of the three technological types identified in the first book (Woodward, 1965) reflect different mixtures of types of control (Figure 3).

Figure 3 shows that small-batch firms are somewhat more likely to rely on fragmented control than are continuous-process firms. The major effect, however, is that as one moves from small-batch to mass and then to process technology, there is a pronounced shift from personal to mechanical control. This newer view suggests that the old measures of technology were really ill-formed surro-

FIGURE 2

4 Types of Control Systems

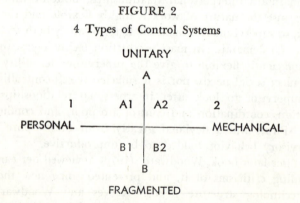

Source: Reeves and Woodward, 1970, p. 53.

FIGURE 3

Control and Technology

	Control System A1 (%)	Control System B1 (%)	Control System B2 (%)	Control System A2 (%)
Unit and Small Batch Production	75	25	....	....
Large Batch and Mass Production	15	35	40	10
Continuous Process Production	....	....	5	95
Total Firms	28	21	18	33

Source: Reeves and Woodward, 1970, p. 54.

gates for control processes. There is no reason for structure to respond directly to one or another technology; the purpose of structure is to achieve control and coordination. If different technologies require different forms of control and coordination, then it is these control and coordination demands of technology which should be studied. The "pure" nature of technology, in an engineering sense, is of little use in understanding organizational structure. This point of view is in accord with the work of Thompson (1967), who, as we shall see, provided a theoretical framework which treats technology as being influential on structure due to the kinds of coordination which it demands and the forms of evaluation or control which it allows.

Perrow. As we saw above, Perrow suggests a two-dimensional view of technology in terms of (1) whether problems are "analyzable" and (2) whether they are familiar (few exceptions) or unfamiliar (many exceptions).

Constructing a matrix (shown below), he argues that organizations (e.g., firms making nuclear-propulsion systems) which are frequently faced with new and uncertain problems that must be handled by unanalyzable search procedures will employ nonroutine technologies, and these will be accompanied by nonbureaucratic organization structures. At the other extreme, organizations (e.g.,

	Few exceptions	Many exceptions
Unanalyzable search	Craft	Nonroutine
Analyzable search	Routine	Engineering

firms making heating elements for electric stoves) which face few
exceptions to their daily routines and have standardized operating
programs will exhibit routine technologies accompanied by bureaucratic organization structures. Between these two extremes
of technology, Perrow identifies a craft technology (used, for example, by firms making fine glassware) and an engineering technology (used by firms building made-to-order machines such as
drill presses or electric motors). As with the routine and nonroutine technologies, the craft and engineering technologies each
have their own associated organization structure. Perrow has not
submitted his theory to empirical test, but he believes that organizations will ". . . wittingly or unwittingly attempt to maximize
the congruence between their technology and their structure"
(1970, p. 80).

The Aston group (1969). We have already mentioned the vast
empirical work done by the Aston group. As many as six of their
dimensions can be interpreted as representing technological variables. While some of these appeared at first to be related to
structure, the relationships disappeared when the effects of size
were controlled (Hickson, Pugh, and Pheysey, 1969; Child and
Mansfield, 1972). The Aston group concluded that there is no
"technological imperative"—there is no evidence that technology
dictates structure. Their argument is not completely convincing, however, despite the large amount of supporting data. For
example, Aldrich (1972) has shown that the data collected by the
Aston group can be used to support a number of causal models
in which technology affects structure, or in which structure affects
technology.

The work of the Aston group reinforces the notion that future
research on the effects of technology on organizational structure
must take explicit account of all of the relationships among size,
technology, and structure.

JAMES D. THOMPSON

Much of the discussion above can be pulled together in a theoretical framework presented by James D. Thompson (1967), and
his work has attracted great attention within the field. Thomp-

son has produced a wholly integrated theory of an active organiza-
ion which deals with the ways in which the organization treats
both its technology and its environment. With regard to the impact of technology, Thompson argues that the structure which will
be taken by the organization is determined by what he refers to
as its "core technology," that is, the process that an organization
employs to adapt or change materials which it then exchanges with
the environment. An organization's technical core can be viewed
as consisting of those processes which define the organization's primary function. (An organization's core can be either mechanical
or intellectual or both. For example, the technical core of an
automobile manufacturing company is represented by its assembly
line, and the technical core of a consulting firm is represented by
the ideas and analytic skills of its staff.)

It should be noted that Thompson never attempts to categorize
technologies in the "engineering" sense, according to their routineness (Hage and Aiken, 1969), their smoothness (Woodward,
1958), their specificity (Harvey, 1968), the hardness of their inputs (Rushing, 1968), or their irregularity (Stinchcombe, 1959).
Instead, he refers only to the degree of interdependence and coordination which a technology demands and to the evaluation
and control systems which various technologies permit—a view consistent with Reeves and Woodward (1970).

Thompson's approach to structure builds on the work of Barnard
(1938), Simon (1957a, 1957b), March and Simon (1958), and
Cyert and March (1963). This approach stressed the role of "decision making" in organizations. It starts with the commonsense
notion that the purpose of organizations is to achieve goals which
are so great in scope that no individual could achieve them alone.
For this reason the organization must subdivide tasks into sufficiently small parts that each individual can assimilate all the information necessary to understand and reach a decision concerning
his part of the overall problem. Thompson points out that in
order to achieve organizational purposes, not only must the task
be subdivided into tractable pieces, but each of the pieces must be
related to the others in some coordinated fashion. Thompson
distinguishes three types of interdependence which might characterize the technology of the organization:

1. *Pooled interdependence.* Thompson describes pooled interdependence as follows:

> The Tuscaloosa branch of an organization may not interact at all with the Oshkosh branch, and neither may have contact with the Kokomo branch. Yet they may be interdependent in the sense that unless each performs adequately, the total organization is jeopardized. . . . We can describe this situation as one in which each part renders a discrete contribution to the whole and each is supported by the whole (p. 54).

2. *Sequential interdependence.* Thompson describes sequential interdependence as follows:

> Interdependence may also take a serial form, with the Koekuk plant producing parts which become inputs for the Tucumcari assembly operation . . . Keokuk must act properly before Tucumcari can act; and unless Tucumcari acts, Keokuk cannot solve its output problem (p. 54).

3. *Reciprocal interdependence.* In reciprocal interdependence, the output of each of the parts becomes inputs for the others.

> This is illustrated by the airline which contains both operation and maintenance units: The production of the maintenance unit is an input for operations, in the form of a serviceable aircraft; and the product (or by-product) of operations is an input for maintenance, in the form of an aircraft needing maintenance (p. 55).

Thompson asserts that all organizations have at least pooled interdependence, all those which have sequential interdependence also have pooled interdependence, and all of those which have reciprocal interdependence also have sequential and pooled interdependence. And, as the degree of interdependence increases, coordination becomes more difficult.

To go along with these forms of interdependence, Thompson proposes three types of coordination: (1) standardization, (2) coordination by plan, and (3) coordination by mutual adjustment. Standardization involves the establishment of rules and procedures which determine the action of each unit and which brings about mutual coordination between all of the units when each follows its standardized directives. Coordination by plan is more loosely defined and consists of "the establishment of schedules for the interdependent units by which their actions may be then governed" (p. 56). Coordination by plan permits somewhat greater flexibility of action than does coordination by standardization. Coordination by mutual adjustment is a process through which plans and actions are adjusted during the transformation process as a result of mutual interaction and exchange of information. This form of coordination is clearly the most flexible.

Thompson suggests that coordination by standardization is best suited to pooled interdependence, coordination by plan is appropriate for sequential interdependence, and coordination by mutual adjustment is called for in reciprocal interdependence. He further points out that the costs of coordination are very great as more complex types of coordination are undertaken.

Thompson's work embodies many of the best features of all that we have discussed above. He sees clearly that the basic function of organizational structure is the maintenance of control and coordination. He focuses on the ways in which technology affects these processes by causing modifications in structure.

Technology and Structure in Perspective

Organizations exist for the purpose of controlling and coordinating the efforts of large numbers of people. This is a lesson twice learned. In the previous section, we learned that structure responds to the pressures for control and for coordination which come with increasing size. Now, we have learned that structure also responds to the pressures for control and coordination which come from technology. Both Woodward (1970) and Thompson (1967) came to the conclusion that technology affects structure through its control and coordination demands. The nature of the goods processed and the routineness of the tasks themselves are unimportant except as they affect coordination.

But this was a lesson learned the hard way. The early studies, from Trist and Bamforth (1951) onward, clung to the "engineering" view of technology. Their crude approach yielded results principally because their simple measures served as effective surrogates for the control and coordination demands of technology. When the Aston group (Pugh, *et al.*, 1969) attempted a complex "engineering" approach, the technological variables became purified, the control and coordination dimensions which had surreptitiously accompanied earlier studies dropped out, and they found no relationships between structure and technology.

Future approaches to studies of technology and structure may well be exemplified by the work of Khandwalla (1974), who draws heavily upon Thompson (1967) and, although he does not cite them, is close to the position of Reeves and Woodward (1970). Khandwalla simultaneously considers the effects of size and of technology on structure and is thus able to assess their unique effects.

As future research explores the effects of size and technology on the elements of structure discussed above, the study of organizational behavior will gain in two ways. First, we will begin to understand in greater depth how technology interacts with control and coordination; and, secondly, we will be able to see how organizations respond when their size and technology make opposing demands on their structure.

Environment and Structure

The next relationship which we will discuss is that between the organization and its environment. No organization is immune to its environment. Outside individuals, institutions, and cultures inevitably provide opportunities, impose constraints, and thus affect the activities of the organization. Thus, the organization is an "open system" (Katz and Kahn, 1966) which must draw sufficient resources from its environment to assure its survival.

Most research dealing with the environment of organizations recognizes not only the impact of the environment on organizations but also the impact of organizations on their environments. According to Weick (1969), the organization is "proactive" rather than "reactive" with respect to its environment. Most organizations actively seek ways to manage their environments in order to bring certainty to an uncertain world.

As the organization actively engages its environment, what changes take place in the structure of the organization? We will begin by considering the question of organizational boundaries, specifying where the organization ends and its environment begins. Next, we will review some perspectives as to how the environment can be described and defined. This will be followed by a discussion of some of the ways in which organizations deal with their environments in order to reduce uncertainty. We will then consider three major studies which examine the environment-structure relationship and close with the presentation of a theoretical framework (Thompson, 1967) which integrates many of the ideas discussed in this section.

ORGANIZATIONAL BOUNDARIES

In order to understand how the environment affects an organization, it is crucial to know the boundary point where the organization ends and the environment begins. Despite years of thought and some valiant research efforts, organization theorists have yet to determine the precise nature of organizational boundaries. Consider, for example, an aerospace company which has as one of its largest customers the United States Air Force. There are a number of Air Force contract officers physically located within the aerospace company, and the contact between the two organizations is dense and frequent. Is an individual on the Air Force payroll a part of the aerospace company, or is he part of the company's environment?

In an attempt to clarify the boundary issue, Evan (1966) has created the concept of the *organization set*. The organization set consists of those organizations which interact with the "focal" organization—that is, those organizations which supply inputs to and receive outputs from the primary organization under consideration. The environment of the focal organization thus consists of those organizations which are a part of its organization set. Clearly, the contract officer in our example is monitoring the aerospace company's performance and is, therefore, part of that firm's environment.

The environment, however, consists of more than just other organizations. Hall (1972) distinguishes between the *general environment* and the *specific environment*. The general environment consists of those conditions outside the organization which confront all organizations, for example, the economy, the legal system, the political system, and the culture. The specific environment refers to those factors which are relatively critical and specific to the focal organization. Elements of the specific environment interact directly with the focal organization.

Weick (1969)—as do many other students of organization—points out that these problems of definition of organizational boundaries can never precisely be settled, at least in part because organizations "enact" their own environments. Organizations do not passively react to conditions which surround them but rather play an active role in shaping or "enacting" the nature of their environments. Thus, the boundary between the organization and its environment is constantly shifting.

Perhaps the critical point to be made is not that organizational boundaries are ill-defined but that organizations actively seek to blur their boundaries. As we shall see, most organizations, if allowed to, would expand their boundaries until there was no environment left.

THE NATURE OF THE ENVIRONMENT

The study of environment and structure is so new that the first widely recognized typology (Emery and Trist, 1965) remains accepted today, although in slightly modified form.

Emery and Trist (1965) distinguished four kinds of environments. These are:

(1) *Placid, randomized.* This type of environment is relatively unchanging and homogenous, and its demands are randomly distributed and change only slowly over time.

(2) *Placid, clustered.* This environment is similarly slow to change, but its threats and its rewards are clustered rather than being randomly distributed. A monopolistic market is an example of such an environment. In this type of environment, the organization's survival depends on its intimate knowledge of the environment.

(3) *Disturbed, reactive.* In such an environment, not only is there competition between similar organizations, but each organization seeks to further its own ends at least in part by hindering the opportunities of its rivals.

(4) *Turbulent field.* A turbulent field is a dynamic, rapidly changing environment. In a turbulent field, organizations must con-

tinually re-evaluate their relationship vis-á-vis governmental agencies, competitors, customers, and suppliers, as well as develop new technologies through the processes of research.

Each type of environment demands more atttention from the organization than does the type listed before it. Emery and Trist suggest that the organizational form which is most successful will be different depending on the environment faced by the organization, although they do not specify the ways in which the structures might differ. Rather than passively reacting to the environment, Emery and Trist suggest that the organization should structure itself in a manner which will facilitate interaction with other systems in the environment. Each organization should provide for maximum surveillance, cooperation, and interchange with elements within its environment.

Emery and Trist concentrated on the organization which exists in the turbulent field, asserting that, ". . . turbulent fields demand some overall form of organization that is essentially different from the hierarchically structured forms to which we are accustomed." Terreberry (1968) asserts that such "turbulent fields" are becoming the predominant type of environment. If this is so, then the majority of future changes in organizational structure will be externally rather than internally initiated. Bennis and Slater (1968) concur, and they furthermore conclude that one result of this increasing rate of change will be the disappearance of bureaucratic organizations.

Duncan (1972), following Dill (1958) and Thompson (1967), used two basic dimensions of the environment which he labeled "simple-complex" and "static-dynamic." The environment is simple if it offers few variables for the decision makers in organizations to consider, complex if it offers many. It is static if these variables change their values slowly, dynamic if they change quickly. Decision makers faced by complex-dynamic environments experience very high perceived uncertainty, while those in simple-static environments experience relatively little uncertainty.

Research on the nature of the environment is just beginning. The formulations of Emery and Trist (1965) and of Duncan (1972) do not empirically relate the nature of the environment to the structure of organizations as we have been treating it. Their common goal is to find ways to describe the kinds of uncertainties which the environment creates.

MANAGING THE ENVIRONMENT

The organization cannot have an easy relationship with its environment. In its natural state the environment creates uncertainty, and uncertainty threatens the rational process which is at the heart of every organization. The organization does not merely accommodate itself to uncertainty, it actively seeks to reduce it (Starbuck, 1965; Katz and Kahn, 1966). That is, organizations do not have to accept or react passively to the conditions which surround them; they can take an active part in shaping these condiions to suit their needs: they can either attempt to blur their boundaries, thus gaining some control or at least some intelligence of their environment, or they seek to seal themselves off from this environment.

Selznick's study (1949) of the development of the Tennessee Valley Authority (TVA) is one of the most vivid examples of how an organization can manipulate its environment. Faced by initial opposition, the TVA co-opted into its membership the dominant agricultural power structure of the Tennessee Valley. Selznick describes the process of co-optation as follows:

> The unacknowledged absorption of nucleuses of power into the administrative structure of an organization makes possible the elimination or appeasement of potential sources of opposition. At the same time, as the price of accommodation, the organization commits itself to avenues of activity and lines of policy enforced by the character of the co-opted elements . . . viewed thus broadly, the process of informal co-optation is a mechanism of comprehensive adjustment, permitting a formal organization to enhance its chances for survival by accommodating itself to existing centers of interest and power within its area of operation (p. 217).

Selznick points out that, although official regulations prohibit the merger of two organizations, one may informally co-opt the other in order to enhance its chances of survival. This technique clearly has dangers, however, for the co-opted members may seek to change the original goals of the co-opting organization.

A more familiar form of co-optation is noted by Pfeffer (1972a), who found that size and composition of the boards of directors in 80 nonfinancial corporations were related to environmental forces. He showed that corporations attempt to co-opt lawyers and bankers by including them on boards when they are subject to governmental regulations and have high needs for capital. Pfeffer claims that co-optation is the chosen strategy when total absorption is " (1) legally proscribed, (2) impossible due to resource constraints, or (3) when partial inclusion is sufficient to solve the organization's problems of dealing with the external organization" (p. 222). Pfeffer (1973a) observed a similar use of boards of directors in a study of 57 hospitals.

A more subtle form of managing the environment is for companies to trade executives (Pfeffer and Leblebici, 1973b). As executives move from company to company, job-hopping within one industry, styles of management become homogenized, thus reducing uncertainty for every firm.

Stronger than co-optation is total absorption, or merger. Pfeffer (1972b) has noted that mergers occur for three reasons: (1) to acquire suppliers or customers, (2) to acquire competitors, and (3) to diversify into new activities. In each case, the goal of the merger is to reduce the dependence of the organization on its environment.

INTERNAL ORGANIZATION TO COPE WITH THE ENVIRONMENT

Turning from the ways in which organizations attempt to manage their environments by establishing boundary-spanning mechanisms, let us now look at three major studies which have examined how an organization's internal structure responds to environmental influences.

The internal structure of the organization is adaptable to different kinds of environmental demands. Because the organization exists in an open relationship with its environment, as the nature of the environment changes, so the internal structure must change in order to maintain communication flows. Several authors have dealt with the nature of these structural changes which are responses to environmental demands.

Burns and Stalker. Hypothesizing that organizations which exist in stable environments take on different structural forms than organizations which exist in turbulent environments, Burns and Stalker (1961) studied 20 industrial firms in Britain. They found striking differences in the form and operation of organizations in each of these kinds of environments, which they described as "mechanistic" and "organismic" systems (Figure 4).

FIGURE 4

Comparison of the Characteristics of Mechanistic and Organismic Systems

Mechanistic Systems	Organismic Systems
1. Differentiation into specialized functional tasks	1. Continual adjustment of tasks through interaction with others
2. Subordinates pursue individual tasks with concern for narrow task completion	2. Generalized responsibility
	3. Commitment to organization as a whole
3. Rigid chain of command	4. Interaction laterally as well as vertically
4. Detailed and exhaustive job descriptions	5. Communication of advice and information rather than orders
5. Overall picture relevant only to those at the top of the hierarchy	6. Sanctions derived from community (peers and superiors) with concern for the whole organization
6. Interaction follows vertical lines along chain of command	7. A network structure of control, authority, and communication
7. Behavior is governed by superiors	
8. Emphasis is on narrow, specific knowledge rather than general, complete knowledge	

Burns and Stalker believed that organizational performance will be optimal when the mechanistic system is combined with a stable environment or when the organismic system is combined with a turbulent environment. If the wrong system is combined with the wrong environment, then they argued that organizational performance would suffer.

Hage and Aiken. In 1967, Hage and Aiken produced evidence which can be interpreted as supporting the Burns and Stalker position. Hage and Aiken studied a set of social welfare organizations which existed in turbulent, rapidly changing environments. As expected, these organizations, in the process of learning to cope with their environment, developed a low degree of job formalization, a high degree of employee participation in agency-wide decisions, and a high degree of employee job satisfaction. These characteristics led to many program changes, and the relationships remained approximately the same even when the size, age, and specific functions of the organization were varied.

Lawrence and Lorsch. Lawrence and Lorsch (1967) presented evidence which again confirmed the view that organizational structure must be properly linked to characteristics of the environment in order for productivity and performance to be high. They studied organizations from three different industries: plastics, packaged foods, and standardized containers. They characterized the plastics industry as being in a rapidly changing, highly turbulent environment, one in which both the nature of technology and the demands of customers were highly unpredictable. Firms in the standardized container industry, on the other hand, were in a highly stable environment, one in which there were few surprises. The packaged foods industry, they felt, lay somewhere between these two extremes.

Lawrence and Lorsch were interested in two primary aspects of organization structure: (1) *differentiation* (differences in cognitive and emotional orientations) and (2) *integration* (quality of collaboration between organization subunits). They expected that the more turbulent the environment which faces an organization, the greater would be the degree of differentiation beween its sub-parts. In an organization which faces a stable environment, they hypothesized, virtually all organization members could operate on the same set of schedules, with the same set of goals and expectations. In a rapidly changing environment, however, some parts of the environment would demand rapid change and flexibility, while other parts of the environment and some internal demands of everyday administration would require much more stable conditions. For this reason, they expected to find a much higher level of structural and normative differentiation within the plastics industry than within the standardized container industry. In addition, they expected that while differentiation may be necessary in a turbulent environment, a high degree of integration then also becomes a necessity. An organization which successfully differentiates its sub-parts but does not manage to coordinate them will fly into a number of pieces with poor performance results.

Lawrence and Lorsch's research supported both hypotheses. By separating the organizations in each of the three industries into high performers, medium performers, and low performers, they were able to test the proposition that the fit between structure and environment determined the performance of the organization. They found, in fact, that in each case, the high performing organizations were those which had a structure which best fit the environmental demands. In the plastics industry, for example, the high performing organizations had the greatest differentiation and also the greatest integration. In the standardized container industry, the highest performing organizations had the least differentiation and consequently the least need for integration.

Reducing Uncertainty: James D. Thompson

Thompson (1967) again provides us with a useful general framework for tying together our discussion of environment, technology, and structure. He views organizations as open systems which are affected by forces frequently beyond their control. All of this contributes to uncertainty.

Because organizations are created for the purpose of achieving a rational distribution of work which no individual could achieve alone, they operate under criteria of rationality and hence require both determinateness and certainty. The locus of the uncertainty which faces the organization lies in its interdependence with other organizations, its organization set. Thompson suggests the strategies which organizations should employ in order to create stability and certainty in their environment:

1. ". . . organizations facing heterogeneous task environments seek to identify homogeneous segments and establish structural units to deal with each" (e.g., Lawrence and Lorsch, 1967; Emery and Trist, 1965).

2. ". . . boundary-spanning components facing homogeneous segments of the task environment are further sub-divided to match surveillance capacity with environmental action" (e.g., Lawrence and Lorsch, 1967; Emery and Trist, 1965).

3. "The organization component facing a stable task environ-

ment will rely on rules to achieve its adaptation to that environment" (e.g., Burns and Stalker, 1961; Emery and Trist, 1956; Terreberry, 1968).

4. "When the range of task environment variations is large or unpredictable, the responsible organization component must achieve the necessary adaptation by monitoring that environment and planning responses, and this calls for localized units" (e.g., Selznick, 1949; Pfeffer, 1972a, 1973a; Lawrence and Lorsch, 1967) (pp. 70–72).

In addition, Thompson refers to techniques such as long-term contracts, mergers, and acquisitions, as devices which the organization can use to buffer itself from uncertainties in its environment. In essence, Thompson's point is that as task environments become more heterogeneous and more dynamic, the need for specialized boundary-spanning components of the organization increases. Boundary-spanning organizational components are those sub-units which deal with the environment, attempting to gain some control over it either through direct manipulation or through observing and learning about the environment in order to be able to anticipate its demands.

The more rapidly the environment changes and the more uncertain it becomes, the greater must be the internal flexibility of the organization. In a stable environment, the organization can employ standardized rules and centralization as modes of coordination and control. As the environment becomes more complex and more unpredictable, the organization must become more decentralized and make more use of coordination by mutual adjustment. As discussed above, the purpose of these structural variations is to protect the technological core of the organization from uncertainty and complexity, in order to assure the continued survival of the organization.

A Convergence

Although the study of organization and environment is relatively young, there already seem to be areas of convergence. The most basic agreement is on the view that the internal technological processes of organizations demand rationality, stability, and predictability, but forces in the environment threaten these conditions. In order to reduce its dependence on the environment, the organization resorts to various means of expanding its boundaries through such means as co-optation (Selnick, 1949), interlocking boards of directors (Pfeffer, 1972a, 1973a), trading employees (Pfeffer and Leblebici, 1973b), and merger (Pfeffer, 1972b).

No organization can absorb all of its environment, however, so organizations change their structure to permit more effective contact with other organizations. Differentiation serves to provide specialization and economies of scale (Blau and Schoenherr, 1971), and one form of this specialization is for each differential unit to specialize in monitoring a different sector of the environment (Lawrence and Lorsch, 1967).

Of course, whether differentiation occurs in response to size, to the environment, or to the control needs of a particular technology (Reeves and Woodward, 1970), it brings with it a need for integrative mechanisms. These integrative mechanisms may take the form of a higher supervisory ratio (Blau and Schoenherr, 1971), a mechanical or automatic control system (Reeves and Woodward, 1970), or specialized department-spanning personnel (Likert, 1961; Lawrence and Lorsch, 1968; Whisler, 1970).

Thus, the organization seeks to deal with its environment by controlling what it can control and by monitoring closely what it cannot. In an attempt to bring stability to its technology, the organization undertakes change in its structure. The point to be remembered is that organizational success depends on the organization achieving the appropriate levels of differentiation *and* integration, with appropriateness being determined by the characteristics of the environment.

Environment and Technology

In order to complete our review of the relationships between structure, technology, and the environment, we must consider the relationship between environment and technology. Of course, environments and technologies may not directly affect each other, but both simultaneously interact with structure. A number of these mutual interactions have already been noted, but we find in the work of Thompson (1967) and of Lawrence and Lorsch (1967) an explicit consideration of these effects.

As we noted earlier, in uncertain, turbulent environments the organization is confronted with constant threats to its survival. Thompson suggests that given these environmental threats the organization will attempt to protect or "seal off" its core technology from the fluctuating demands of the environment. In order to accomplish this, organizations surround their core technology with input and output components. Examples of these buffering activities include stockpiling on the input side and warehousing inventories on the output side. Additionally, organizations attempt to "smooth" environmental demands by offering inducements to use services at "nonpeak" times. For example, the telephone company offers lower rates during nonbusiness hours for long-distance calls in an effort to smooth phone demand. Airlines and other transportation firms offer special reduced fares on "light days" and during slow seasons.

As Lawrence and Lorsch (1967) point out, organizations in dynamic, changing environments (e.g., the plastics industry) must constantly be concerned with meeting environmental demands. Since their marketing and research departments are unable to "protect" the technology (production) from the environment, constant changes must be made in this technology itself.

The organization utilizes various means to minimize environmental fluctuations and demands on its technology. However, the more "powerful" the environmental pressures, the less likely are organizations to be able to "seal off" their technical core. Though the environmental pressures on technology are often only indirect, they nonetheless are powerful and cannot be ignored.

The Dynamic Organization

The study of organizations has made great progress since Gulick and Urwick published their *Papers on the Science of Administration* (1937). In the search for the one best model of organization, our thinking has evolved from Weber's bureaucratic model (1947) based on impartiality and rationality, through human relations and participative management (Likert, 1961; Argyris, 1964) to the present acceptance of contingency views (see Chapter One). The earlier perspectives that the task and people components of the organization should be the primary determinates of organizational structure and that organizational success was solely the result of the people-task linkage have been shown to be inadequate—inadequate in the sense that such simplistic views are neither descriptive of the complexities of organizational dynamics nor predictive of organizational success.

We no longer believe that there is one ideal administrative ratio, one best form of departmental structure or one best way to organize. We have brought technology and the environment explicitly into the domain of organization research, and we have begun to see how these forces are simultaneously articulated in the structure of the organization as it seeks to achieve control and coordination. Last but not least, we can now provide to those who study individual and group behavior a better understanding of the organizational context in which humans act out their roles.

It would be unfair to characterize even the early students of administration as being uniformly of the belief that one best form of organization exists, for Luther Gulick noted in 1937 that,

> Students of administration have long sought a single principal of effective departmentalization just as alchemists sought the philosopher's stone. But they have sought in vain. There is apparently no one most effective system of departmentalism (taken from Lawrence and Lorsch, 1967, p. 168).

In the 1970's it is the rule rather than the exception to encounter Gulick's point of view. Blau and Schoenherr (1971) describe an internal structure that is properly quite different for small organizations than for large ones. Lawrence and Lorsch (1967) demonstrated that a high degree of differentiation is suited to complex, turbulent environments but not to simple, stable environments. Thompson (1967) held that standardization is an entirely appropriate mechanism for control and coordination where pooled interdependence exists but not for sequential or for mutual interdependence. Reeves and Woodward (1970) found unitary, personal control systems to be suitable for some technologies but not others. Our view of organizations has become more elaborate, more complex, and it admits a larger number of alternative forms of structure.

In addition to considering more alternative forms of structure, we can now consider more influences on structure than before.

The work of Emery and Trist (1965) and of Lawrence and Lorsch (1967) provide us explicit means of relating structure to environments. The works of Trist and Bamforth (1951) and Woodward (1965, 1970) connect structure to technology. Thompson's comprehensive review (1967) shows us how structure, technology, and environment simultaneously affect the processes of control and coordination.

One major influence on organizational structure that is just now beginning to receive attention is the effect of culture. Azumi (1973) has shown that the "usual" relationship between large size and the division of labor did not hold in his study of 25 Japanese manufacturing organizations. According to Johnson and Ouchi (1974), this absence of specialization in large Japanese organizations is due to the common Japanese practice of rotating managers to different divisions and different functional areas every three to five years. This practice provides control and coordination mechanisms which rely on subordinates to "see the whole picture" and to coordinate their efforts through lateral communication, rather than relying on direction from above. This major alternative to the Western approach is supported by the Japanese practice of "lifetime commitment" (Abegglen, 1958), which guarantees that people who have gained wide experience in an organization will stay with it and thus be able to provide coordination and control. Although Likert's (1961) "linking pin" coordinator serves the same purpose in some American organizations, this form of coordinaton is the exception in the U.S. and the rule in Japan.

It is expected that in the next few years we will see a significant interest in research examining the impact of culture and of subcultures on organizational behavior.

Conclusion

The organization, formerly a dull, static collection of organization charts, spans of control, suppliers and clients, is now revealed as a dynamic system whose parts constantly must be adjusted. To those who study the social psychology of the worker and the work group, we can now give some help. We can refer to the clear need that organizations have for "rational" behavior, where friendship and blood are of no concern (Barnard, 1938; Weber, 1947 translation; Thompson, 1967). We can explain that organizations fail to satisfy individual needs (for example, social and self-actualization needs) not because they are arrogant but because their very nature as "rational" creations (Udy, 1962; Litwak and Meyer, 1966) requires this. Thus, the conflict between individual and organization remains one of the major problems to be faced by all modern industrial nations.

To those whose concern is with job design or participative schemes, we can give a warning that work arrangements are not completely flexible. Managements do not resist job design changes just because they are jealous of their power, although that may sometimes be the case. Rather, technological, environmental, and size conditions dictate the fairly specific structural forms that should evolve (Blau and Schoenherr, 1971; Thompson, 1967; Lawrence and Lorsch, 1967). Resolving the conflict between the organization's "rational" demands for particular forms of structure and people's needs for other forms of structure is a problem faced by all those who manage, work in, or study organizations.

The next two chapters speak directly to the problems mentioned above. The immediately following chapter is concerned with conflicts which occur in organizations and with specifying alternative mechanisms which might be employed to resolve them. The final chapter deals with a question we have left unanswered—how can management make the process by which the organization adjusts to its environment more effective and less painful?

Chapter 6

Conflict and Conflict Resolution

Donald Nightingale*
Queen's University, Ontario

In the introductory chapter of their pioneering work on game theory, Luce and Raiffa (1957) point out that conflict is a theme that has occupied the thinking of man more than any other—with the exception of God and love. Social conflict has fallen within the purview of the historian, the novelist, the philosopher, and the theologian, and has been treated systematically by authors in all of the biological and social sciences. Conflicts between nations, political parties, and ideologies have been examined by the political scientist; conflicts in the market place have been studied by the economist; group conflicts of various kinds—familial, racial, religious, and social class—have been investigated by the sociologist; and the struggle for survival by species of differing genetic endowments has been studied by the biologist.

The subject of conflict is obviously of central importance to collective bargaining in particular and to organizational behavior in general. But although impressive strides in the study of conflict have been made by some scientific disciplines, only the beginning of a systematic theory of social conflict is emerging in the field of organizational behavior. We will explore this emerging theory by offering, first, a definition of conflict and then proceeding to examine two contrasting approaches to the study of social conflict— the "human relations" and the "pluralist" approaches. The origins of each approach, the unique way each views the nature and causes of conflict, and the resolution strategies offered will provide the background necessary to evaluate some of the recent attempts to develop a broader, integrative framework. This review should offer suggestive leads to those who advise on matters of public policy in this area and to those who seek more viable resolutions of conflict in any setting—be it marital, racial, organizational, or international.

* The author wishes to acknowledge the assistance of two colleagues, Bryan Downie and Robert Crandall, of Queen's University.

What Is Conflict?

In common usage, conflict includes race riots, donnybrooks in hockey games, jockeying for the right of way with a taxi driver, strikes and lockouts, elections, competition in the market place, family quarrels, separation and divorce, revolution and civic disorder, war, and a variety of other human and social relationships where the interests of parties are, or appear to be, opposed. For purposes of this discussion, therefore, we will adopt a broad definition of conflict compiled by Stern (1970; see also Fink, 1968):

> Conflict . . . may be viewed behaviorally as a form of opposition which is opponent-centered; based on incompatibility of goals, aims, or values of opposing parties; direct; and personal; in which the opponent . . . controls the goal or object desired by both parties. (p. 1)

This broad conceptualization of conflict can be differentiated into two useful constructs: (1) A *conflict situation* refers to the pursuit of incompatible, or at least seemingly incompatible, goals by two or more parties such that the gains to one party come at the expense of the other. (One party need not lose in absolute terms, but may lose when compared to the other party.) (2) A *conflict episode* refers to the behavior of the parties which results from the conflict situation. A common conflict situation exists between labor and management during contract negotiations. The behavior of the parties, such as threats, attempts to arouse public sympathy, strike action, and the like, are all conflict episodes. Our concern in this chapter is a rather wide-ranging discussion of conflict, and we will consequently be less concerned with precise theoretical definitions of the concept.

The Two Views of Conflict

Practitioners and researchers who concern themselves with social conflict can be divided into two camps: (1) those who believe that conflict is an inevitable and, if managed properly, desirable part of human interaction (the pluralists), and (2) those who believe that conflict signifies the breakdown of normal and "healthy" interaction among individuals and groups (the human relationists).

The separation of all behavioral scientists into these two camps is admittedly an oversimplification of a complex and legitimately controversial area. The separation, however, highlights the fundamental influence that a priori assumptions play in the way people react to conflict situations and in the means they use to reduce or resolve conflict. The two extremes of the spectrum of underlying assumptions about conflict are presented below:

UNDERLYING ASSUMPTIONS ABOUT CONFLICT

Human Relations Approach	Pluralist Approach
(1) Conflict, by and large, is "bad" and should be eliminated or resolved;	(1) Conflict is good and should be encouraged; conflict must be regulated, however, so that it does not get out of hand.
(2) Conflict is not inevitable;	(2) Conflict is inevitable;
(3) Conflict results from breakdowns in communication and lack of understanding, trust, and openness between parties;	(3) Conflict results from (a) a struggle for limited rewards, be they food, status, responsibility, or power, and (b) to a lesser extent, from innate aggressive and competitive instincts in man;
(4) The environment plays a major role in shaping behavior. Thus, any inappropriate or "bad" behavior, such as aggressiveness or competitiveness, results from circumstances in the environment which can be altered;	(4) The importance of the environment has been overplayed; there are many determinants of behavior including genetic and physiological, which program individuals to act aggressively;
(5) Man is essentially good; trust, cooperation, and goodness are givens in human nature.	(5) Man, if not essentially bad, is nevertheless driven by aggressive, self-seeking, and competitive instincts.

The human relations view of conflict found its first and most articulate spokesman in Mayo (1933, 1947), and the theory has acquired other supporters over time such as Lewin (1948), T-group trainers, and modern-day theorists such as Likert (1961, 1967).

The pluralist view, of course, arises from social and political philosophers who were primarily concerned with structuring society so as to make it more responsive to the diverse interests within it. According to the pluralist view, there should be as many power centers as possible, consistent with the effective functioning of society, and these power centers should be roughly balanced in strength. Follett (see Metcalf and Urwick, 1940) was among the first to propose that organizations might benefit from the open expression of differences among members. She felt that if some "joint" responsibility to the unity of the larger system existed, it would be safe for labor and management to take "sides." In fact, she felt that it was important to have sides in an organization because it is helpful to know what each group says is good for the whole as seen from a particular viewpoint. Kerr (1964) has been a leading figure in the application of pluralist political theory to the study of organizational conflict.

Related approaches. The classification of conflict proposed here is hardly unique. Harbison and Coleman (1951) divided union-management relationships into three categories: armed truce, working harmony, and cooperation. Armed truce is characterized by (a) a feeling on the part of management that unions are at best necessary evils, and a belief on the part of labor leaders that the union's main purpose is to challenge management; (b) rivalry for the loyalty of workers; and (c) a desire to work out orderly and mutually acceptable procedures for limiting conflict and compromising differences. Under working harmony, union and management recognize the legitimacy of each other and are aware that although differences of objectives frequently occur, it is nevertheless possible for each side to advance its interests. Union-management cooperation, as the name implies, is a relationship in which both parties are willing to pursue cooperative activity, and mutual trust, confidence, and respect exist between parties. The armed truce relationship is roughly equivalent to the pluralist approach, and the cooperative relationship is subsumed under the human relations view.

Walton and McKersie (1965) compare "distributive" and "integrative" bargaining—similar to the pluralist and human relations approaches, respectively. Distributive bargaining is based on a zero-sum contest between parties ("what you win, I lose"), and integrative bargaining is a problem-solving process which identifies, enlarges and acts upon the common interests of the parties.

SOURCES OF CONFLICT

The human relations and pluralist views tend to treat the sources of conflict differently, and, as we will see shortly, this discrepancy leads to different strategies and techniques for coping with conflict.

Sources of conflict in the human relations approach. Human relations theorists and consultants typically focus on interpersonal and organizational conflicts which arise from (a) misunderstandings; (b) insensitive and nonsupportive relationships; (c) failure to communicate openly and honestly; and (d) a climate of distrust, unreasonable pressure, or competition.

The best statements of the human relations theory of conflict are provided by the classic studies of Sherif and Sherif (1953) and Blake and Mouton (1964). Both studies have made a significant contribution to our understanding of the causes as well as the dynamics of intergroup conflict. In both of these researches, the authors' conclusions are based on experiments with rival teams. Sherif and Sherif conducted their studies in a natural field setting at a boys' camp; the Blake and Mouton study involved managers taking part in a management training seminar. In each case, the experimenters were easily able to develop strong competition between the teams, resulting in the following behaviors: (a) group cohesion mounts rapidly, a "we-they" feeling emerges; (b) disagreements and diverse viewpoints are discouraged within the group, consensus and unanimity are demanded; (c) the more aggressive group members establish control over their groups; (d) there arise stereotyped and derogatory perceptions of the "enemy" and positively distorted perceptions and judgments of one's own group; and (e) confidence and trust between groups disappear.

In the Blake and Mouton experiment, the representative or spokesman for the winning group was received as a hero; the defeated representative was typically greeted by his group with dismay and derision.

Studies such as these show that conflicts which create winners and losers (so-called "win-lose" conflicts) display predictable patterns of interaction and have predictable effects on perceptual, intellectual, and emotional processes. As each side becomes committed to winning, its members endeavor to have their solution to the confrontation accepted, and there is no search for constructive or integrative solutions. Because win-lose conflict creates winners and losers, a residue of hostility remains. Accurate and candid communication between the parties decreases, suspicion of the other party continues, and "conflict traps" emerge such that any further interaction between the groups, regardless of how benign, will be interpreted as hostile by the parties.

Sources of conflict in the pluralist approach. Pluralists, on the other hand, regard conflict as a natural (and desirable) part of life. Some proponents of the pluralist view argue, like the "new biologists," that man has inherited aggressive instincts from his primal ancestors. Others suggest that inequality is an ineradicable aspect of life, and the pursuit of equality leads inevitably to conflict. Conflict is thus seen as the balance wheel of society and as the primary vehicle of social change and justice. Conflict between parties within organizations is not seen as destructive but as facilitative of the interests of all parties. As Cyert and March (1963) have observed, "most organizations most of the time exist and thrive with considerable latent conflict . . ." (p. 117). Apparent harmony can be obtained only at the cost of independence and vigor.

According to the pluralist view, subsystems within the organization should be encouraged to compete with one another, and the interests of all parties will be best served through the dialectical process. This approach accepts conflicts of interest as an inevitable aspect of organizational functioning and seeks to distribute power within the organization in such a manner that ultimate authority rests in no one group. This principle applies most clearly to the bargaining relationship between labor and management. Neither the company-dominated union nor the union-dominated enterprise is desirable if contending positions are to be expressed freely and resolved.

Pluralist theory requires that the membership in each power center should be able to exert at least a minimum amount of control over the leadership. Union members should have ultimate, though not day-to-day, control over their officials and stockholders over the management of their companies. In this way, the organization is maximally responsive to all parties.

Although pluralist theory, like human relations theory, subsumes a number of different viewpoints, a common theme emerges: conflicts within groups and organizations can be functional and can enhance the effectiveness of these systems (Coser, 1956). Pluralists argue for a climate which encourages a tough, open exchange of viewpoints and in which the basic underlying issues between the parties are understood, accepted, and hence not subject to disagreement. Pluralists concede, however, that there is as yet no acceptable definition of an "optimal" amount of conflict within a system (Boulding, 1962), and they recognize that excessive conflict can be dysfunctional. Thus, as Boulding (1961) suggests, it would be desirable to develop conflict-resolution machinery which could prevent system participants from making "pathological" moves toward each other in a conflict situation.

Techniques for Coping with Conflict

The contrasting assumptions of each of the two approaches to conflict lead to different strategies and techniques for coping with conflict. Although each view contains a variety of techniques, we will examine only the more generally accepted ones here.

Some techniques of the human relations approach are designed to prevent conflicts through the development of diagnostic skills which increase interpersonal awareness and sensitivity. Others are designed to resolve conflicts once they have occurred through the development of curative ("third-party") skills.

Blake, Shepard, and Mouton. One interesting technique for coping with conflict has been proposed by Blake, *et al.* (1964). They have reported remarkably successful results in generating a cooperative, problem-solving relationship between antagonistic parties, whether they be unions and management or groups within management. The Blake *et al.* approach includes the following steps: (1) The two groups must express an interest in improving their relationship. (2) The groups are separated and each group writes down its perception of itself and the other group. (3) The two groups are brought together and a representative from each presents his group's perceptions of itself and the other. The purpose of this step is simply to present and share perceptions; rebuttals, denials, and questions are not permitted at this point. (4) The two groups separate again and begin to analyze the discrepancies between their perceptions of themselves and of the other group and the corresponding perceptions of the other group. The groups, with the help of a consultant, explore the reasons why each group sees things differently and how these differences might be reduced. (5) The groups are brought together in order to share their analyses of why different perceptions exist and how they can be reduced. This step becomes a problem-solving session where interaction between all group members is encouraged.

The goals of this technique are to reduce misperceptions, to stimulate accurate and reassuring communications, and to develop trust and confidence in members of other groups. Blake *et al.* state that when applied to industrial relations their "orientation is based on recognizing union and management disputes as symptoms of pathology in the problem-solving area" and view their approach as "diagnosing the causes which produce the symptoms and treating the causes directly" (p. 144).

Sherif. Sherif's work has led to a rather different approach to coping with intergroup conflict. He has proposed that conflicts be resolved through the search for "superordinate goals"—goals which are compelling for both parties and cannot be ignored but which cannot be achieved by the efforts and resources of one group alone. For example, the threat of reduced domestic automobile sales caused by the energy shortage and foreign imports has stimulated serious discussion between the UAW and the auto manufacturers to find ways of reducing absenteeism and of improving workmanship. Likert (personal communication) has suggested that hostilities in the Middle East might be reduced if the Arabs and Israelis were to find salient and significant superordinate goals that would require joint effort if they were to be achieved—for example, exploration for petroleum resources and the irrigation of arid areas.

One disadvantage of this strategy, however, may be that conflict reappears after the accomplishment of the superordinate goal. Blake, Shepard, and Mouton (1964) have noted that:

> The condition under which superordinate goals will produce cooperative effort, *without resolving the intergroup relations* problem, is when the assumed *superordinate goal*

> *is really a superordinate threat.* . . . In this circumstance, the groups put aside their own conflict until the greater enemy has been annihilated. But, the differences that were set aside earlier return once the threat or superordinate need has been removed. In truth, then, the problem has not been solved. It has only been deferred under conditions of more pressing need for cooperative effort. (p. 89)

Hopefully, in the interim of cooperation, the opposing parties may change their attitudes and behavior toward each other as a result of their cooperative efforts. The conflict situation is not likely to be fully resolved, however, until the parties seriously explore the underlying causes for their conflict and attempt to deal with them directly.

Walton. One of the more promising of the human relations conflict resolution techniques is the "third-party" or "peacemaker" role described by Walton (1969). A typical case requiring the services of a third party might concern two managers who, for reasons of organizational pressure, competition, or misunderstanding are caught in an escalating cycle of reciprocal distrust and destructive interpersonal conflict. A third party who is skilled in interpersonal peacemaking brings the two together, stimulates a reappraisal of viewpoints through candid dialogue and confrontation and thereby creates a new basis for an enduring relationship between the parties.

The skills required of the third party are not unlike those demanded of the T-group trainer or the labor mediator. Since conflicts may be waged in indirect ways and since the parties may focus on some ostensible but not fundamental issue between them, the third party must be skilled in diagnosing the real causes of the conflict. Skill is also required in bringing the parties together and in choosing the proper time, place, and issue for the confrontation and dialogue to begin.

Rogers. Another approach seeks to give the parties to the conflict the interpersonal skills necessary to resolve the conflict themselves. Carl Rogers (1961), a distinguished clinical psychologist, proposes the following:

> What would happen to a labor-management dispute if it were conducted in such a way that labor, without necessarily agreeing, could accurately state management's point

of view in a way that management could accept; and man-agment, without approving labor's stand could state labor's case in a way that labor agreed was accurate? It would mean that real communication was established, and one could practically guarantee that some reasonable solution would be reached. (p. 333)

Unlike the human relationists, the pluralists approach conflict as an interpersonal and organizational process that can be ex-ploited for purposes of effecting change and enhancing organiza-tional performance. Pluralists view conflict as a normal (even healthy) rather than a pathological organizational state. Whyte (1967) states the case well:

Harmony is an undesirable goal for the functioning of an organization. The objective should not be to build a harmonious organization, but to build an organization ca-pable of recognizing the problems it faces and developing ways of solving these problems. Since conflicts are an in-evitable part of organizational life, it is important that conflict-resolution procedures be built into the design of the organization. (p. 25)

The pluralist, thus, looks upon conflict as a means of generating agreements and of creating agreed upon terms of collaboration. Threats of violence are employed to accommodate differing in-terests rather than to produce actual violence. Conflict becomes an instrument of social change and influence rather than a symp-tom of a breakdown in social relationships. In fact, conflict be-haviors must occur from time to time in order to demonstrate the will and capability of action.

Leaders often orchestrate conflicts as a means of enhancing their bargaining power. Violence, disorder, and militancy among lower level members have been used by leaders in the civil rights and labor movements as a means of demonstrating possible out-comes for their opponents if concessions are not made.

Conflict management. Although pluralist theory encourages conflict, the emergence of unrestrained conflict is prevented by proper "management" of the conflict situation. The pluralist approach is most effective when (1) neither party dominates the other, (2) both parties see some advantage to continued association and interaction regardless of how the basis of their relationship may change as a result of the conflict, (3) neither party wishes (nor is able) to annihilate the other, and (4) cross-loyalties or affiliations exist which prevent polarization of all parties into two camps.

In the realm of labor-management relations, the human relationist would call for the greater commitment by labor to the public good and greater corporate responsibility when conflict between the parties is inevitable. The pluralist would be concerned only that neither party has unfair advantage over the other and would then let the conflict run its course.

Counterplanning. An interesting application of pluralist theory to the decision-making process in organizations has been suggested by Churchman (1968). The strategy, called "counterplanning," recognizes the indispensable role of choice in any planning and decision-making process. The counterplanning strategy requires that a given plan be opposed by its "deadly enemy." It can be accepted as axiomatic that in any statement of organizational objectives, there will exist some goals that are not shared by all members. Counterplanning in such a situation is accomplished in the following way: whenever a decision maker proposes a course of action or supports the advisability of a particular policy, a counterplan is generated by other decision makers who are charged with the responsibility of questioning the appropriateness of the initial plan of action. In this way, the basic assumptions underlying each proposal are identified, conflict is generated, and the decision makers' sensitivity to the situation is increased.

Churchman's ideas are supported by many other thoughtful observers. Harlan Cleveland (1965) puts the matter thus:

> It is too easy to get people to cooperate. People are, if anything, too conformist. This is why the executive's most difficult task is almost precisely the reverse of inducing cooperation. It is to maintain an adequate degree of tension within the organization—enough fruitful friction among its members so that all possible points of view are weighed before important decisions are made. No executive worth his salt wants staff members that are so bored with the agency's work or so undifferentiated in function that they never argue with each other or with the boss.

In a counter to counterplanning, however, Reedy (1971) relates an interesting anecdote which suggests that this technique may not lead to improved decision making in organizations:

> During President Johnson's Administration I watched George Ball play the role of devil's advocate with respect to foreign policy. The Cabinet would meet and there would be an overwhelming report from Robert McNamara, another overwhelming report from Dean Rusk, another overwhelming report from McGeorge Bundy. Then five minutes would be set aside for George Ball to deliver his dissent, and, because they expected him to dissent, they automatically discounted whatever he said. This strengthened them in their own convictions because the Cabinet members could quite honestly say: "We heard both sides of this issue discussed." Well they heard it with wax in their ears. I think that the moment you appoint an official devil's advocate you solidify the position he is arguing against" (pp. 12–13).

This sort of outcome is, of course, precisely what human relations theory would predict.

EVALUATION OF THE TWO APPROACHES

Human relations. The research and practice generated by the human relations approach have had an enormous impact on modern-day thinking about conflict and its resolution. Techniques suggested by the human relationists have been profitably employed in many conflict situations. Walton (1970), for example, reports partial success in getting representatives from three African countries to begin the search for solutions to a border dispute on the basis of a two-week workshop utilizing his "third-party" technique. Such techniques are also frequently part of executive development programs and are widely used in labor-management negotiations.

Human relations theory alerts the practitioner to important psychological processes which are known to affect the relationship between parties in a conflict situation. One such process—the parties' perceptions of each other—determines the kinds of behaviors which are likely to emerge. A decision by management to subcontract plant work may be perceived by the union as an attempt to take work out of the bargaining unit and to undermine the collective agreement when, in fact, the decision may have been made because the plant was operating at full capacity. The parties have the choice of perceiving the issue as large or small. A conflict can be made more manageable by, for example, perceiving or defining it as a conflict between two individuals of different races rather than as a racial conflict, or as a conflict over the application of a principle rather than as conflict over a principle.

When a conflict situation is defined in terms of absolutistic values or in terms of ideological principles, parties have little room to maneuver. Beliefs about human rights, moral precepts, and ideology cannot be sacrificed piecemeal to an opponent. There is an "all-or-nothing" quality to such conflict situations which makes resolution difficult. Labor-management conflicts centering on the issue of union recognition, for example, have typically been bitter and prolonged, while conflicts over "bread-and-butter" issues have been much easier to resolve.

Perceptions of relative strength are also important in determining the quality of the relationship between parties. (Pluralist theory states that parties should have roughly equal power but ignores perceptions of power.) Research evidence suggests that perceptions of power inequality can undermine trust, inhibit dialogue, and can decrease the likelihood of a constructive resolution of conflict. Inequality tends to undermine trust on both ends of the imbalanced relationship, directly affecting both the party with the perceived power inferiority and the party with perceived superiority (Solomon, 1960; Thibaut and Riecken, 1955).

Perhaps the most basic reason why another's power advantage undermines trust is the general appreciation of the tendency for power to be used by those who possess it. Experimental studies of interpersonal bargaining have indicated that the weaker party in an asymmetric power relationship expresses more negative attitudes toward the stronger party as the power differential between the parties increases. Also, the existence of a power advantage may make a party more likely to interpret cooperative behavior by another as compliant rather than volitional, with a consequent reduction of the stronger party's trust in the weaker (Walton, 1965).

Weaknesses of the human relations approach. But while human relations theory identifies important processes in conflict situations, it also ignores others. Perhaps the essential point overlooked by human relations theorists is the realistic basis for much conflict. There are scarce resources which lead parties to compete. Thus conflict becomes inevitable and, in fact, may be desirable so long as it does not produce prejudiced, stereotyped, and hostile relationships which broaden the conflict and make it more difficult to resolve.

Also, human relations theory suggests techniques for coping with conflict such as openness, flexibility, and willingness to listen and consider opposing viewpoints which run counter to many of our cultural and organizational values. One might argue that these techniques are morally superior and that they might be more effective than pluralist techniques, but is it realistic to expect these techniques in the current organizational climate? Competitiveness is considered to be normal and healthy in our culture and high value is placed on aggressiveness. When executives were asked: "What does it take to get ahead in this company? "What are the kinds of things the company is most looking for?", and "What type of person 'makes it' in this company?", the most frequently mentioned traits were aggressiveness, self-confidence, assertiveness, dominance, and self-assurance (Quinn, Kahn, Tabor, and Gordon, 1964).

Furthermore, the application of human relations theory to organizational life frequently leads to the excessive conformity and rigidity of Whyte's (1956) "Organization Man" and to the practices of "managerial social psychology" described by Thompson (1961). The human relations emphasis on eliminating conflict tends (a) to direct attention away from the need for change by emphasizing the desirability of adapting the individual to existing structures, and (b) to eliminate the discipline and clarity of thought the conflict between ideas and policies fosters. Finally, Eric Hoffer (1955) expresses the following reservations about the human relations view of labor-management conflict:

> The important point is that this taking of the worker for granted occurs not only when management has unlimited power to coerce, but also when the division between management and labor ceases to be self-evident. Any doctrine which preaches the oneness of management and labor— whether it stresses their unity in a party, class, race, nation, or even religion—can be used to turn the worker into a compliant instrument in the hands of management. Both

communism and fascism postulate the oneness of management and labor, and both are devices for the extraction of minimum performance from an underpaid labor force.

Pluralist. The pluralists point to the free enterprise market system and the long-standing American political system with its checks and balances as demonstrating the strengths of their approach. There is also a growing body of research evidence which points to the advantages of intra-organizational conflict. Sociometric studies of sports teams, for example, indicate that in-group conflict or rivalry (if it is kept within bounds) contributes to team effectiveness and provides an additional stimulus for high achievement (Lenk, 1964). Research and development scientists are found to be most productive in organizations with a certain amount of "dither" or intellectual conflict (Pelz and Andrews, 1966). Similarly, in a study of local unions, Tannenbaum (1956) found that conflict between local members was positively correlated with union power and with member loyalty, conformity, and participation in union affairs. Conflict within the union local thus appears consistent with a strong rather than a weak local.

Experimental studies of creativity and innovation suggest that groups are more productive when a dissenter is present than when dissenters are absent. (Interestingly, when group members are asked to throw out members, the dissenters are routinely thrown out. When forced to work with a dissenter, the group will do so—with creative results—but when given an opportunity, the group prefers to function without the member who forced the confrontation and integration of conflicting views.)

Crosscutting affiliations, multiple loyalties, and cross-pressures generated by intra-organizational conflicts play a critical role in pluralist theory. Whenever one of the opposing parties in a system finds itself opposed to another on *all* possible issues, there is no reason why it should not attempt the destruction of the other, and it can be expected to do so. But as soon as there are some divisions of loyalties, neither party can destroy the other without jeopardizing some of the interests of its own members. For example, hostility between various ethnic groups in this country, such as between the Irish and the Italians, has prevented the emergence of a class consciousness reflecting common economic interests.

The legitimation of differences has other, perhaps less obvious, benefits to organizations. Tolerance of differences has the effect of encouraging working or cooperative agreements among different interest groups who might otherwise consistently align themselves on different sides of issues and thereby precipitate violent confrontation. The Teamsters, for example, have demonstrated a closer degree of cooperation with the trucking employers on many issues than they ever have with their brothers in the railroad unions. Similarly, the maritime unions and shippers have collaborated to obtain increased federal subsidies against the opposition of other labor groups, while the steel producers and the steel workers have cooperated in efforts to restrict imports of foreign steel.

Weaknesses of the pluralist approach. It is obvious that conflicts of interest and diversity of viewpoints do not always lead to desirable outcomes. The dysfunctional effects of pluralism can be seen most clearly in the case of conglomerates which engage in many different activities spanning a number of industries. On occasion, subsidiary divisions of a company may be direct competitors having unrelated or even antithetical political and economic interests. For example, the shipbuilding division of a conglomerate may be well served by particular federal policies or industry subsidies that are contrary to the welfare of a sister subsidiary in the aerospace business (Bauer, Pool, and Dexter, 1963).

Dissension and consequent reduced effectiveness also exist in the labor movement. Within the ranks of the AFL-CIO, there are competition and hostility among the constituent international unions and their leaders which have hampered unions in their efforts to organize particular industries. In the electrical industry, for example, the deep split between the International Union of Electrical Workers (IUEW) and the International Brotherhood of Electrical Workers (IBEW) has impeded labor's effectiveness in dealing with General Electric and Westinghouse. This example illustrates the frequent unwillingness of unions to cooperate even to protect their vital economic interests. These intraunion conflicts dissipate union energies and resources and weaken the effectiveness of the union in its bargaining with management.

The work of Blake and Mouton discussed earlier documents some further dangers of pluralist theory. Differences between groups or persons can easily become ritualized (as in collective bargaining), and the overdramatization of what might be moderate differences can make resolution of the conflict difficult to achieve.

NEWER PERSPECTIVES

To this point, we have discussed the human relations and pluralist approaches as two different and opposing perspectives on social conflict. The discussion mirrors a very real division in the field of organizational behavior, and only recently have attempts been made to formulate a theory of conflict and conflict resolution which draws upon the strengths of the two traditional views. We will now examine three significant attempts to reconcile the human relations and pluralistic views of conflict.

Game theory. An extension of the pluralist approach is game theory, and its application to the study of social conflict has been pioneered by Luce and Raiffa (1957) and Rapoport (1970). According to game theorists, conflict stems neither from instincts nor psychological frustrations and misunderstandings, but rather results from the pursuit of scarce resources by parties acting within a defined framework of rules. The belief that conflict results from scarce resources follows from pluralist theory, but game theory can be employed to test the validity of either human relations or pluralist views.

In simplest terms, game theory is a branch of mathematics that analyzes various problems of conflict and decision by considering alternative strategies parties might adopt in the pursuit of their self-interest. A strategy is a set of guidelines a party establishes which determines how he will respond should his opponent act in any given way. Neither party in the game controls the choices of his opponent nor can the parties on their own affect any particular outcome. Each party makes a choice from among several alternatives and is unaware of the choice that the other party is going to make. The parties are assumed to act rationally and are assumed to pursue their own interests (or in game theoretical terms, to maximize utility or expected payoff).

This can be best illustrated with the game known as the Prisoner's Dilemma. The situation is as follows:

Two suspects are being held incommunicado and questioned separately by the district attorney. Although the suspects

are guilty of a serious crime, there is insufficient evidence
to convict both of them on the charge, but there is sufficient evidence to convict them on a lesser offense. The
district attorney points out to each prisoner that he has
two alternatives: confess or not confess. If both suspects
do not confess, they will be charged with a lesser crime
(such as possession of a weapon), and both will receive
short sentences. If both confess, they will be prosecuted
for the serious crime, but the sentences will be partially
commuted because of the guilty plea. If one confesses and
the other does not, the confessor will receive a light sentence, and the other will "get the book thrown at him."

Since the prisoners are separated, neither is aware of the other's
decision. Each prisoner's choice depends on his trust of the other
(and very likely on his level of trust toward people in general).
Both prisoners would be better off refusing to confess. Yet if one
prisoner is sure that the other will not confess, he might confess
and thereby reduce his sentence, according to the district attorney,
from a year to three months. By opting for mutual benefit, each
prisoner runs the risk of being exploited by the other. If both
prisoners choose to exploit the other, the result is mutually cata-
strophic. The table below illustrates the payoff matrix for the two
prisoners.

		Prisoner A	
		not confess a_1	confess a_2
Prisoner B	not confess b_1	1 year each	3 months for A 10 years for B
	confess b_2	10 years for A 3 months for B	8 years each

The game is of interest because the most rational choice each
suspect can make—maximizing the chance for gain and minimizing
the chance for loss, the so-called minimax strategy—is also the one
which is most harmful ("exploitive") to the suspects taken together. Clearly were the parties allowed to communicate with each
other, a solution more in their common interest could be derived.

And yet, according to human relationists, too many of the problems in our society are dealt with destructively within Prisoner's Dilemma terms.

The Prisoner's Dilemma illustrates a "zero-sum game" in which the gains of one party equal the losses of the other. Greater reality and different solutions are possible when different assumptions are introduced. The game may involve several people or groups; chance can enter the game such that the outcome of a particular play of the game is not completely determined by the other player's choices (expected payoffs are entered into the payoff matrix) ; what one player wins, the other does not necessarily lose (non-zero-sum games) ; the players can recognize that outcomes can be allocated in different ratios and must choose between increasing their own immediate gain or increasing the total gain of both players (mixed-motive games) , and parties can influence their opponent's choice with the use of threats, commitment to an irrevocable course of action, expressing appreciation, and the like.

Walton. A theory offered by Walton (1965) states that groups entering into contact with other groups may carry two basic objectives with them: (1) they may seek concessions on substantive matters from the other group, and (2) they may desire improvement in their relationship. Pluralist theory is primarily concerned with the first goal, the more favorable allocation of scarce resources (such as money, status, or power) between the groups. Human relations theory, on the other hand, focuses on factors such as trust, openness, and supportiveness which define the type of relationship between the parties.

The prescriptions of each approach for coping with conflict are, as we have seen, quite different. For example, human relations theory emphasizes direct and undistorted communication between parties, minimizing perceived differences between members of opposing groups, minimizing perceived differences between the groups' goals, and creating a climate of trust between the parties. Pluralist theory, on the other hand, implies the usefulness of purposeful manipulation of communication such that one party conveys strength of purpose or irrevocable commitment to a course of action. Kerr (1964) , for example, states: "In fact, misunderstanding and the misuse of words have probably made a substantial contribution to industrial peace" (p. 233) . Diplomatic language often dismissed as double talk makes possible "planned misunderstandings" which keep tensions down and permit opportunity for clarification prior to ultimate or aggressive measures.

Rather than minimizing the differences between parties, pluralist theory suggests that the exaggeration of differences by one group may enable it to obtain concessions from the other. Trust *between* conflicting parties, according to pluralist theory, may undermine *internal* group loyalty and solidarity and a willingness to make sacrifices for a cause.

There are some types of conflict situations where one approach is more helpful than the other. In wage negotiations, out-of-court settlements, negotiations with an insurance claims representative or in other types of "distributive" conflicts—where gains to one party entail losses to the other—the parties might be well advised to follow the pluralist theory. On the other hand, if the parties to the conflict are marketing and manufacturing representatives of the same firm, and thus operating in a continuing relationship, the parties ought to seek a resolution through use of the human relations theory.

But what theory should parties follow when they seek both an improved relationship *and* a reallocation of scarce resources between them? Since most conflict situations involve both objectives, parties to such conflict situations face a dilemma. By following pluralist theory, for example, one group maximizes the likelihood of achieving substantive concessions from the other, but may at the same time minimize the likelihood of developing a more positive relationship with the other party.

Walton proposes some tactics for coping with this dilemma. First, activities can be sequenced in such a way that gains are made in one area first and then in the other. For example, minority groups may first seek concessions through application of the pluralist approach, and through the self-respect and confidence thereby acquired, gain the respect of the majority community. Or conversely, a group may first seek trust and respect from the other and subsequently gain concessions.

There are obviously some problems associated with this strategy, however. Once a party has employed pluralist bargaining tactics with another, that party may find that it cannot subsequently appeal to the other for increased trust or understanding. Also, for tactical reasons, a party may appear to be seeking a resolution of the conflict through application of human relations theory when in fact he is employing pluralist theory. In other words, it is to a party's advantage to get an opponent to pursue a strategy of improving their relationship while he pursues substantive concessions from his opponent.

A second strategy assigns a different technique for coping with conflict to different members of the group. For example, in international relations, pluralist tactics can be employed in the United Nations, while human relations tactics can be employed through cultural and scientific exchanges.

Lawrence and Lorsch. A novel approach to the resolution of interdepartmental conflicts in organizations (and an approach which attempts to synthesize the human relations and pluralist approaches) has been proposed by Lawrence and Lorsch (1967). According to their framework, organizational subunits (e.g., production, marketing, R & D) require different degrees of *differentiation* (differences in cognitive and perceptual orientations), but all require a high level of *integration* (high quality collaboration) with other subunits.

The differences that are of interest to Lawrence and Lorsch concern attitudes and ways of thinking, and those differences are believed to arise from the specialization of skills and abilities and the segmentation or departmentalization of organizations. People may have (1) different goals (e.g., the sales manager is interested in increasing sales volume while the production manager is interested in lowering manufacturing costs); (2) different time orientations (the production manager is more pressed by immediate problems than is the research and development scientist who deals with long-range questions); and (3) different interpersonal orientations (some people are primarily interested in getting the job done while others are primarily interested in maintaining good relationships with fellow workers). A fourth dimension of differentiation is called "formality of structure" and refers to the emphasis placed on the management hierarchy and on reward and control systems in the organization.

Companies operating in a highly volatile environment with a highly specialized technology must be highly differentiated to survive. But at the same time, they must avoid being torn apart by internal differences and dissension—that is, they must also be highly integrated. This seemingly paradoxical state of high differentiation and high integration allows an organization to enjoy the fruits of both the pluralistic expression of differences and the human relations atmosphere of high trust and consensus.

How is this state achieved? The firms studied by Lawrence and Lorsch typically created a role of "integrator" to act as a liaison between departments (such as sales and R & D). Ideally, the integrator's way of thinking and approach to the job (goals, time orientation, and interpersonal orientation) should be approximately half-way between the members of the departments in question. In addition, integrators must be perceived by the relevant departments as having sufficient power and influence to enforce decisions, and the integrators must be rewarded for the overall performance of the departments in question.

Successful integrators in the Lawrence and Lorsch study would openly "confront" parties with whom they disagreed rather than "smooth" over differences or unilaterally "force" a decision on another party. This open confrontation of differences requires considerable emotional energy, a high degree of interpersonal skill on the part of the integrator, and an organizational climate where people do not fear that their careers will be jeopardized by disagreeing with superiors.

A final condition for a state of high differentiation and integration is a feeling among managers that their ideas are always considered and that no department has undue influence in the decision-making process.

Although Lawrence and Lorsch do not go as far as they might in integrating human relations techniques into their theory, their work is an important step in the development of a theory of conflict and conflict resolution which not only generates further research ideas but is at the same time useful to the practitioner who seeks viable strategies for coping with conflict. Their concept of "confrontation" is an especially useful one, since in the long run this may be more useful than the "smoothing" (covering over, ignoring) implied by some of the more simplistic versions of human relations or the purely power-oriented "forcing" implied in some of the more simplistic versions of the pluralistic approach. Confrontation at its best takes on elements of both human relations and pluralism.

SUMMARY

This chapter has examined two major views of conflict which begin with different assumptions about the causes of social conflict and has explored the resulting strategies and techniques proposed by each approach. We have looked at the historical origins of the two approaches and have attempted to show how modern-day thinking about conflict has evolved. Finally, we discussed three attempts to synthesize the human relations and pluralist views into a single theory of conflict and conflict resolution.

There seems to be a growing recognition in the field of organizational behavior that parties who frequently find themselves in conflict situations should be trained and equipped to employ both the pluralist and human relations views. Parties should become skilled at diagnosing the basic character of a relationship and at perceiving the appropriateness of different tactics in achieving their goals. They should be flexible enough to shift from pluralist to human relations tactics as circumstances dictate. Further, researchers and practitioners should continue to search for new ways of looking at social conflict and experiment with new techniques of coping with conflict. The continued effectiveness of our organizations, and perhaps their survival, depend on this search. Organization Development—a technique discussed in the next chapter—is designed especially to facilitate conflict resolution and to "confront" organizations with their problems.

CHAPTER 7

Organization Development

RAYMOND E. MILES
University of California, Berkeley

The previous chapters discuss circumstances under which managers may wish to redesign jobs, move toward a more participative style of supervision or decision making, attempt to realign the structures of their organizations to meet changing environmental conditions, or adopt different approaches for reducing conflict. These discussions imply that changing any of these organizational features is an extremely complex process involving a host of individual and situational variables and that change in any one area—for example, job design, leadership, interdepartmental conflict—has implications for all the others. How, then, are such changes to be made?

The answer that has been voiced most frequently over the past ten years is OD—Organization Development, a term which has swept into prominence perhaps as pervasively as did "human relations" and "participative management" in earlier eras. Broadly defined as the effort to improve organizational effectiveness through long-term, planned, systematic applications of behavioral science knowledge and techniques with the collaborative aid of skilled consultants, OD has a complex lineage. While some key components of the OD movement (e.g., sensitivity training and action research) can be traced back to the 1940's, the term Organization Development itself was probably not used with any distinct meaning until the late fifties, and much of the broader conceptualization associated with the movement has occurred within the last ten years (French and Bell, 1973, Chap. 3). Numerous academic programs and courses focusing on OD have emerged within the last few years and the final academic annointment—the appearance of textbooks using Organization Development in their title—occurred in the 1969 Addison-Wesley Series (Beckhard, 1969; Bennis, 1969; Blake and Mouton, 1969; Lawrence and Lorsch, 1969; Schein, 1969; Walton, 1969).

Despite its youth, however, and despite the lack of substantial hard evidence attesting to its value, OD has already acquired most of the accoutrements of an established field. Many leading firms and agencies have OD departments (French and Bell, 1973), practitioners have their own accrediting agency, the field is represented by several professional associations and divisions (Friedlander and Brown, 1974, p. 314; French and Bell, 1973, pp. 28–29), and the Conference Board has prepared two bulletins surveying prominent OD accomplishments (Rush, 1969, 1973). Perhaps most significantly, it is becoming increasingly common in articles, in texts (Margulies and Raia, 1972; French and Bell, 1973), and in reviews (Friedlander and Brown, 1974) to find established areas of concern such as leadership, job design, conflict resolution, etc., incorporated within the framework of OD theory and concepts.

OD is thus an evolving field whose boundaries and issues are not yet precisely defined. In this chapter, therefore, we attempt to define OD, outline and trace the origins of its major approaches and their underlying theories, consider the major criticisms which have been raised, and weigh the available empirical evidence as to its utility.

THREE MAJOR OD APPROACHES

While I will argue below that OD in practice seldom matches the definition cited earlier, three approaches incorporating many of these "ideal" characteristics have been designed. It may be useful to look briefly at these as illustrations of the scope and methods of OD efforts before we turn to a comprehensive discussion of the issues.

The Managerial Grid. As discussed in Chapter Four, the Grid approach (Blake and Mouton, 1968) is based largely on a "style" of management which attempts to jointly maximize concern for production and concern for people. (The "Grid" itself refers to a graph with two perpendicular axes, each of which is marked off in nine intervals. One axis is labeled "concern for people" and the other "concern for production." An ideal manager is one who rates high on both scales; that is, one who is at the 9,9 position on the graph.) Building on this framework, instruments and exercises have been developed through which managers can appraise their own managerial styles. In addition, the exercises permit managers to receive feedback from and provide feedback to their peers concerning these appraisals. These analyses and discussions, plus training in problem solving, communication, and group process skills are included in Phase 1 of the six-phase Grid OD program, which moves from development of the immediate work group to improvement of intergroup processes, to an organization-wide improvement plan, to the implementation of this plan, and finally to a review of the total effort and planning for new action steps.

Survey feedback. The survey feedback approach, pioneered and developed at the Survey Research Center at the University of Michigan, is built around the collection and discussion of perceptual and attitudinal data concerning organizational processes and relationships between and across hierarchical levels. The first step in this approach involves orienting the top management group and obtaining their support along with that of various internal "resource" persons (change agents). Following this, preparations are made for the administration of a detailed questionnaire to employees at all levels. Survey findings are processed so that the data for each work group are available only to that group. Feedback of these data is handled on a group-by-group basis in sessions run by the group leader with the assistance of an outside consultant (Mann, 1961). Feedback is intended to stimulate discussion of the work group's behavior and to suggest areas for immediate action or further analysis. Subsequent administrations of the questionnaire provide opportunities for measuring improvement on key behavioral dimensions both within and between work groups.

Team training. The system-wide team development approach provides "group problem-solving" and "interpersonal process" training for work teams throughout an organization. Utilizing a variety of techniques, team development specialists lead a superior and his immediate subordinates through analyses of "how" and "why" they relate to one another as they do as they carry out their work assignments. The focus is on identification of and removal of barriers (e.g., unexpressed feelings, miscommunications, conflicting priorities, etc.) to effective performance and the development of behavior patterns which will aid the group in dealing with present and future problems.

Advocates of this approach (Schein, 1969; Davis, 1967) argue that team development training and consultation should usually begin with the top executive teams and then flow down the hierarchy. With high-level groups, it is typical for the outside consultant first to interview top managers and then to use data gathered from these interviews to stimulate discussion of group processes in one or more initial training sessions. The consultant then meets regularly with the group as they address current organizational problems, "intervening" to encourage insight and learning concerning the ongoing dynamics of the group. As the program moves toward lower levels, training efforts usually become shorter and more heavily structured (i.e., they take on the appearance of traditional leadership training courses) and more use is made of "inside" OD consultants—members of the organization's OD department or training staff.

A synthesized example. In order to visualize these approaches in action (and capture their common features) consider the following synthesized example:

> A top manager of organization A hears about a presumably successful utilization of behavioral science concepts and techniques in another firm. He arranges a meeting with (or attends a seminar held by) the consultant involved and is further intrigued (convinced, sold). He and the consultant plan an initial conference (meeting, seminar, learning session, demonstration) with the executive team of organization A. Entry of the OD effort thus occurs at or near the top of the organization with a level of involvement (and, hopefully, a level of understanding) that goes well beyond that associated with most training and development programs. Out of these initial meetings a *change strategy* emerges (jointly designed or simply approved) which may begin with either the top executive team or some other receptive unit or department.

> Change strategies vary around a central theme—data on attitudes toward and perceptions of current policies, practices, and processes are collected ("surfaced") through interviews, questionnaires, group meetings, or experiential learning formats and are discussed and analyzed by the group involved with the aid of the consultant (who frequently provides an interpretive framework of concepts and theory).

These data and their discussion provide targets for change which may include individual or group behaviors which impede decision making or coordination, role pressures or reporting relationships which have dysfunctional consequences, policies which require rethinking, etc. The group, with the aid of the consultant, determines how these changes will be introduced, implemented, and evaluated. Evaluation may include further data collection at periodic intervals, a series of sequenced review and planning sessions, or some other *sustaining mechanism.*

By this point, an internal OD group or department has frequently been created (developed, expanded), and OD work in subsequent areas (usually modeled after the initial efforts) may rely heavily on these resources, with the outside consultant returning for planning (and learning sessions) with top management and with the internal OD staff.

Basic OD Concepts

The Managerial Grid, survey feedback, and team training represent only three of the more advanced and widely known OD approaches. In practice, the term OD is regularly applied to a host of training and development activities which fit only *poorly* my definition of "real" OD, including traditional programs such as classroom training for middle managers and the use of standardized job satisfaction surveys. In some organizations new high-level groups have been formed which are headed by heavily credentialed professionals (frequently Ph.D.'s) with substantial experience in one or more approaches to system-wide development; in others, however, the scrape of a blade and a few strokes of a lettering brush have transformed what were previously known as management training departments into "OD units" without other changes. Most OD practitioners have their own set of prescriptive concepts, definitions, and change or training strategies. To this point, the field has applied far more energy to the development of techniques than to the structuring of descriptive theory and research.

Nevertheless, out of the confusing array of techniques, approaches, and concepts labeled OD there seem to be some emerging areas of agreement, especially as to (1) the kind of organization

OD should develop, (2) the critical necessity of change, (3) the means to be utilized in effecting change, and (4) the role of OD consultants.

The Normative Model of Effective Management

As French and Bell (1973) note, the assumptions, values, and concepts of Argyris (1962), Likert (1967), Maslow (1970), McGregor (1960, 1967), and others have become an integral part of the OD literature. Out of the writings of these theorists has been gleaned not only a common image of the main processes characterizing an ideal organization but also a set of specific, desirable underlying behavioral mechanisms. For example, trusting, open relationships are viewed as essential to meaningful participation in decision making and goal setting. Similarly, the provision of nonevaluative feedback and the sharing of feelings as well as thoughts and facts are deemed crucial to cooperative, self-directed performance. Further, openness to feedback and the willingness to confront issues are required if conflicts are to be creatively and thoroughly resolved.

While various terms have been used to identify the end state toward which OD aspires—for example, a "Theory Y" organization (McGregor, 1960, 1967) or a "System IV" organization (Likert, 1961, 1967)—the key dimensions are seldom dissimilar. For many if not most OD theorists and practitioners, OD is development toward an organization characterized by wide employee participation in decision making and goal setting, individual and group self-direction and self-control based on jointly decided goals and objectives, and creative resolution of conflict between and across hierarchical levels—a setting which is expected to provide the opportunity for individual growth and fulfillment while at the same time removing barriers to effective performance. In sum, OD seeks to develop the kind of organic organizational structure discussed in Chapter Five.

Turbulent Environments and the Necessity of OD

A second area of convergence among OD theorists relates to OD's justification. The environment, as they see it, is becoming increasingly turbulent and this, they argue, makes it especially important that organizations adopt the kinds of structure and processes mentioned above. As do the open-systems theorists discussed in Chapter Five (Burns and Stalker, 1961; Emery and Trist, 1965), OD writers tend to believe that the linkage among the elements in most organizational environments are becoming more numerous and more complex, that the rate of change in environmental conditions is increasing, and that traditional bureaucratic structures are becoming less and less adequate. It is argued that new and more adaptive structures and processes are required and that these in turn demand new levels of interpersonal skill and awareness which OD can best provide.

As mentioned earlier, Bennis (1964) went beyond most of his predecessors, holding that changing organizational environments and societal values doomed all bureaucratic organizations to extinction within a few decades. Bennis (1969) completed the argument a few years later in his pioneering book on OD by stating that "basically, organization development is one of the few educational programs I know of that has the potential to create an institution vital enough to cope with the unparalleled changes ahead" (p. 82). Some variation of this theme appears in most recent OD texts (e.g., French and Bell, 1973, pp. 197–200), which imply an urgent need for fundamental changes in organizational systems, their components, and their relationships, a sweeping mandate not claimed by earlier management and employee development proponents.

ACHIEVING EFFECTIVE MANAGEMENT THROUGH TRAINING

There is a third area of convergence in OD writing: a faith in the value of training as a means of obtaining the changes desired. OD can be viewed as an outgrowth from what had previously been known as "management training and development." The techniques now associated with OD—such as those discussed earlier—have themselves developed over the years, in part as a result of trial and error, as training and development experts struggled to make their programs more effective. For this reason a brief history of organizational training and development efforts may help put OD in perspective.

Technical and human relations training. In the early part of this century, training efforts were aimed almost exclusively at the shop-floor level and at the immediate job skills required to operate an emerging rationalized organizational technology. The bulk of the training was done on the job, augmented by apprenticeship programs incorporating some classroom sessions.

Once the organizational structure was operating, attention turned to maintaining it—keeping friction down and promoting stable performance. With this need, the training spotlight moved up a rung on the organizational ladder and focused on the foreman or first-line supervisor. Beginning in the twenties and thirties and expanding dramatically during World War II, the bulk of this training effort focused on human relations problems—leadership, discipline, the handling of complaints and grievances, etc. Much of this training was carried out in classroom settings, and as effective performance in these areas required major changes in the trainees' attitudes and behavior, it quickly became apparent that training approaches other than the traditional lecture and discussion modes would be required. Case studies, and later role-playing situations, were early products of this search for more intensive forms of training and gained wide usage in the forties and fifties. However, research on the efficacy of these training efforts soon documented a second dilemma that has proven to be strong and persistent—the problem of transfering changes in attitude and behaviors from the training sites (e.g., the classroom) back into the work setting. While supervisors might learn to express consideration toward their subordinates during a leadership training course, once out of the supportive atmosphere of the classroom and back on the job, a supervisor's attitudes and behaviors might well revert back to whatever pleases his boss (Fleishman, 1953).

Management training. While the problems of how to change supervisory behavior and transfer these changes back to the work setting were being debated, major development attention began to shift upward again. In many organizations, work procedures at the lower levels had long been rationalized, and the line was at least being held with regard to work group problems. The most visible problems were no longer those of building and maintaining large-scale production processes but the coordination of increasingly complex organizations and the facilitation of orderly growth. Thus, while training of rank-and-file employees and their supervisors continued to expand in scope and quality, the leading edge of training and development efforts moved into the middle and upper management ranks.

Reflecting this shift in attention, executive development programs spread through major universities across the country during the fifties. The purpose of these usually lengthy (three weeks to six months) programs was to increase the manager's awareness of and ability to respond to the increasing complexity of his organizational world; their curricula included both human relations topics and new techniques for planning and problem solving.

Sensitivity training. Paralleling these developments, a group of psychologists (most notably Kurt Lewin, Kenneth Benne, Leland Bradford, and Ronald Lippitt) were also experimenting with new training approaches aimed specifically at increasing awareness and responsiveness to immediate interpersonal relations. Working from a base of theory and experience created by Kurt Lewin (Marrow, 1969), these psychologists argued that the improvement of interpersonal skills required attitudinal and behavioral changes that could best be accomplished through experiential learning in unstructured "laboratory" settings, where the participant's own behavior served as the curriculum. Out of these experiments was born the T-group (the "T" is for training) (Bradford, 1967; Bradford, Gibb, and Benne, 1964), perhaps the most influential training development in recent decades and the cause of a least a minor social movement.

The original T-group design called for 10–12 participants (called "stranger" groups) from different work or life arenas and one or more "trainers," psychologists skilled in intrapersonal and interpersonal dynamics. Participants gathered in an informal setting with no set agenda of activities—a purposely created vacuum which their own behaviors were to fill. These behaviors then became topics for consideration by the group. Group members were encouraged, by discussion and by the behavior of the trainer, to provide open, direct feedback to one another concerning their "here and now" feelings and responses. Such feedback fulfilled the "unfreezing" step of Lewin's three-phase change model which called for "unfreezing" old attitudes and behaviors, "changing," and then "refreezing" the newly adopted patterns. That is, members first receive feedback which frequently "disconfirms" the image they hold of themselves and how others respond to them. This feedback, hopefully, then motivates them to search for alternative behaviors to which more positive responses will be forthcoming—the "change" phase in the Lewinian model. If new behaviors are positively reinforced by the group, then the final Lewinian phase is accomplished—the new behaviors are "refrozen."

Organization executives followed teachers and counselors as T-group participants, and through the fifties and sixties the T-group phenomenon spread in ever varying formats (Strauss, in press; Back, 1974) across the country and across occupational, sex, and status categories—housewives in Texas, ministers in Kansas, and ex-drug addicts in California attempted to help one another gain insights into themselves and their impacts on others and to experiment with behaviors which were more effective and rewarding.

Almost from the beginning, the T-group movement came under criticism on two counts. The first of these was the charge that T-groups might well be too powerful—that participants risked real emotional damage from direct feedback, unmediated by the usual social amenities, concerning their attitudes and behavior (Odiorne, 1962; Strauss, in press). Allied with this indictment was the charge that even for those for whom T-group training did not prove unhealthy, it was still immoral. That is, this criticism holds that organizations have no right to "brainwash" members' basic attitudes and values—to manipulate changes in their patterns of relating to others and thus in their total life style. This criticism notes that there are few true volunteers for attitudinal and behavioral training—that most members are at least subtly coerced into attendance and even more subtly led to the belief that they have freely chosen new attitudes and behaviors.

T-group advocates responded that participants, under the guidance of an accomplished trainer, might well be in less emotional danger during supportive training sessions than in their typical work-life space (McGregor, 1967). Further, they argued, if training is mandatory and manipulative, it is little more so than any other aspect of managerial life—a process which always demands that the individual sacrifice some freedoms in the interest of effective joint action. Concern over possible damage from participation in a T-group continues to be raised periodically, particularly with regard to some of its more intensive variations and the frequent use of poorly qualified trainers. The concern over trainer qualification is widely acknowledged, and accrediting procedures are available (Friedlander and Brown, 1974, p. 314). Concern regarding the more exotic variants of the T-group format can only be verified or dispelled, by major, difficult-to-design research which is unlikely to be forthcoming. Finally, the issue of manipulation has been repeatedly raised and has subsequently been applied to all OD actvities. Most OD consultants are sensitive to this issue, as we shall see in a later section, but the underlying ethical questions remain unanswered.

A second, essentially unrefuted criticism holds that traditional T-group formats have not proved effective in providing a carryover of behavioral changes from the protective atmosphere of the training group and site to the harsh realities of the organizational world. More specifically this charge holds that there is little evidence of increased group and organizational effectiveness directly resulting from attitude and behavior changes acquired in T-group type sessions outside the organization (Campbell and Dunnette, 1968). This is essentially the same criticism that was leveled earlier at human relations courses for supervisors.

A number of early T-group supporters were concerned with this "transfer dilemma" and clearly recognized the difficulty that participants might have in maintaining their newly adopted posture of openness, directness, and willingness to acknowledge feelings as well as facts unless their peers, subordinates, and particularly their superiors were also trained along the same lines. Thus, in the 1950's McGregor, Shepard, Blake, and others took T-group concepts inside organizations and began working directly with actual superior-subordinate management teams (French and Bell, 1973, pp. 23–29). By the late sixties, traditional "stranger" T-groups had given way to "family groups" consisting of managers in a single or related set of departments. Greater concern was also shown for improving managers' relations with each other in their *managerial* roles, with less attention being given to individual feelings as such. (The critical question is whether managers can work together; whether they like or respect each other is a related but subsidiary consideration.) This new approach, which has been discussed above, is often called team training and is designed to minimize the transfer dilemma. Here the focus is on the work group as it deals with its ordinary, day-to-day problems, as the consultant seeks to direct the group members' attention to the kinds of social and psychological processes which may be preventing the group from reaching its maximum potential.

As a consequence of all these developments, today it is not uncommon to find organizations which may have moved step by step from the practice of sending individual executives to off-site T-groups, to the practice of placing numerous executives from different organization units in the same T-group, to the current practice of on-site team training (Davis, 1967; Rush, 1969).

Organization development. The training evolution took its most recent step with the growing recognition through the fifties and sixties of a broader, though more subtle, version of the transfer dilemma. The work team, like the individuals in it, is embedded in a larger system. And, just as individual atttitudinal and behavioral changes acquired through intensive, experiential learning may be discouraged by the responses of other work group members, modifications in the attitudes and behavior of a work team may also be rejected by other organizational units and levels. A host of incidents in which work group development efforts were damaged if not destroyed by organizational forces external to the group (e.g., Strauss, 1955) led to widespread agreement among training specialists that the development target should not be the individual manager or even the work group, but must be the organization as a whole—thus the term, in its current meaning, Organization Development.

THE ROLE OF THE OD CONSULTANT

The final area of convergence relates to the role of the OD consultant. OD consultants have adopted a view of their role which differs greatly from that associated with many accepted consultancy practices. Traditional consultants frequently operate under what I have called the Syndicate Model (Strauss, 1973; Miles, in press). Under this model, someone in the organization "lets a contract" on some portion of the organization (other than his own). Unobtrusively clad outsiders arrive carrying the ominous tools of their trade, briefcases. Units (victims) are studied (cased), briefcases are opened and closed (the report is filed), and the outsiders leave as silently as they arrived. Frequently in their wake are missing names in the organization chart and perhaps major realignments of power and processes.

The new concept of consultancy rejects, in theory if not always in practice, the prescriptive, solution-oriented role of the traditional consultant. Instead, the OD consultant describes his role as (1) *collaboration*, working *with* the client rather than for him; (2) *research*, assisting the client in collecting the information necessary to diagnose and solve his *own* problems; and (3) *process expertise*, focusing on *how* decisions are made (the dynamics of work group behavior) rather than on the nature or quality of the decisions themselves (Schein, 1969; Bennis, 1969).

These values, as suggested, are built into the role of the T-group trainer, who is presumed to teach by example and by participating with the group, rather than by unilaterally diagnosing problems and prescribing solutions. Similarly, close ties can be seen between this emerging concept of consultancy and the role of the behavioral scientist engaged in "action research" (French and Bell, 1973, pp. 84–95). As discussed in Chapter Three, action research attempts to "bring together in a single cooperative adventure the skills and resources of both men of science and men of action . . ." (Lippitt, 1951, p. ix). The concept of action research crystallized in the 1940's—Kurt Lewin (1946) was again a leading figure—out of work in the area of ethnic and community relations. Complex attitudinal and behavioral phenomena, it was reasoned, could only be changed if they were understood—and understanding could be achieved only through collaborative research. The action researcher's role was defined as that of helping the client system (a community, a social work agency, an organization, etc.) to (1) assess existing patterns or attitudes, perceptions, and behavior (through interview, questionnaire, and observational methods); (2) set targets or goals for change or further learning; and (3) monitor (feedback) evidence related to progress toward these goals.

Note that in this role the behavioral scientist aids rather than directs; he gathers information for but does not determine action steps. Similarly, the OD consultant utilizes a full range of behaviorally sound techniques to help clients understand their own behavior and that of their organizational unit, surfacing unspoken concerns such as "no one listens to anyone else around here," or "priorities are never really made clear, we just guess and go."

Finally, since training and development efforts focus on the enhancement of the capabilities of organization members and groups, and since OD advocates hold that interpersonal skill turns largely on the extent to which trustworthiness, supportiveness, and openness are displayed, it follows that these behaviors must be key elements of the consultant's role. Therefore, if the new consultant is to gain and build trust, he must protect those he works with from damage (e.g., the work group being studied must have the right to decide how information collected about it will be used). He must share freely of all that he learns and knows, for his effectiveness does not center on the quality of *his* solutions to organizational problems but on the extent to which those he works with develop their own capabilities for solving present and future problems.

In practice, this new concept of consultancy is compromised by the consultant's own ego (his need to prove his expertise in solving as well as clarifying problems) and the demands of clients accustomed to the more comfortable roles prescribed in the traditional model (which allows them to delegate problem solving to the consultant and then simply accept or reject his solutions). Nevertheless, to the extent that the new model is approached in practice, it represents one of the most distinctive and unique features of Organization Development.

Some Areas for Debate

Is OD a Distinct Field?

Despite the accumulation of the paraphenalia associated with a field and despite considerable agreement among its supporters as to its aim and techniques, OD's first and continuing problem is that of proving that it represents something really new. Cynical observers allege that OD is little more than human relations, participative decision making, and management development banded together and marching under a new banner; OD advocates, in response, insist that OD is not merely a passing fad but a substantive, lasting field of research and practice (French and Bell, 1973, p. 198). Yet identifying the nature of this field is difficult.

If, for example, OD is defined simply in terms of techniques such as attitude surveys or participative/group problem-solving, then, according to the recent Conference Board survey, many organizations not listed by experts as involved in OD look much like their "OD" counterparts (Rush, 1973, pp. 18–41). On the other hand, if OD involves more than a specific set of techniques, as most of its advocates would argue, but is instead "a process," "a system of values," "applied behavioral science," etc. (Rush, 1973, p. 2; French and Bell, 1973, Chap. 4), it is even more ephemeral and difficult to identify. Finally, if OD, as at least some of its proponents suggest, encompasses or can encompass all organizational change activities aimed at improving performance (Friedlander and Brown, 1974), it runs the risk of falling into the category of concepts such as "communications" which are so all-pervasive as to become almost useless, unless strictly delimited, for theory building or research.

The question of OD's identity as something distinct and different is one of more than merely academic or professional interest. OD, its supporters and critics agree, demands a level of managerial support (time and money) well beyond that given to "human relations" and other training movements and involvement which cannot be delegated or assigned to some staff unit or department and forgotten. This support and involvement is unlikely to occur if OD is viewed as simply this year's model of an old training vehicle.

At this point, there is probably no adequate response to the criticism that OD is essentially an amalgamation of earlier concepts and some variations on existing training techniques. The key leadership and decision-making models and concepts which OD attempts to implement on a system-wide basis have, as indicated above, been around for at least a decade and have been "sold" under a variety of titles other than OD. Moreover, these universalistic theories have come under heavy attack in recent years for their failure to take into account situational and individual differences (Perrow, 1972; Fiedler, 1967), a point to which we will return later.

Similarly, the principal development methods utilized in OD, particularly the T-group and its variants, are (a) no longer new and (b) were originally offered as techniques for developing *managers* rather than *organizations*. In fact, as stated above, one of the major difficulties faced by OD advocates is that of differentiating OD as a body of theory and practice from the change techniques it employs. The term Organization Development was probably first used by consultants employing variations of T-groups with existing management teams and has since been eagerly adopted by almost everyone who has engaged in any form of experiential training with one or more managers from any organization. Thus, to many, T-groups and OD are synonymous, and the criticism of and disillusionment with T-groups (now widespread in organizations and within the OD fraternity) carries over to OD. Finally, many OD practitioners are essentially technique-oriented and have continued the practice of referring to whatever training methods they are currently employing (at the moment it appears that transactional analysis (Rush and McGrath, 1973) is in vogue) as OD.

To further compound the problem of establishing OD's identity, the two distinguishing characteristics which apply somewhat exclusively to OD, the collaborative role of the OD consultant and the requirement of a long-term investment in the self-renewal capacity of the organization to meet changing environmental demands, are most often missing in OD practice. The typical OD activity in most organizations is still a training effort begun without the full, uninfluenced endorsement of all its participants and carried out by someone unlikely to have a long-term collaborative relationship with the individuals or unit involved. The image of consultant and client jointly defining problems and utilizing a wide range of behavioral science research techniques to generate and evaluate their solution is more often honored from the podium than in practice. To the extent that this is the case, it is difficult to defend the claim that OD is a special field existing apart from a collection of training activities. Moreover, the same set of problems hampers efforts to demonstrate that OD, whatever it may be, is in fact helping to make organizations more effective.

DOES OD DELIVER ON ITS PROMISES?

The question of whether OD leads to improved organizational performance is almost impossible to answer unless there is an agreed upon, sharply defined concept of what constitutes OD. The Weldon Company case illustrates this dilemma. In the midst of economic distress, the Weldon Company, a sleepware manufacturer, was acquired by the Harwood Company, a competitor known for its highly participative management philosophy and for its sponsorship of behavioral science research. The new management embarked on an ambitious program to develop, or, if you will, redevelop the Weldon Company's work processes, control and reward systems, and other managerial processes. Subsequent to these efforts, there was a clear-cut change in the organization's "profile" toward Likert's System IV (see Chap. Three). These changes have been exhaustively documented by Marrow, Bowers, and Seashore (1967).

Nevertheless, even with this evidence in hand, it is difficult to obtain agreement that Weldon represents a triumph for OD. At Weldon, not only were a series of efforts made to change managerial attitudes and behaviors through experiential learning techniques, but in addition equipment was updated, work procedures were revised, skill training was provided for many work group members, and some poor performers were "weeded out" (discharged). The simultaneous change of so many variables made it impossible to identify separate effects, and thus unless the total effort, including changes in structure, process, procedure, rewards, personnel, and managerial style is accepted as OD, then the Weldon data are open to a number of interpretations.

At the other extreme, efforts to measure the effects of more limited, "accepted" components of OD, such as team development, also tend to produce findings which are hard to interpret. Many of the components are difficult to define or to measure, a conceptual fuzziness which makes research much harder and also provides a built-in excuse for the OD man who fails to attain his objectives. It is very easy for him to claim that OD was unsuccessful in a given situation because the parties just didn't develop a sufficiently high degree of trust.

Case study evidence detailing attitudinal and behavioral changes, coupled in many instances with improved output and/or profit figures, have been offered in support of each of the major OD approaches described in the beginning of this review, i.e., Managerial Grid (Blake, *et al.*, 1964), survey feedback (Marrow, Bowers, and Seashore, 1969; Waters, 1971), and team training (Davis,

1967, 1971). Case studies are highly vulnerable to criticism, however.

They seldom provide adequate controls for Hawthorne effects and "external" causation. Moreover, most OD case studies have been carried out and reported by those involved with or supportive of the development efforts. Acknowledging these shortcomings, along with the fact that successes are probably reported more frequently than failures, it is still almost impossible to deny the fact that major performance improvements have accompanied many of these efforts. Friedlander and Brown (1974), reviewing a number of studies, conclude:

> Though none of the research designs is flawless, there is convergent evidence that group development activities affect participant attitudes and sometimes their behavior as well. These effects may also "spill over" in some fashion to other organization members. It remains unclear, however, what mechanisms operate in successful team development activities, or what critical conditions must be satisfied for successful generalization of learning outside the team, or what effects group development has on actual task performance (p. 329).

As Friedlander and Brown (1974) also point out, performance improvements may also come from non-OD approaches, and definitive research to fairly compare the efficacy of OD vs. non-OD change efforts is extremely difficult, if not impossible, to design and carry out. This fact alone probably accounts for Kahn's (1973) critical assessment of the OD literature: "Of the 200 items in Franklin's (1973) bibliography of organizational development, only 25% include original quantitative data; the remaining 75% consist for the most part of opinions, narrative material, and theoretical fragments" (p. 4).

Which approach? These criticisms notwithstanding, if one believes that OD can and does produce desired attitudinal and behavior changes and performance results, the subsequent research question is which approach is most effective and/or efficient. Perhaps the most detailed analysis of various change techniques to date is that of Bowers (1973). His findings appear to indicate that the survey feedback approach and interpersonal-process consultation had more positive effects on the attitudes of organization members than did task process consultation and T-group related techniques. Moreover, survey feedback appeared to lead more directly to perceived changes in the total organization climate (decision making, communications, willingness to change, acceptance of influence from below, etc.) than did any of the other approaches, and perceptions of changes in these areas were, in turn, crucial to the success of any of the change techniques. Still, the question of whether each of the change techniques had an equal opportunity to succeed in the settings covered by the Bowers review cannot be answered definitively.

In sum, the evidence to date does not provide reliable answers to questions concerning OD's effectiveness or the comparative advantages which one OD approach or change technique may have over another. This is not an unusual situation, however, in the field of organizational behavior, where cause-effect relationships are extremely complex and where few concepts are ever definitively proven or rejected. Some measure of acceptance is evident, however, when the main thrust of criticism moves from a theory, concept, or approach as a whole to issues of its limitations or misapplications. On the basis of such evidence, the basic concept of OD may well be near acceptance, for much of the most recent criticism in and outside of the field has been directed at the variables which OD tends to neglect, most prominently structure and power and the question of under what conditions OD may be most successful. These criticisms are our next concern.

Criticisms of OD

STRUCTURAL CHANGE

Does OD give too little emphasis to structure? The question of whether and/or how OD leads to changes in organization structure is one of the more interesting issues facing the field today. Few of the OD critics have been as pointed in their comments regarding this concern as has one of its chief advocates, Warren Bennis, who states:

> I have yet to see an organization development program that uses an interventional strategy other than an interpersonal one, and this is serious when one considers that the

most pivotal strategies of change in our society are political, legal, and technological. . . (Bennis, 1969, pp. 78–79).

While Bennis, who has never been known for excessive moderation, may overstate the case, it is clear that early OD advocates placed too much emphasis on the primacy of interpersonal (as opposed to structural) change strategies. As noted earlier, the OD consultant tends to reject the idea of prescribing structure and process changes, the solutions to organizational problems most often offered by traditional consultants. Instead, the original OD approach, stated or implied, was to attack attitudes and perceptions first, working toward actual changes in interpersonal behavior patterns; then, if necessary, changes in roles, procedures, and perhaps structure would follow as their need was recognized by enlightened organizational members. This was in direct opposition to the socio-technical approach which was emerging during the same period at the Tavistock Institute in England and which sought to work with organization members in the redesign of roles and man-machine systems, assuming that this would lead to changes in attitudes and behavior (Trist and Bamforth, 1951; Rice, 1958).

More importantly, perhaps, the emphasis on interpersonal issues has appeared "soft" and ambiguous in the face of a rebirth of interest in structural determinancy—the search for lawful relationships between types of task environments, types of technology, and particular patterns of organization structure and process discussed in Chapter Five. In fact, OD's emergence may have widened the already visible gap between primarily social psychological investigations of organization behavior (e.g., Likert, 1967; McGregor, 1960) and concepts offered primarily by sociologists and political scientists (Perrow, 1970, 1972).

While this interdisciplinary debate continues (Argyris, 1972), probably having reached the point where acrimony rather than clarity is the primary outcome, the dialectic has already produced its synthesis, at least in the case of the recent OD literature which considers job and socio-technical systems design as part of its domain. Friedlander and Brown (1974) include both technostructural change efforts and human-processual development approaches as appropriate forms of Organization Development. And they conclude that "increased integration of the two approaches, we feel, will increase the present capacity of OD to influence organizational effectiveness toward both human fulfillment and task accomplishment" (p. 334). More pointedly, they specify the need for this integration in their citations of resistance and failure resulting from an attempt to change structure, technology, or human behavior alone, without considering other factors (p. 314). What they do not specify, however, is how and on what basis this integration is to proceed, which leads us to the question of power.

THE PROBLEM OF POWER

The allocation of power and its use presents problems for OD theorists and practitioners which may not be as easily dealt with as those associated with the issue of structure. The OD consultancy model, described earlier, eschews the use of coercive power and instead aims at a collaborative relationship in which experiential learning rather than prescription produce the desired changes. The key question is, How is such a relationship established? How does an OD consultant create a collaborative relationship with someone who does not share his expertise and who, even if concerned about some aspect of performance may see little need to change his own behavior or the structure and processes within his unit?

Most prominent OD consultants claim to work "only by invitation" (Schein, 1969; Bennis, 1969), but many others, if not actively "selling" their approaches and services, are in no sense shy about having their availability widely known. All but the most naive are aware that the conditions under which they begin their work with a client (entree) are crucial to their relationship and the overall success of their approach and thus struggle hard to establish enlightened endorsement and approval from key people in the client system, particularly top management. True collaboration is difficult even at this point, however, because the client ordinarily does not know enough to evaluate alternatives, if indeed any are presented. The more formalized the consultant's approach (e.g., survey feedback, the Grid, etc.), the fewer the alternatives available, other than acceptance or rejection of the total effort. Moreover, even if the consultant makes an elaborate effort to build a base for informed collaboration with top management, as I have advocated he should (see Strauss, 1973), the sheer number of individuals and situations involved makes it increasingly difficult to obtain purely voluntary participation as OD moves down the hierarchy. At the lower levels, members sense the implicit if not explicit power of higher management behind the OD effort, and many persons are coerced into participation despite any tactic which the consultant may employ to prevent this from occurring. Finally, organization members well schooled in the "advancement" game utilize their usual political ploys around an OD effort just as they have learned to do around any organizational activity.

While the use of power or coercion by top management may at times be functional—for example, where reluctance to participate in an OD program is based on apathy rather than on fear or conviction—many unintended dysfunctions may occur if the consultant deemphasizes OD's "learning" goal. Recall that a key objective of OD is not simply one-time behavioral and process change but the development of increased capacity for continuous, self-directed, organizational renewal (Bennis, 1969). While all OD theorists and most practitioners pay homage to this goal, the pressure to move ahead, to show results, and to prove one's expertise is seductive even to a financially secure consultant—and frequently overpowering to members of an OD unit inside an organization. Unchecked, these forces push OD efforts toward the status of "just another management program" aimed at short-term results, dependent on pressure, and devoid of much learning. My current belief is that every major OD effort should have an outside consultant who takes no part in the effort, is not employed for his expertise in change strategies or to verify performance goals, but is simply there to raise questions and concerns regarding the pace of the effort and the extent to which learning is maintained as a goal (Miles, in press).

The second point at which power issues are raised with regard to OD concerns intergroup relations. Early OD theorists and practitioners, particularly those who emerged from the T-group movement, tended to view most conflict, whether between individuals or between adjacent groups or hierarchical levels, as failures in communication and understanding. Presumably, persons or groups who understood one another's situations and were aware of the impacts of their behaviors would choose more mutually rewarding alternatives. Where alternatives exist for increasing the gains to all concerned ("variable sum games"—see Chapter Six) and where interdependence is real and lasting, it makes sense to prescribe "problem solving" approaches to conflict resolution (Lawrence and Lorsch 1967). However, where such alternatives do not exist (zero-sum situations) or where interdependence is either not recognized or not valued, efforts to create understanding and improved communication may either be repulsed or simply serve to raise the conflict to a more sophisticated level.

WHEN DOES OD SUCCEED?

The statements here (and in Chapter Six) that conflict resolution is probably most amenable to productive solution when it is contained, when the issues are discernible, and when alternatives are available (Walton, 1969) leads us to a final question: When and under what conditions is OD most likely to succeed? Despite OD's emphasis on feelings and emotions and despite its claimed value in creating coping capability, OD probably requires a moderately stable set of organizational and environmental conditions if it is to succeed. The principal reason for this requirement is that OD takes time. Friedlander and Brown (1974), reviewing the available reports of major (system-wide) OD efforts, note that "these cases took years to bear fruit" (p. 333), a point generally made by OD advocates though not sufficiently stressed in practice. All but the most shallow or limited OD efforts require extensive, time-consuming interventions at various levels and across numerous units. The development of awareness of organizational processes beyond simple face-to-face interactions cannot be accomplished quickly, nor can collaboration in the choice of new procedures and structures be maintained in the face of intensive internally or externally generated pressures for immediate action.

The organization whose very existence is threatened can probably not afford to wait for a long-term payoff. Potentially disastrous market threats must be countered, all but the most necessary operations curtailed, and other similar dramatic actions must be taken rapidly and often unilaterally, simply to survive. Such crises, of course, are frequently manufactured by managers (Miles and Ritchie, 1971), but when they are real, OD is unable to produce a quick solution.

Furthermore, any successful change effort, including OD, probably requires that the parties involved strongly recognize the need for change (Griener, 1967). In line with the Lewinian change model mentioned earlier, some discontent with present processes and performance is probably necessary before managers will begin to search for alternative modes of behavior. Most successful major OD efforts appear to have occurred in organizations which were already successful by most standards, but which recognized that growth, market change, or some other anticipated events might be likely to exacerbate existing problems and create new dilemmas requiring new capabilities (Rush, 1969). (The Weldon Company example discussed earlier may be viewed as an exception, but there the OD effort emanated from its stable, successful purchaser, Harwood). Of course, the fact that successful OD programs may require a relatively stable organizational and environmental setting does not destroy the argument that OD can lead to greater responsiveness under conditions of uncertainty. One can argue that a long history of OD activity during stable periods can make an organization much more successful in anticipating and coping with future turbulence. Proof of this argument awaits that rarest form of research, comparative longitudinal studies.

OD's Future

Just as with the weather, the best short-run prediction for the future of OD is that of "little change." The amazing growth and adaptiveness of Organization Development have already belied the here today, gone tomorrow predictions of its most cynical critics. At the same time, there is little sign that OD is likely to move quickly toward fulfilling the promises of its more extreme supporters. Instead, there are competing trends and forces which, in combination, appear likely to keep OD alive and even growing, but not in the flourishing, forceful fashion that it advocates desire.

On the positive side, OD has momentum. It has accumulated the accoutrements of a professional field, and those who are associated with the field are, logically enough, devoted to its growth and expansion. OD has a firm foothold in the private sector and growing acceptance in the public, where problems are in abundance and where established, guaranteed solutions are at a minimum. In corporations, public agencies, schools, and hospitals, OD is an accepted if frequently misunderstood term, and OD practitioners are busily accumulating clients. Further, many of the techniques and approaches associated with OD have spread to organizations which do not have full OD efforts (Rush, 1973), and this spillover may prepare the way for further expansion.

On the negative side, OD's momentum may be its own worst enemy. As Burke puts it, OD has a future if ". . . it can avoid premature formulation [of concepts and methodology] . . . and avoid being co-opted by traditional organization pressures" (in French and Bell, 1973, p. 195). OD is a continuing and evolving process that requires substantial investments of resources (especially management time and energy) over a lengthy period of time in order to produce major results. But it is particularly vulnerable to being oversold as a quick, painless solution for every organizational problem and thus being naively purchased. The search for quick solutions, particularly to "people problems," is a way of life in most organizations and is fueled by managers' needs to demonstrate accomplishments rapidly in order to move on and up. The troublesome possibility is that the sellers of OD will attempt to meet the buyers' demands, resulting in the further proliferation of shallow, limited efforts. To the extent that this occurs, OD will grow, but its accomplishments will be limited. Ineffective OD is unlikely to do the organization major damage; rather, it may lead to what I have called an "inoculation effect"; that is, groups and organizations which engage in short-term, ineffectual OD "programs" will be unlikely to engage in more serious efforts in the future. This phenomenon is neatly summarized in the statement a manager made to me recently. "OD?" he said, "we went through that a couple of years ago."

The Conference Board survey cited earlier (Rush, 1973) identified fewer than fifty major organizations which experts agreed were substantially involved in OD (i.e., in which there was a level of involvement likely to lead to sustained, long-term accomplishments). Given the problems mentioned above, I think it unlikely that this number will increase substantially. The growth of genuine OD programs probably does not depend on the development of improved training approaches. Instead, it is more likely to be a function of the extent to which (a) high-level officials in organizations become knowledgeable about what OD can and cannot do, and (b) practitioners move beyond an exclusive focus on interpersonal processual change to a concern with structural questions.

These two determinants of meaningful OD growth are by no means independent. One reason why OD efforts have focused so closely on interpersonal rather than structural or policy issues is because this is exactly as far as many organizations want them to go. In the minds of many managers, OD should not go beyond a concern for improvements in communication, trust, cooperation, etc. In other words, managers too often look upon OD as a means for improving the present system—not for changing it. To the extent that OD practitioners accept the notion that OD produces a need for and an approach to major changes in roles, procedures, departmental reporting relationships, etc. and demand similar awareness from the top administrators with whom they are working, they are likely to achieve fewer, though perhaps more productive, opportunities to engage in OD.

If nothing else, the current focus on OD's failure to take structural and power issues sufficiently into account could have an unanticipated positive effect. That is, it could be that the attention given to structure and task processes, for example, will focus greater attention on the behavioral effects of changes in technology, procedures, roles, reporting relationships, etc. If managers and consultants who regularly prescribe unilateral change in major organizational variables began to take interpersonal processual issues into account to the same extent that OD's critics demand that it focus on organizational variables, OD's impact may well be great.

Concluding Comments

In their review of the Organization Development literature, Friedlander and Brown (1974) offer a most important observation: "We have generally failed to produce a theory of change which emerges from the change process itself" (p. 336). They note that instead of focusing on the change process, the bulk of research to date has sought to "prove" the efficacy of OD or its components (an effort that is no more likely to succeed than attempts to prove or disprove the value of participative management, mediation, job enrichment, or any other complex process influenced by a wide array of difficult to measure and control forces). OD's basic thrust, particularly as it incorporates concern for organizational variables, is, I believe, behaviorally sound, but this belief is likely to remain beyond definitive proof.

This comment is not intended to place OD beyond criticism or to discourage research, for many of its concepts and practices merit concern and are researchable, though at a high cost. Instead, it is intended to focus attention on what we can learn from the successes and failures, in practice, of essentially sound concepts. Friedlander and Brown (1974) call for a closer merging between research and practice and particularly for research which illuminates the processes of change as well as its results. As they point out, we still have much to learn if we are to make effective use of the behavioral sciences in solving problems in either work organizations or in society generally. We still know very little about how to initiate change, about the roles which change demands of those who participate in it, or about how change energy may be sustained. OD may not be the answer to improving organizational and societal change processes, but it is perhaps the best arena for learning and experimentation presently available.

CHAPTER 8

Implications for Industrial Relations

GEORGE STRAUSS
RAYMOND E. MILES
University of California, Berkeley
AND
CHARLES C. SNOW
Pennsylvania State University

The previous chapters covered a variety of research issues. Some of these related merely to methodology and definition, but much of the work in this area has far-reaching economic, social, and even political significance. This final chapter will deal, albeit fairly disjointedly, with some of the implications of this work for management, unions, and collective bargaining and will close with a final statement on some value issues.

CONVERGENCES

If nothing else, the previous chapters have demonstrated that OB offers numerous competing explanations of (and prescriptions for) behavior in organizational settings. Despite this competition, the perceptive reader may have discerned considerable convergence both between and across subject matter areas: regardless of how one approaches organizational behavior—whether through the portal marked leadership or that marked conflict resolution or formal participation—he is likely to find similar explanations and prescriptions for organizational problems. Through the forties and fifties, convergence occurred around the need for and means of humanizing the work place; there was widespread agreement as to the desirability of objectives such as being more considerate of employees' feelings, making the job environment more pleasant, and finding means of preventing or smoothing over conflict. The late fifties and sixties saw convergence around the notion that merely treating people decently was not enough; it was also important to provide opportunities for them to utilize their untapped capabilities for creative self-direction and self-control. Currently convergence appears to be occurring around the idea of contingency—around the search for theories which take into account the human and situational variables which *moderate* expected general behavioral patterns.

By and large, however, the key concepts in the emerging contingency models have been derived from the writings of earlier Human Relations and Human Resources theorists. To take one example, Human Relations and Human Resources theory have frequently dealt with the broad relationship between participation and performance. Contingency theory is concerned with how this relationship is affected by various personality and situational characteristics. For instance, it is now reasonably well established that participation is more likely to have a positive effect on performance when workers have a high need for achievement and less likely to have such an effect when work is highly programmed.

Implications for Management

Although few contingency models have been fully validated, the contingency approach introduced a note of realism which should be welcomed by practitioners. After all, the typical practitioner distrusts universalistic prescriptions; he evaluates OB writings in terms of the people and situations in his own organization and so applies a contingency model of his own. Where possible, we will use the contingency notion as we derive implications for management from the research discussed in the previous chapters.

ORGANIZATIONAL STRUCTURE, TECHNOLOGY, AND ENVIRONMENT

The implications of the research reviewed in Chapter 5 are rather clear. For example, Human Resources prescriptions seem to be appropriate in organizations where large numbers of skilled professionals and technicians are employed and in which environmental conditions (e.g., markets, products, technologies) are changing rapidly. That is, "organic" organization structures—where jobs permit high levels of self-direction and control, communication across departmental lines is relatively unrestricted, and leadership approaches are essentially facilitative (advice and consultation) rather than directive (commands)—are apparently more likely to result in both effective performance and high job satisfaction than are more mechanistic, routinized, and controlling structures and practices. Conversely, there are organizational settings where little opportunity exists to follow Human Resources prescriptions, whatever managers' or rank-and-file members' beliefs, needs, or abilities. In these situations, stable environments and technological constraints seem to dictate structural rigidity, job routinization, and tight controls.

Only a small percentage of organizational situations fit either of the extremes described, however; most organizations face environments which are neither completely stable nor highly turbulent. For managers in these "in-between" situations, the choices are not as clear; their organizational settings neither demand organic structures and processes nor severely limit the extent to which these could be applied. For these managers, therefore, the question becomes: should we leave well enough alone, or should we consider restructuring our organizations along either more mechanistic or more organic lines?

In answer to this question, management can be reasonably certain that, on balance, events will push them in the organic rather than the mechanistic direction. As workers' material standards of living improve, as they become better educated, and as their expectations change, they can be expected to show increasing preference for freedom on the job. If, in addition, as some OB theorists predict, the organizational world of the future is likely to be characterized by increasingly unpredictable markets, regulatory pressures, and interorganizational relations, then management can also expect that tasks which are uncertain and difficult to program will become relatively more common.

But what about today? Since there is little reliable evidence that workers' job satisfaction is declining or that demands for more challenging work (and similar organic practices) are increasing, should those managers whom we have described as in "in-between" situations simply do nothing with regard to creating organic organizational structures? We think not. Organizations are slow to change. If the future requires organizational adaptation (certainly *some* changes are inevitable, even if they turn out to be less dramatic than OB writers suggest), then managers holding Traditional or Human Relations viewpoints are likely to cling to outmoded practices far too long, and such inertia may dangerously slow down adaptation even when it becomes necessary.

Managers may logically respond that it would be unwise to invest scarce resources in programs designed to make their organizations more organic when there appears to be little current need to do so. However, we believe that limited-scale investments in such programs might produce valuable insurance against a potential collision between future environmental changes and an unprepared organization. Managers might experiment with more organic technological and structural features, perhaps in selected pockets of their organizations, in order to learn *where* and *how* to introduce them more widely if future conditions appear to require this. Although such high-technology companies as TRW, Inc. and Syntex (Rush, 1971) commonly experiment in this fashion, possibly the most extensive experiment of this kind took place in the sleepwear manufacturing company discussed in Chapter 7—hardly an organization in a turbulent environment. We should stress, however, that these experiments should be carried out in a portion of the organization which is relatively autonomous and constitutes an organizational system of its own. Otherwise, unanticipated and potentially harmful effects on other organizational processes could occur, obscuring the results of the experiment and perhaps causing it to be scrapped by top management.

There is another reason why management should consider enlarging the scope of its participative, organic practices. Worker dissatisfaction aimed at mechanistic organizational practices may be expressed in a number of ways, among others through demands for higher wages, for longer vacations, for early retirement, for safer working conditions, for flex-time, and for more challenging work. From management's point of view, most of these represent just a cost item. Of these, flex-time and job redesign are about the only ones which give any substantial promise of lowering rather than raising labor costs. Surely there must be many cases, for example, where it would be cheaper to alter mechanistic practices to make jobs more satisfying than to pay for early retirement.

SUPERVISION

OB research on leadership and supervision has yielded relatively few findings useful for practitioners, among other reasons because of an overemphasis on discovering a simple relationship between a supervisor's leadership "style" and his subordinates' performance and satisfaction. Despite the arid nature of the leadership terrain, however, there are a few oases which contain important implications for management.

Higher managers should first clearly recognize the bind in which they frequently place their lower managers and supervisors. In the vast majority of organizations, such supervisors are expected to obtain results through the performance of their subordinates. And yet, as Chapter 3 pointed out, supervisors—individually—have less impact on subordinate performance than they have on subordinate satisfaction. This is because the supervisor's impact on his subordinates' *satisfaction* is primarily dependent on his attitudes and face-to-face interactions with these subordinates (e.g., whether he trusts them and behaves accordingly). *Performance,* on the other hand, is mostly determined by a much wider range of supervisory behaviors (e.g., his ability to provide materials and information, to plan, or to maintain good relations with other departments). These behaviors, in turn, are heavily influenced by how higher management itself behaves; indeed, Chapter 3 concluded that behavior subject to the supervisor's own control may account for only 15–20 per cent of his subordinates' performance. For these reasons, the first step in improving supervisory effectiveness is for management to undertake a thorough and critical self-examination of its own behavior, with the goal of identifying the barriers it places on effective supervisory performance.

This conclusion has some further implications for lower level managerial and supervisory training programs. These programs are not likely to be effective when they emphasize changing supervisory attitudes yet ignore the constraints on supervisory behavior placed by higher management. This is especially true when changed attitudes are not rewarded in the "back home" organizational setting. Instead training programs might focus on helping supervisors develop criteria which they might use to select alternative behaviors which in turn could actually be employed on the job while, at the same time, seeking to identify those higher managerial constraints which might be modified or even eliminated.

ORGANIZATION DEVELOPMENT

The discussion of OD in Chapter 7 produced several conclusions of importance to management. First, there is evidence that OD can be useful to management if properly supported and conducted—though this is not universally so and OD should not be considered a panacea. Secondly, to date OD has emphasized people issues over structural and power issues, but this emphasis is changing, and OD efforts in the future may be of even greater value as they begin to deal with more of management's traditional concerns (e.g., organization design). Finally, an OD program may provide the best available means for learning about and experimenting with new organizational and managerial practices.

Let us enlarge on this last point. OD represents a means for introducing change in an organization and for increasing the organization's capacity for self-renewal. It helps make organization members more perceptive of environmental changes; it helps make the organization's structure and processes more responsive to these changes; and it develops a variety of sustaining mechanisms to insure that future changes can be identified and accommodated by the organization. OD stresses the importance of collecting accurate, timely data about aspects of the organization not normally closely monitored—evidence as to employee job satisfaction, the accumulation of specialized knowledge and skills, signs of interdepartmental conflict, and the like. With these data, management can better evaluate the impact of its decisions on the human resources of the organization and can make more informed plans for the future.

Lastly, because OD views the organization as a total system, it asks the appropriate questions about achieving an effective and satisfying organization: What are the goals of the overall organization and its major subunits? What resources are available for meeting these goals? What areas of the organization need to be improved, and what effects will improvements in these areas have on others? What strengths and weaknesses are evident in the organization's human resources? How can data be collected to assess these conditions? And how can mechanisms be designed which will continuously sustain the organization's strengths and aid in remedying its weaknesses? It may well be that managers who can answer these questions about their organizations have taken effective, system-wide action steps that OB scholars cannot at this point capture in their contingency models.

SOME CONCLUSIONS FOR MANAGERS

Organizational Behavior has come a long way since the day of the early Human Relations evangelists with their clear-cut answers for every organizational problem. Today, we are fully aware that organic, participative techniques are by no means of universal value to management. Quite the contrary. But, following our contingency approach, we suggest that such techniques are not being utilized in a number of situations where they are already appropriate and that the number of such situations may increase in the future. In any case, management should give serious thought to the use of *appropriate* OD techniques to increase organizational readiness for change. And it should also carefully consider the implications of its own behavior—especially in designing communications and reward systems—for the behavior of lower level supervisors. These are only a few of the implications of OB research, but they are the ones most heavily stressed in recent years.

Implications for Unions

Assuming that our previous hypotheses, based on contingency theories, are correct—that is, organic, participative practices will become economically more feasible in the future and workers' desires for meaningful, challenging work will grow—what are the implications of these for unions? In particular, what problems will demands for job redesign or for formal participation create for unions? And what are the implications for unions of research on organization structure and OD? Let us consider these issues in turn, stressing the point that our conclusions are highly tentative and designed more to raise questions than to present prescriptions for action.

JOB REDESIGN

Job redesign issues, particularly those surrounding the increasing use of job enrichment and self-managing work teams (Chapter 2), raise some important questions as to union collective bargaining goals. In the past, union objectives have been primarily concerned with higher wages, greater job security, less autocratic supervision, and generally with what Herzberg calls "hygienic" or around-the-job factors. Over the years, unions have won significant rights for their members in the area of hygienic job factors—the right for health benefits, for a decent retirement income, for layoffs only in accordance with seniority, for protection against unjust discipline, and the like. Should American unions follow the lead of their European counterparts (Mire, 1974) who now argue for a new right—a right to challenging work?

Is there a demand for job enrichment? Note that job enrichment demands are already being made by unions and professional associations in some fields. Teachers, librarians, social workers, and engineers are among those seeking greater freedom to determine the content and methods of their work. Here the demands are cast in terms of "professionalization," but the difference between this and various forms of job redesign is largely a matter of semantics. (Cynics may argue that these "professional" concerns merely represent an attractive new packaging for such traditional union demands as reduced work loads and protection of jurisdictional claims. Though there is some truth in this cynical view, there is no question that professionals are asking for greater control over the *quality* as well as quantity of work. And unions seeking to organize professional and white-collar workers are paying increasing attention to these demands.)

Although Chapter 2 concluded that there is little solid evidence to date indicating that the *expressed* demand for job enrichment has spread to blue-collar workers, it leaves open the possibility that authors such as Terkel (1974) may be partly right: though so far poorly articulated (except by Terkel's carefully selected respondents) and largely unfocused, the demand for more challenging work may be festering below the surface, and it may just possibly break out into the open in the near future.

But how can we be sure? Demands for higher wages are easier to articulate than demands for more challenging work. Money earnings are tangible; psychic earnings are not. Workers might feel foolish demanding that their bosses provide them with interesting work, but a demand for a pay increase can be put into writing and negotiated.

The union's role in assessing the demand for job enrichment. How are union leaders to recognize this mostly unexpressed demand (which may even be nonexistent)? Should they take the initiative to stimulate it and bring it out in the open? Or should they wait until it is more clearly developed?

We may ask, is the union hierarchy sufficiently close to the membership (particularly the younger membership) to recognize such an unconventional demand? Or, is it as blind today as early AFL leaders were, for example, to the organizing potential in mass-production industries during the early thirties? And, is this an issue where the union leadership should wait for rank-and-file awareness to break through—or should the leadership play an educational role? Certainly there have been some issues where the leadership has been unafraid to march considerably ahead of the membership (e.g., the Guaranteed Annual Wage in the automobile industry).

Can a meaningful analogy be drawn between the area of job enrichment and occupational health and safety? Until quite recently, unions looked upon safety as primarily a management function, and workers (particularly those engaged in piecework) viewed the safety man as a management snoop whose chief function was to make workers do uncomfortable things, such as wear safety glasses. Today unions are generally taking a more active role in the area of safety. Educational programs have been developed to make workers more conscious of possible job hazards as well as to elicit support for giving greater priority to health and safety demands, and unions are even hiring their own health and safety representatives (perhaps twenty years too late). Should they also hire behavioral science and mental health experts?

We as editors have few specific answers to these questions. Union leaders differ considerably in their sensitivity to rank-and-file desires. By and large, they react most quickly to well organized pressure groups (Sayles and Strauss, 1967) and to well defined issues. Upward communications are sometimes distorted in unions, as they are in other organizations, and union leaders, as leaders elsewhere, may be slow in sensing some of the immediate problems faced by the rank and file.

Traditional means of upward communication within the union may need to be supplemented. The local meeting may be an inadequate vehicle for such communication, especially in large locals (Sayles and Strauss, 1967). Some unions have taken imaginative steps to sample rank-and-file opinion and to establish forums in which younger workers will feel unafraid to speak their mind, uninhibited by agenda, parliamentary procedures, or the presence of old timers. Such experiments should be encouraged. In addition, union leaders might be well advised to explore the applicability of attitude survey techniques for their own organizations. It would be ironic if companies were to do a better job than unions in keeping track of rank-and-file desires.

The union's role in implementing job enrichment programs. Assuming that the union is able to discern some membership sentiment for more challenging work, how should this desire be translated into issues for collective bargaining? Should unions simply use the normal grievance procedure to police job enrichment experiments instituted by management—or, as in Scandinavia, should they take the initiative in demanding that jobs be improved? If the latter, should the union demand that specific jobs be changed in certain ways or merely that a mechanism be created for joint consultation?

Sometimes changes are desirable from the workers' point of view, even if they are not particularly desirable from management's. For this reason, it may not be enough for the union to wait quietly for management to make the first move. If job redesign programs are good for workers, then unions should take the initiative in getting them introduced (as some professional unions have done).

Impact of job redesign on collective bargaining practices. Regardless of how they are introduced, job redesign programs will have an impact on a number of collective bargaining practices. The thrust of collective bargaining in many industries has been to define job classifications ever more strictly and to insist that no one work outside his classification. Job enrichment obviously requires movement in the opposite direction: the combination of some jobs, the blurring of the boundaries between others, and even the blending of worker and supervisory functions. Job redesign efforts may also disturb established promotional ladders and seniority provisions. And, finally, where job redesign efforts involve raising job qualifications, this may conflict with affirmative action programs designed to make jobs easier for untrained, hard-core workers.

Difficult problems such as the above, however, are constantly being resolved through the process of collective bargaining; for example, work rules exist in many plants to deal with problems of job assignment. Once union leaders discern a clear mandate for job enrichment from their membership, job redesign problems may well be solvable within this work-rule context.

Impact on union governance. The appropriate locus of job redesign efforts, if these are to occur, is at the shop level. Thus, a shift from an emphasis on uniform company-wide (or even industry-wide) wage and salary benefits to shop-level job design questions might also lead to a shift in the power balance between the union's international leadership and the shop steward (though the likelihood of dramatic change should not be exaggerated).

Narrowly defined, job redesign merely involves the one-shot redefinition of job descriptions. But more broadly defined (as discussed in Chapter 2), it involves the creation of self-managing work teams and continuing worker participation in resolving such previously managerial problems as supply, production, planning, and quality control.

Will greater participation on the job lead to greater worker participation in union affairs? Or, because job redesign provides an alternative means for the resolution of work place problems, will this reduce union loyalty? The answer to this question depends largely on whether the union itself actively participates in decisions concerning job redesign—or whether it only reacts to the actions management takes. However, as the next section on formal participation schemes suggests, nowhere in the world has the role of the union in participative management been adequately resolved—and this may be a continuing problem, even with such relatively minor changes in traditional union-management power relationships as those required by job redesign.

WORKERS' PARTICIPATION IN MANAGEMENT

Workers' participation has received far more attention elsewhere than it has in the United States. Participative schemes overseas range from weak shop councils in the United Kingdom to formal Workers' Self-management in Yugoslavia, but in one form or another they have received widespread support from both unionists and intellectuals. The U.S. and Canada may be the only Western countries in which participation has not become a significant social, economic, and political issue.

There are at least three reasons why the United States is seemingly out of step with much of the industrialized world.

The first reason is ideological. Workers' participation is happily consistent with both Socialism and the papal encyclicals and so has enlisted support from such widely divergent people and groups as President de Gaulle, Marshall Tito, the German Social Democrats (and, at one time, the Christian Democrats), and the Israeli Histradrut. In Europe, formal participation performs a significant symbolic ideological role, with the nature of this role differing somewhat among countries (Strauss and Rosenstein, 1970). None of these ideological motives exists in the United States.

Secondly, among the purposes of European workers' participation is that of extending U.S.-style collective bargaining to the plant level. As Chapter 4 pointed out, unionized workers in the U.S. already participate in many decisions important to them, and plant grievance committees take on many of the functions performed by European workers' councils.

Finally, one of the major differences between the participation movements in Europe and the U.S. is that the former has emphasized what Chapter 4 called "legal systems" while in the latter it relates to a management style. Although hard evidence is not available, American management may be more Human Relations (if not Human Resources) oriented than its European counterpart. This, combined, with the greater strength of U.S. unions at the shop level, may help explain recent findings that American employees feel they have greater influence on what goes on in the plant than do employees in Austria, Germany, or Italy (Tannenbaum, *et al.*, 1974).

For these reasons, the extension of European-style workers' participation (beyond those few plants under the Scanlon Plan) to the United States seems unlikely in the near future. For the longer run we are less sure, although two possible developments may eventually change the picture.

Planning. In the first place, U.S. unions may wish someday to follow the lead of European unions by seeking to become directly involved in corporate-level planning regarding such issues as plant size and location, level of investment, pricing, and distribution of profits. All these are of at least indirect concern to workers as well as to society as a whole. There are already some American precedents: the UAW offered to share management decisions during World War II (there were no takers), and the construction and garment unions have been heavily, though informally, involved in shaping the directions of their respective industries. Possibly, by the turn of the century, American unions may wish to participate in corporate planning directly rather than wait to react to policies once they have been announced.

Job and process redesign. The second approach to formal union participation may be via the job redesign route. As mentioned in Chapter 2, for job redesign to be effective, broad organizational changes are usually required which go beyond the confines of a given department. For example, for workers to be really successful in planning how their work is to be scheduled, they may also have to participate in developing schedules for the plant as a whole, in improving the flow of critical supplies, in developing inventory policies, and the like. Once the momentum of participation has begun, it may be difficult to confine it to problems affecting only individual departments.

While participation within a small department can simply involve individual workers, once interdepartmental problems are dealt with, it becomes less feasible for each individual to participate directly, and some sort of representative participation is required. But representative participation raises a host of new problems. If an organization desires to expand participation beyond the small group level, it may have to adopt one of three approaches.

1. According to Likert's (1961) version of participative management, the supervisor of each work group is to act as a "linking pin" who fulfills the dual role of representing his group's needs to higher management (and other work groups) and of presenting higher management's needs to the work group. Sometimes called "System 4," this form of participation is based on the "human relations" (rather than "pluralistic," see Chapter 4) assumption

that the supervisor can somehow effectively represent both his subordinates and his superiors without suffering a great deal of role conflict. Such participation also seems to assume that the supervisor will not distort his subordinates' desires as he carries them upward or otherwise ineffectively represent them. Such assumptions may be naive in many cases.

2. Individual workers may be elected or otherwise selected to serve on consultative bodies. This is how workers' councils are created in most European countries; it is also the method used in many U.S. companies to form committees to deal with such varied tasks as collecting money for the United Fund, regulating the parking lot, and planning the annual picnic. But once these committees gain significant decision-making clout, they threaten existing unions.

3. The third model, of course, is for the union officers themselves to assume the representative role. They can perform this task regardless of whether participation concerns long-range planning or improving day-to-day production processes.

Problems with formal workers' participation. Regardless of its motivation, however, formal workers' participation creates a number of serious political and human relations problems for all concerned, especially unions. These problems have been the subject of considerable research (e.g., Slichter, 1941; Strauss and Rosenstein, 1970) resulting in the following conclusions, among others:

. . . Workers' representatives on joint participative bodies may be coopted: the more they learn about management's problems and the more they become involved in managerial decision making, the more likely they will become insensitive to rank-and-file needs. There is considerable evidence that this alienation is a continuing problem wherever union-management cooperation occurs.

. . . Workers may lack the knowledge and technical skills to make significant inputs.

. . . Unless exactly the same union officers are involved in participation as are involved in bargaining, there is a strong possibility that the individuals performing these two functions will clash. Yet concentration of both sets of responsibilities in a single set of individuals substantially reduces the number of workers who enjoy a genuine sense of participation.

. . . Though formal participation schemes are designed to increase the autonomy and involvement of every worker, in practice active participation (in the sense of contributing ideas or speaking at meetings) is limited to relatively few individuals, regardless of the system (e.g., Obradovic, in press) —with the possible exception of the kibbutz.

Thus, the impact of European-style formal workers' participation (called "legal systems" in Chapter 4) can be summarized as follows:

> It has involved top leadership far more than the rank and file, and it has almost ignored lower and middle levels of management. It has not brought power and influence to the ordinary worker; nor has it unleashed workers' creativity or even actively involved the leadership in making production decisions. The division of labor between decision makers and those who carry out decisions has not been abolished. . . . There is little evidence that participation has resulted in workers working harder or even smarter. A major reason why formal participation schemes have had such limited success in raising production is that they are focused on the wrong level and on the wrong subjects (Strauss and Rosenstein, 1970, pp. 212–213).

The last sentence poses a major dilemma: workers may find that participation confined to the shop level is too constricting but that representative participation, whether through union auspices or otherwise, tends to alienate the representative from his constituents and to deal with problems of little direct interest to the average worker. As mentioned earlier, this dilemma is not easy to resolve.

The concept of workers' participation in management is becoming increasingly attractive to left-wing and labor-oriented intellectuals throughout the world. Despite growing interest in this area on the part of behavioral scientists—and numerous international conferences—the problems involved in transforming workers' participation from dream to reality are still immense.

ORGANIZATIONAL STRUCTURE, TECHNOLOGY, AND ENVIRONMENT

The discussion of structural problems in Chapter 5 is very relevant to unions. A union's structure has much to do with its leaders' ability to perceive and react effectively to environmental influences. In the early 1930's, the AFL's structure, organized along craft lines, prevented it from reacting quickly to organizational opportunities. On the other hand, the CIO's centralized structure may have reduced its ability to organize and service small plants, especially those in the service industries. Only a brief historical glance is necessary to show that unions have a tendency to retain their organizational forms long after they have lost their utility; when change does occur, it is only in the face of the strongest of environmental pressures.

Today unions are dealing simultaneously on the governmental and economic fronts and with problems at the national and local levels; in many cases, economic conditions are changing rapidly in the industries within which they operate. This plethora of problems—each at a different level and each requiring different managerial skills—suggests that the union movement would be wise to re-examine its organizational structure. Given the growing importance of political questions, for example, should the role of state and local federations be strengthened, as well as that of the AFL-CIO itself? Should multi-industry unions encourage the development of industrial coordinating councils (perhaps at the expense of regional bodies) ?

Should unions become more centralized or less so? In some ways, unions are becoming more centralized while the thrust of the management literature seems to be toward decentralization. As early as 1953 (Sayles and Strauss, 1953), it was clear that the power of the shop steward had eroded from its position during "the primitive revolutionary democracy" of the 1930's and 1940's. The process seems to be continuing today, with power being concentrated in full-time porkchoppers (and a growing number of staff experts who never worked in the shop). Arguably, increasing concentrations of power are inevitable as unions become more complex and technical; however, the process makes leader-member communications more difficult (and at times less successful). There seem to be some counterpressure at work, however; the new collective bargaining agreement in the steel industry provides some measure of decentralization. Should similar experiments be encouraged elsewhere? As Bok and Dunlop (1970) convincingly argue, unions have given too little attention to the problems of union structure and administration.

ORGANIZATION DEVELOPMENT

Structural change requires acceptance by the affected parties. Organization Development (OD) deals with the problems of introducing internal change and also of building organizational readiness for change tomorrow. Every large company worth its salt has an OD consultant today (as do many governmental and nonprofit agencies). There are few formal union equivalents to the management OD consultant, although occasionally this role is played in fact by an international representative, an educational director, or even a university labor education center. As described by Bok and Dunlop (1970, Chapter 5), the Laborers International Union went through what was, in effect, a major OD effort which resulted in skill training for its leaders, a complete restructuring of the union's goals and structure, and substantial personnel turnover. Especially in some unions, considerable efforts have been made to train leaders at the rank-and-file, local, and international levels. However, as Chapter 7 pointed out, individual development is not the same as *organization* development; in this sense, union training programs are at about the same stage as management training programs of the early 1950's.

Miles's (1968) study of union officials' leadership philosophies suggested that these leaders were, if anything, less trusting of the capabilities of their subordinates than their management counterparts. This is a somewhat surprising finding for a type of organization so reliant on the democratic support of the rank-and-file member. For these and other reasons, unions would seem to be especially appropriate candidates for OD efforts. To some extent, outside OD consultants might be used, but it might be wiser to train present union staff people in OD skills, perhaps through an AFL-CIO Organization Development training center.

To conclude, with its emphasis on "freeing up" crusty organizational practices, OD is an area where behavioral scientists could perform a significant service for the union movement.

Implications for Collective Bargaining and Conflict Resolution

Research by Organizational Behavior specialists on conflict and conflict resolution is still in its early stages, and most of the work has been concerned with conflict among managerial groups within organizations. Already, however, some insights have appeared which are relevant to collective bargaining. Perhaps the most useful of these arise out of the work of Lawrence and Lorsch (1967), although Walton (1969), Blake, Shepard, and Mouton (1964), and a number of others concerned with Organization Development have also made significant contributions. The paragraphs below provide a sampling of the possible implications of this work for collective bargaining. They are offered with considerable hesitance and with full recognition that they may have practical value in only a limited number of situations. But even if their implications are somewhat tentative and limited at this point, they may help formulate questions of mutual interest to OB scholars and collective bargaining practitioners. Other than Walton and McKersie's (1965) major work, very little has been done to span the gap between the two fields.

THE VALUE OF CONFLICT

OB theorists are coming to increasing agreement as to the value of what might be called "structured conflict." Structured conflict, it is argued, permits the surfacing and systematic confrontation of interpersonal differences as well as the consideration of alternative solutions to organizational problems. The objective should not be to repress conflict but to permit it to be more effectively expressed and resolved. However, the optimal degree to which conflict should be structured may differ widely among situations.

According to Lawrence and Lorsch (1967), organizations differ in the extent of their differentiation, that is, the extent to which organizational subunits (e.g., production and sales) differ in terms of their values, objectives, length of work cycle, organizational life styles, and the like (see Chapter 6). Furthermore, the degree of "optimal" differentiation differs among organizations. Too much or too little differentiation are both counterproductive. The most effective organizations seem to be those in which subunits are best structured to face the specific problems of their respective environments.

The implications of this research are fairly obvious. Just as it is desirable for the production and sales departments of large organizations to preserve their distinctive patterns of behavior, unions and managements also have different functions to perform, and so it is desirable for each to represent its own position vigorously. On the other hand, we should not expect the degree of differentiation between labor and management to be the same throughout society. Lawrence and Lorsch found that the optimal degree of differentiation between departments to be less in container making (a stable industry) than in plastics (a changing industry). Similarly, the optimal degree of differentiation between labor and management in professional organizations may be less than it is in mass-production manufacturing organizations. There is a far greater overlap in objectives (and life styles) between employees and management in a university, for example, than in an automobile assembly plant. Negotiations can be more easily focused on shared objectives in the first than in the second. For these reasons, it might be unwise for either managements or unions in professional organizations to model themselves too closely on their mass-production counterparts—in terms of either their internal organizations or their relations with each other. Similarly, one might also question the wisdom of applying the same principles of labor law to all industries.

INTEGRATIVE PROCESSES

Lawrence and Lorsch suggest that the greater the degree of differentiation among organizational subunits, the more elaborate the integrative mechanisms required to maintain control. To provide such integrative functions, many highly differentiated organizations make use of full-time "integrators"—"neutral" individuals or groups whose full-time job it is to manage conflict. Applying this managerial analogy to collective bargaining would suggest the desirability of extending the preventive mediation services of the Conciliation Service, of encouraging arbitrators to enter the grievance process as mediators prior to deadlock, or perhaps of the parties themselves jointly hiring full-time go-betweens (some with behavioral science backgrounds) who would intervene as low as the steward-foreman level.

Lawrence and Lorsch suggest that integrators should operate at the level where the conflict occurs. If a foreman and a steward have trouble getting along together, perhaps it might be best for the integrator (i.e., the mediator) to work with the two individuals directly, with representatives of higher levels being absent, at least part of the time.

The literature on conflict appears also to support the principles of continuous negotiations, of viewing the contract as a "living document," and of plant-level (and even shop-level) agreements.

The Negotiations Process

Organization Development specialists have developed a number of principles for resolving conflict once negotiations begin. While these principles may be useful with rival managerial groups, there is considerable doubt as to their value in labor relations, except where the parties have already developed considerable harmony.

The first principle is that conflict should be brought out into the open. By and large, collective bargaining accomplishes this admirably. A second principle is that the parties should "level" with each other; that is, they should reveal their real goals and withhold neither feelings nor information. For this reason, bluffing and exaggerated demands are viewed as counterproductive. Another key OD principle is that the parties should try to understand each other's position fully before seeking solutions. A common OD exercise is to require each party to state as best it can what it views as the *other* party's position and then to spend considerable time correcting what misunderstandings may arise—*before* trying to reduce substantive differences.

OD practitioners stress the importance of having the parties explore all problems at length before proposing solutions (and among the problems are the parties' own feelings and interests). This would suggest that it is highly unproductive for the parties to begin negotiations with each submitting a shopping list of demands (at least unless the parties recognize that these are purely ritualistic) prior to full problem exploration.

OD experience would also suggest that once the parties enter the bargain-seeking stage, the full range of possible solutions should be explored for each problem (not just one solution each from union and management) and that the implications of *every* possible solution should be explored before any effort is made to choose among alternatives.

Ideally, once the parties understand each other, bargaining should be viewed as a joint exercise in which the union helps management solve management's problems, management helps the union solve the union's problems, and both parties work to establish conditions under which employees can satisfy their own economic, social, and egoistic needs through working creatively toward organizational objectives.

OD also teaches the desirability of the parties in conflict periodically stepping back from their daily activities to assess the quality of their relationship. For example, after an organization has gone through a period during which interpersonal relations have been under particular strain, it may be desirable to go through a post-mortem in which the parties analyze their past mistakes with the objective of learning how to avoid these next time around. Joint post-mortem analyses might also be useful after each contract has been signed, with the objective of learning how to improve negotiating abilities during future negotiations. The convergence of interests is clear: if the parties could reach the same agreement in a few weeks of relatively stressless negotiations as they could in three months after a strike, why not take the easier route?

Some cautions. The principles and techniques discussed above have been used widely among managerial and community groups, often (but not universally) with considerable success. As we stressed earlier, we are cautious about their present applicability to perhaps the majority of collective bargaining relations. In the first place, there is the proverbial chicken-and-egg problem: when the principles listed above are applied in good faith, the parties normally learn to trust each other more (note that trust need not imply agreement); however, these principles are not likely to be tried in the first place unless a certain minimum of trust already exists. Secondly, collective bargaining involves not just negotiators themselves but also their principals, the rank-and-file members of union and management. Shopping lists, bluffing, and exaggerated demands are used to impress these organization members and serve the psychological purpose of mobilizing support for making concessions when these become necessary. These facts of life make collective bargaining more power oriented and complex than most situations dealt with by OD scholars, though some (e.g., Blake, Shepard, and Mouton, 1964) take third-party relationships (and the representative function of the parties) explicitly into account. Finally, OD principles and methods would seem easier to apply to variable-sum issues (e.g., designing a new seniority system which benefits both parties) than to such fixed-sum issues as the size of wage increases (where what labor gains the company loses). (However, even wage negotiations may be converted into variable-sum issues in the context of productivity bargaining or union-management cooperation, where the parties discuss how to increase the size of the pie as well as how to divide it.)

In conclusion, conflict-resolution research to date may be more useful in helping to understand the psychological processes involved in collective bargaining than in developing methods to resolve industrial relations disputes. Nevertheless, we believe that this is an area for much fruitful research and that scholars and practitioners from both disciplines—collective bargaining and organizational behavior—have much to learn from each other. There is much room for cross-fertilization here.

Beyond the Negotiations Process

OB research can be of value to collective bargaining in two areas related to the negotiations process but somewhat broader in scope.

Organizational structure and communications. As Walton and McKersie (1965) stressed, collective bargaining actually consists of three sets of relations: besides the main, interorganizational bargaining that occurs between the union and management, there is also a great deal of intraorganizational bargaining which occurs within the two parties. Since the rules for intraorganizational bargaining are considerably less formalized (and probably the conflicts of interest are somewhat less clear-cut) than they are in interorganizational bargaining, OB can possibly contribute more to the former relationship than the latter. As mentioned earlier, OB research can help design organization structures and communications processes which (1) may improve upward communications so that union and management representatives can better understand what union members and lower level managers really want; and (2) may facilitate the process of commitment, so that contracts laboriously bargained over are neither rejected by the rank and file nor sabotaged by lower levels of management. (And, note that within public-sector management, the recent growth of unionism has introduced a new area of intraorganizational bargaining).

Behavioral impact of bargaining choices. OB research may also increase the sophistication of the parties with regard to the probable behavioral impact of alternative bargaining choices. Unions and management today generally recognize that effective bargaining over wages requires the parties to possess (or have available to them) considerable sophistication in economics and the law. Especially if bargaining turns to matters concerned with job redesign, similar sophistication is required in OB. For example, there is some evidence that at least in some circumstances the following conditions prevail:

1. Workers do not consciously know (or at least are unwilling to freely verbalize) what they really want from the negotiations process. Specifically, there is some tendency not to articulate genuine discontent with the nature of one's job.

2. When offered more challenging job tasks, the first reaction of many workers is to turn them down (at least unless they are accompanied by substantial wage increases). Furthermore, for the first few months after being given more challenging work, a considerable number of workers express preference for their previous, simpler jobs. However, once they have served on the new job for a year or so, workers' job satisfaction increases and they indicate a strong preference for the new job.

3. Satisfaction with pay and satisfaction with the intrinsic nature of the job are often correlated. If two workers earn the same pay, the individual with the more satisfying (and perhaps objectively more difficult) job may also report greater satisfaction with pay (unless there is "coercive comparison").

None of the above conditions occurs universally. Quite the contrary. There is conflicting evidence as to each proposition stated. But where these conditions do occur—and OB research may help determine this—then it would seem that job redesign would be more in the workers' interest than a simple poll of workers' present desires might reveal.

Similar research might help management determine the likely impact on quality, productivity, and turnover of such policies as voluntary overtime, early retirement, or changes in reward systems.

None of the above is to suggest that OB research can (or should) offer sure-fire guaranteed remedies (there have been too many of these already). Nor does it suggest that unions and management do not possess considerable sophistication in the area already—they do. But note that economists and lawyers were at one time excluded from the collective bargaining process, and their advice is now routinely sought (as is that of actuaries and even occupational health specialists). OB may be increasingly able to play a similar role.

Some Value Choices

Underlying all of the issues discussed in this volume is an important factor which has not yet been addressed directly: the question of values. A brief discussion of some value choices may aid practitioners in evaluating the research presented in the previous chapters.

As mentioned earlier, there seems to be considerable agreement among authors as to the merits of a related series of activities *under the proper circumstances*. These activities include job enrichment, general supervision, organic organization structures and processes, the use of OD techniques to introduce change, and so on. For convenience, let us call these related—but by no means identical—activities "participation."

Increased use of participation may have an effect on both organizational performance and worker satisfaction. According to contingency theory, it may increase both, decrease both, or increase one and decrease the other. At first glance, the central issue appears to boil down to two main questions:

1. What will be the impact of greater participation on organizational performance (especially unit labor costs)?

2. What will be the impact of greater participation on worker satisfaction, particularly the kinds of satisfaction derived from feelings of self-determination, achievement, and the like? Or, to put the question in economists' terms, we can call feelings which are derived from participation "nonpecuniary goods" and then ask, what are the terms under which workers would be willing to trade pecuniary goods (e.g., pay) for nonpecuniary goods?

If participation increases both performance and satisfaction, then obviously participation will benefit both the organization and the individual at the same time. If the opposite holds true—if participation reduces both performance and satisfaction—then it is in no one's interest. But what is the solution at intermediate points, especially where increased participation will increase satisfaction but reduce performance? In other words, what is the tradeoff between human happiness and growth on the job and organizational performance (which in turn can be translated into higher wages and a higher material standard of living).

Economists can provide a formal answer to the question (for an early statement, see Flanagan, Strauss, and Ulman, 1974). Noneconomists are not likely to be impressed by this exercise, especially since the variables involved are extremely difficult to measure accurately. Furthermore, the simple choice between human happiness and organizational performance may oversimplify the issue. There may be a third area where values play a part—human growth. It can easily be argued that even if workers' present preferences could be mapped, these might bear no meaningful relationship to the real welfare of workers. Why? Because the society in which workers live has conditioned them to lower their expectations, to accept instrumental orientations toward work (see Chapter 2), and generally to develop what Argyris (1958) has called "immature" personalities. Working under participative conditions, however, would permit workers to develop their unrealized (and presently unimagined) potential. Therefore, the preference for participation may be greater in the long run than in the short run. And, as noted above, as workers grow in capacity they may also become more productive.

Thus, human growth may contribute in the long run to both satisfaction and performance. But human growth can be valued in itself. Our educational system is often justified on the grounds of its contribution to GNP and to human happiness. However, our society supports its school system because it views education as valuable *per se*, regardless of its other benefits. And if formal schooling is independently valuable, should we look upon the learning and growth obtained through work in the same way?

Let us pose the question even more directly: what does society want from its work organizations? As a whole, society expects management to emphasize performance. Only through controlled and steady growth in all sectors of the economy can we expect to obtain a higher quality of life—at least as measured in terms of better goods and services at reasonable prices. If economic performance is in any way de-emphasized—particularly if it is subordinated to a concern for increasing individual self-expression at work—then society will pay in the long run through more unemployment and an impaired standard of living.

On the other hand, there is a growing segment of our society which is asking whether organizational effectiveness, productivity, and an increasingly higher material standard of living should continue to enjoy their present high priorities—or whether greater priority should be given to individual happiness and development. Thus, the question of Quality of Work Life may inevitably involve broader issues. Philosophically, at least, the supporters of participation may have an affinity with representatives of the counter-culture and environmentalists. All place the Quality of Life generally over rapid economic growth, and the first two place great value on individual expression.

There are three reasons why we would expect society to place greater emphasis on participation in the future. All three have been mentioned before. First, we believe that even at present there are a large number of jobs which could be more effectively performed were workers given greater opportunities for participation. Secondly, we expect that technological change will increase the number of these jobs over time. Finally, we anticipate at least some pressure for a change in the tradeoff between organizational performance and material goods on the one hand and individual satisfaction and development on the other.

Since two of us are at Berkeley, our vision may be somewhat blurred. Nevertheless, we predict that unions and management will have to give increasing attention to the issues which we have grouped together as "participation" and that both parties may well wish to give higher priority to individual development at work as a complement rather than a substitute for high wages and organizational performance.

Bibliography

Abegglen, James C. 1958. *The Japanese Factory: Aspects of its Social Organization.* Glencoe, Ill.: The Free Press.

Adams, J. Stacy. 1963. "Wage Inequities, Productivity, and Work Quality." *Industrial Relations* 3 (October), 422–436.

Aldrich, Howard. 1972. "Technology and Organizational Structure: A Reexamination of the Findings of the Aston Group." *Administrative Science Quarterly* 17 (March), 26–43.

Allport, Gordon W. 1937. *Personality: A Psychological Interpretation.* New York: Holt-Rinehart.

Alutto, Joseph A. and James A. Belasco. 1972. "A Typology for Participation in Organizational Decision Making." *Administrative Science Quarterly* 17 (March), 117–125.

Anderson, Theodore and Seymour Warkov. 1961. "Organizational Size and Functional Complexity: A Study of Administration in Hospitals." *American Sociological Review* 26 (February), 23–28.

Andrews, Frank M. and George F. Farris. 1967. "Supervisory Practices and Innovation in Scientific Teams." *Personnel Psychology* 20 (Winter), 497–515.

Argyle, M., G. Gardner, and F. Cioffi. 1958. "Supervisory Methods Related to Productivity, Absenteeism, and Labor Turnover." *Human Relations* 11, (February), 23–40.

Argyris, Chris. 1957. *Personality and Organization.* New York: Harper.

————. 1962. *Interpersonal Competence and Organizational Effectiveness.* Homewood, Ill.: Dorsey.

————. 1964. *Integrating the Individual and the Organization.* New York: Wiley.

————. 1971. *Management and Organizational Development.* New York: McGraw-Hill.

————. 1972. *The Applicability of Organizational Sociology.* New York: Cambridge University Press.

————. 1973. "Personality and Organization Theory Revisited." *Administrative Science Quarterly* 18 (June), 141–167.

Azumi, Koya. 1973. "Bureaucracy East and West: A Comparative Study of Japanese and British Factories." Unpublished revision of a paper presented at the Annual Meeting of the American Sociological Association, 1972.

Back, Kurt W. 1974. "Intervention Technique." *Journal of Applied Psychology* 59 (July), 367–387.

Barnard, Chester I. 1938. *The Functions of the Executive.* Cambridge, Mass.: Harvard University Press.

Bauer, Raymond Augustine, Ithiel De Sola Pool, and Lewis Anthony Dexter. 1963. *American Business and Public Policy.* New York: Atherton.

Baumgartel, H. 1956. "Leadership, Motivation, and Attitudes in Research Laboratories." *Journal of Social Issues* 12, 24–31.

Beckhard, Richard. 1969. *Organization Development: Strategies and Models.* Reading, Mass.: Addison-Wesley.

Bell, Daniel. 1958. "Two Roads from Marx." Paper presented at the International Seminar, Workers Participation in Management, under auspices of the Congress for Cultural Freedom. Vienna, September 19–25.

Bennis, Warren G. 1966. *Changing Organizations.* New York: McGraw-Hill.

————. 1969. *The Nature of Organization Development.* Reading, Mass.: Addison-Wesley.

————. 1973. "Organizational Development and the Fate of Bureaucracy." In W. E. Scott an dL. L. Cummings, editors, *Readings in Organizational Behavior and Human Performance.* Revised edition. Homewood, Ill.: Irwin.

————, K. D. Benne, and R. Chin. 1961. *The Planning of Change.* New York: Holt, Rinehart, and Winston.

————, and Philip E. Slater. 1968. *The Temporary Society.* New York: Harper and Row.

Beynon, H., and R. M. Blackburn. 1972. *Perceptions of Work: Variations Within a Factory.* Cambridge: Cambridge University Press.

Blake, Robert R., and Jane S. Mouton. 1961. "Reactions to Intergroup Competition Under Win-Lose Competition." *Management Science* 4 (July).

———. 1964. *The Managerial Grid.* Houston, Texas: Gulf.

———. 1968. *Corporate Excellence Through Grid Organization Development.* Houston, Texas: Gulf.

———. 1969. *Building a Dynamic Corporation Through Grid Organization Development.* Reading, Mass.: Addison-Wesley.

———, L. B. Barnes, and L. E. Greiner. 1964. "Breakthrough in Organizational Development." *Harvard Business Review* 42 (November), 133–155.

———, Herbert Sheppard, and Jane Mouton. 1964. *Managing Intergroup Conflict in Industry.* Houston, Texas: Gulf.

Blau, Peter M. 1968. "The Hierarchy of Authority in Organizations." *American Journal of Sociology* 73 (January), 453–467.

———, W. Heydebrand, and R. Stauffer, 1966. "The Structure of Small Bureaucracies." *American Sociological Review* 31 (April), 179–191.

———, and Richard A. Schoenherr. 1971. *The Structure of Organizations.* New York: Basic Books.

———, and W. R. Scott. 1962. *Formal Organizations.* San Francisco: Chandler.

Blauner, Robert. 1964. *Alienation and Freedom.* Chicago: University of Chicago Press.

Bluestone, Irving. 1974. "Comments on Job Enrichment." *Organizational Dynamics* 2 (Winter), 46–47.

Bok, Derek E., and John T. Dunlop. 1970. *Labor and the American Community.* New York: Simon and Schuster.

Boulding, Kenneth E. 1961. "Opening Remarks." In Elise Boulding, editor, *Conflict Management in Organizations.* Ann Arbor: Foundation for Research in Human Behavior.

———. 1962. *Conflict and Defense.* New York: Harper and Brothers.

Bowers, David G. 1973. "OD Techniques and Their Results in 23 Organizations: The Michigan ICL Study." *Journal of Applied Behavioral Science* 9 (January), 21–43.

———, and Stanley Seashore. 1966. "Predicting Organizational Effectiveness with a Four-Factor Theory of Leadership." *Administrative Science Quarterly* 11 (September), 238–263.

Bradford, Leland P. 1967. "Biography of an Institution." *Journal of Applied Behavioral Science* 3 (April-May), 127–143.

———, Jack R. Gibb, and Kenneth D. Benne. 1964. *T-Group Theory and Laboratory Method.* New York: Wiley.

Brayfield, Arthur H., and William H. Crockett. 1955. "Employee Attitudes and Performance." *Psychological Bulletin* 52 (November), 396–428.

British Trade Union Congress. n.d. *Trade Unions and Productivity.* London.

Brown, Julius. In press. "How Many People Have Jobs Which Permit Discretion?" *Industrial Relations.*

Burns, Tom and G. M. Stalker. 1961. *The Management of Innovation.* London: Tavistock Publications.

Business Week. 1973. "Productivity Still Has a Bad Name." No. 2261 (January 6), 28.

Business Week. 1973. "GM Zeroes in on Employee Discontent." No. 2279 (May 12), 140–144.

Campbell, John P., and Marvin D. Dunnette. 1968. "Effectiveness of T-Group Experiences in Managerial Training and Development." *Psychological Bulletin* 70 (February), 73–104.

Campbell, J. P., Marvin D. Dunnette, Edward E. Lawler, III, and Karl E. Weick, Jr. 1970. *Managerial Behavior, Performance, and Effectiveness.* New York: McGraw-Hill.

Caplow, Theodore. 1957. "Organizational Size." *Administrative Science Quarterly* 1 (March), 484–505.

Chandler, Alfred D., Jr. 1966. *Strategy and Structure*. Garden City, N.Y.: Doubleday Anchor.

Chaney, Frederick B., and Kenneth S. Teel. 1972. "Participative Management—A Practical Experience." *Personnel* 49 (November/December), 8–19.

Child, John and Roger Mansfield. 1972. "Technology, Size and Organization Structure." *Sociology* 6 (September).

Chinoy, Eli. 1955. *The Automobile Worker and the American Dream*. New York: Doubleday.

Churchman, C. West. 1968. *The Systems Approach*. New York: Dell.

Clark, A. W., and S. McCabe. 1970. "Leadership Beliefs of Australian Managers." *Journal of Applied Psychology* 54 (February), 1–6.

Clarke, R. O. and D. J. Fatchett. 1972. "Worker Participation in Management in Great Britain." *International Institute for Labor Studies Bulletin* 9, 173–208.

Cleveland, Harlan. 1965. *Jump-McKillop Memorial Lectures in Public Administration*. U.S. Department of Agriculture.

Coch, L. and John R. P. French, Jr. 1948. "Overcoming Resistance to Change." *Human Relations* 1, 512–532.

Cohen, L. B. 1955. "Areas of Worker Decision Making." *Proceedings of the Industrial Relations Research Association*, Madison, Wisconsin, 298–312.

Coser, Lewis A. 1956. *The Functions of Social Conflict*. Glencoe, Ill.: Free Press.

Cotgrove, Stephen. 1972. "Alienation and Automation." *British Journal of Sociology* 23 (December), 437–451.

Cummings, Lawrence L., and Stuart M. Schmidt. 1972. "Managerial Attitudes of Greeks: The Roles of Culture and Industrialization." *Administrative Science Quarterly* 17 (June), 265–272.

Cyert, Richard M., and James G. March. 1963. *A Behavioral Theory of the Firm*. Englewood Cliffs, N.J.: Prentice Hall.

Davis, Louis E. 1971. "Job Satisfaction Research: The Post-Industrial View." *Industrial Relations* 10 (May), 176–193.

Davis, Louis, and James C. Taylor, editors. 1972. *Design of Jobs*. Middlesex, England: Penguin.

Davis, Sheldon A. 1967. "An Organic Problem-Solving Method of Organizational Change." *Journal of Applied Behavioral Science* 3 (January), 3–21.

———. 1971. "Laboratory Training and Team Building." In *Organizational Development, The State of the Art*. Ann Arbor: Foundation for Research on Human Behavior.

Day, David R., and Ralph M. Stogdill. 1972. "Leader Behavior of Male and Female Supervisors: A Comparative Study." *Personnel Psychology* 26 (Summer), 353–360.

Derber, Milton, William E. Chalmers, and Morris T. Edelman. 1961. "Union Participation in Plant Decision-Making." *Industrial and Labor Relations Review* 15 (October), 83–101.

Dill, William. 1958. "Environment as an Influence on Managerial Autonomy." *Administrative Science Quarterly* 2 (March), 409–443.

Douglas, Paul H., and A. W. Kornhauser. 1922. *Cases and Problems in Personnel Administration*. Chicago: University of Chicago Press.

Dowling, Willam F., Jr. 1973. "Job Redesign on the Assembly Line." *Organizational Dynamics*, 51–67.

———, and Leonard R. Sayles. 1971. *How Managers Motivate: The Imperatives of Supervision*. New York: McGraw-Hill.

Dubin, Robert. 1959. "Industrial Research and the Discipline of Sociology." *Proceedings of the Industrial Relations Research Association*, Madison, Wisconsin.

———, George C. Homans, Floyd C. Mann, and Delbert C. Miller. 1965. *Leadership and Productivity*. San Francisco: Chandler.

Duncan, Robert B. 1972. "Characteristics of Organizational Environments and

Perceived Environmental Uncertainty." *Administrative Science Quarterly* 17 (September) , 313–327.

Dunlop, John T. 1960. "Structural Changes in the American Labor Movement and Industrial Relations System." In W. Galenson and S. M. Lipset, editors, *Labor and Trade Unionism*. New York: Wiley.

Emery, Fred, and Einar Thorsrud. 1969. *New Designs for Work Organization*. Oslo, Sweden: Tannum Press.

———, and E. L. Trist. 1960. "Socio-technical Systems." In C. West Churchman and M. Verhult, editors, *Management Science Models*. Vol. 2. London: Pergamon.

———. 1965. "The Causal Texture of Organizational Environments." *Human Relations* 18 (February) , 21–32.

Etzioni, Amatai. 1961. *Complex Organizations*. Glencoe, Ill.: Free Press.

Evan, William M. 1966. "The Organization-Set." In James D. Thompson, editor, *Approaches to Organizational Design*. Pittsburgh: University of Pittsburgh Press.

Evans, Martin G. 1970. "The Effects of Supervisory Behavior on the Path-Goal Relationship." *Organizational Behavior and Human Performance* 5 (May) , 277–298.

Fein, Mitchell. 1973. "The Real Needs and Goals of Blue Collar Workers." *Conference Board Record* 10 (February) , 28–33.

Ferguson, Lawrence L. 1964. "Social Scientists in the Plant." *Harvard Business Review* 42 (May) , 133–143.

Fiedler, Fred E. 1967. *A Theory of Leadership Effectiveness*. New York: McGraw-Hill.

Fiedler, Fred E. 1970. "Leadership Experience and Leader Performance—Another Hypothesis Shot to Hell." *Organizational Behavior and Human Performance* 5 (January) , 1–14.

———. 1973. "The Trouble With Leadership Training Is That It Doesn't Train Leaders." *Psychology Today* 6 (February) , 23 ff.

———, and Martin M. Chemers. 1974. *Leadership and Effective Management*. Glenview, Ill.: Scott, Foresman.

Filley, Alan C. and Robert J. House. 1969. *Managerial Process and Organizational Behavior*. Glenview, Ill.: Scott, Foresman.

Fink, Clinton F. 1968. "Some Conceptual Difficulties in the Theory of Social Conflict." *Journal of Conflict Resolution* 12 (December) , 412–460.

Flanagan, Robert, George Strauss and Lloyd Ulman. 1974. '(Worker Discontent and Work Place Behavior." *Industrial Relations* 13 (May) , 1–23.

Fleishman, Edwin A. 1953. "Leadership Climate, Human Relations Training, and Supervisory Behavior." *Personnel Psychology* 6 (Summer) , 205–222.

———. 1958. "A Relationship Between Incentive Motivation and Ability Level in Psychomotor Performance." *Journal of Experimental Psychology* 56 (July) , 78–81.

———, E. F. Harris, and H. E. Burtt. 1955. *Leadership and Supervision in Industry*. Columbus, Ohio: Ohio State University, Bureau of Educational Research.

Ford, Robert N. 1969. *Motivation Through the Work Itself*. New York: American Management Association.

Forehand, Garlie A. 1968. "On the Interaction of Persons and Organizations." In Renato Tagiuri and George H. Litwin, editors, *Organizational Climate*. Boston, Mass.: Harvard University, Graduate School of Business Administration.

Form, William H. 1973. "Autoworkers and Their Machines: A Study of Work, Factory and Job Satisfaction in Four Countries." *Social Forces* 52 (September) , 1–14.

Franklin, J. 1973. *Organizational Development: An Annotated Bibliography*. Ann Arbor: University of Michigan, Institute for Social Research, Center for Research on the Utilization of Scientific Knowledge (CRUSK) .

French, John R. P., Jr., and Robert D. Caplan. 1972. "Organizational Stress and Individual Strain." In Alfred J. Marrow, editor, *The Failure of Success.* New York: Amacom.

French, John R. P., Jr., Joachim Israel, and Dogfin As. 1960. "An Experiment in a Norwegian Factory." *Human Relations* 13 (February), 3–20.

French, John R. P., Jr., E. Kay, and H. H. Meyer. 1966. "Participation and the Appraisal System." *Human Relations* 19, 3–20.

French, Wendell L., and Cecil H. Bell. 1973. *Organization Development.* Englewood Cliffs, N.J.: Prentice Hall.

Friedlander, Frank and L. Dave Brown. 1974. "Organization Development." *Annual Review of Psychology* 25, 313–341.

Furstenburg, Fredrick. 1969. "Workers' Participation in Management in the Federal Republic of Germany." *International Institute for Labor Studies Bulletin* 6 (June), 94–148.

Garson, G. D. 1973. "Beyond Collective Bargaining." In G. Hunnius, G. D. Garson, and J. Case, editors, *Workers' Control.* New York: Random House.

Georgopoulos, Basil S., and Floyd C. Mann. 1962. *The Community General Hospital.* New York: Macmillan.

Ghiselli, E. E. 1971. *Explorations in Managerial Talent.* Pacific Palisades, Calif.: Goodyear.

Goble, Frank. 1972. *Excellence in Leadership.* New York: American Management Association.

Goldthorpe, John H. 1966. "Attitudes and Behavior of Car Assembly Workers." *British Journal of Sociology* 17 (September), 227–244.

———, David Lockwood, Frank Bechhofer, and Jennifer Platt. 1968. *The Affluent Worker: Industrial Attitudes and Behavior.* Cambridge: Cambridge University Press.

Golembiewski, Robert T., and Stokes B. Carrigan. 1970. "The Persistence of Laboratory-Induced Changes in Organization Styles." *Administrative Science Quarterly* 15 (September), 330–340.

Goodman, H. G. 1958. "Work Simplification." *Factory Management and Maintenance,* 72–106.

Goodman, Paul S., and Abraham Friedman. 1971. "An Examination of Adams' Theory of Inequity." *Administrative Science Quarterly* 16 (September), 271–288.

Goodman, R., J. Wakeley, and R. Ruh. 1972. *What Employees Think: An Evaluation of the Scanlon Plan.* Midwest Scanlon Associates and Michigan State University.

Goodstadt, B., and D. Kipnis. 1970. "Situational Influences on the Use of Power." *Journal of Applied Psychology* 54 (June), 201–207.

Gouldner, Alvin W. 1954. *Patterns of Industrial Bureaucracy.* New York: Free Press.

Graen, G., K. Alvares, J. B. Orris, and J. A. Martella. 1970. "Contingency Model of Leadership Effectiveness." *Psychological Bulletin* 74 (October), 285–296.

Graicunas, V. A. 1937. In Luther Gulick and L. Urwick, editors, *Papers on the Science of Administration.* New York: Columbia University, Institute of Public Administration.

Greiner, Lawrence E. 1967. "Patterns of Organizational Change." *Harvard Business Review* 45 (May), 119–128.

Gulick, Luther. 1967. "Notes on the Theory of Organization." In Paul R. Lawrence and Jay W. Lorsch, *Organization and Environment: Managing Differentiation and Integration.* Cambridge: Harvard University, Graduate School of Business Administration.

———, and Lyndall F. Urwick, editors. 1937. *Papers on the Science of Administration.* New York: Columbia University, Institute of Public Administration.

Hackman, J. Richard, and Edward E. Lawler, III. 1971. "Employee Reactions to Job Characteristics." *Journal of Applied Psychology* 55 (June), 259–286.

Hage, Jerald and Michael Aiken. 1967. "Relationship of Centralization to

Other Structural Properties." *Administrative Science Quarterly* 12 (June), 72–92.

————. 1969. "Routine Technology, Social Structure, and Organizational Goals." *Administrative Science Quarterly* 14 (September), 366–376.

Haire, Mason, Edwin Ghiselli, and Lyman W. Porter. 1963. "An International Study of Management Attitudes and Democratic Leadership." In *Proceedings CIOS XIII, International Management Conference*. New York: Council for International Progress in Management (USA), 101–114.

————. 1966. *Managerial Thinking: An International Study*. New York: Wiley.

Hall, Richard H. 1972. *Organizations: Structure and Process*. Englewood Cliffs, N.J.: Prentice Hall.

Hall, Richard H., J. Eugene Haas, and Norman J. Johnson. 1967. "Organizational Size, Complexity, and Formalization." *American Sociological Review* 32 (December).

Halpin, A. W., and D. B. Croft. 1963. *The Organizational Climate of Schools*. Chicago: University of Chicago.

Harbison, Frederick H., and John R. Coleman. 1951. *Goals and Strategy in Collective Bargaining*. New York: Harper.

Hartmann, Heinz. 1970. "Codetermination in West Germany." *Industrial Relations* 9 (February), 137–147.

Harvey, Edward. 1968. "Technology and the Structure of Organizations." *American Sociological Review* 33 (April), 247–259.

Haythorn, William. 1956. "The Effects of Varying Combinations on Authoritarian and Equalitarian Leaders and Followers," *Journal of Abnormal and Social Psychology* 52, 210–219.

Hedges, Jamie N. 1973. "New Patterns for Working Time." *Monthly Labor Review* 96 (February), 3–8.

Heneman, Herbert G., III, and Donald P. Schwab. 1972. "Evaluation of Research on Expectancy Theory Predictions of Employee Behavior." *Psychological Bulletin* 78 (July), 1–9.

Henle, Peter. 1974. "Economic Effects: Reviewing the Evidence." In Jerome Rosow, editor, *The Worker and the Job*. Englewood Cliffs, N.J.: Prentice Hall.

Herzberg, Frederick. 1966. *Work and the Nature of Man*. Cleveland, Ohio: World Publishing.

————. 1968. "One More Time: How Do You Motivate Employees?" *Harvard Business Review* 46 (January), 53–62.

————, Bernard Mausner, R. Peterson, and Dora Capwell. 1957. *Job Attitudes: A Review of Research and Opinion*. Pittsburgh: Psychological Service of Pittsburgh.

Hickson, David J., D. S. Pugh, and Diana C. Pheysey. 1969. "Operations Technology and Organizational Structure: An Empirical Reappraisal." *Administrative Science Quarterly* 14 (September), 378–397.

Hill, Paul. 1971. *Toward a New Philosophy of Management*. Tonbridge, Kent: Tonbridge Printers.

Hinings, C. R. and Gloria Lee. 1971. "Dimensions of Organization Structure and Their Context: A Replication." *Sociology* 5 (January).

Hoffer, Eric. 1955. "The Workingman Looks at His Boss." *Atlantic Monthly*.

Holter, Harriet. 1965. "Attitudes Towards Employee Participation in Company Decision-Making Processes." *Human Relations* 18 (November), 297–321.

Homans, George C. 1949. "The Strategy of Industrial Sociology." *American Journal of Sociology* 54 (January), 330–337.

House, Robert J. 1968. "Leadership Training: Some Dysfunctional Consequences." *Administrative Science Quarterly* 12 (March), 356–371.

————. 1971. "A Path-Goal Theory of Leader Effectiveness." *Administrative Science Quarterly* 16 (September), 321–339.

———, Alan C. Filley, and Steven Kerr. 1971. "Relation of Leader Consideration and Initiating Structure to R and D Subordinates' Satisfaction." *Administraitve Science Quarterly* 16 (March) , 19–30.

Hulin, Charles H. and Milton R. Blood. 1967. "Alienation, Environmental Characteristics and Worker Responses." *Journal of Applied Psychology* 51 (June) , 284–290.

———. 1968. "Job Enlargement, Individual Differences, and Worker Responses." *Psychological Bulletin* 69, 41–55.

Hunnius, G., G. D. Garson, and J. Case, editors. 1973. *Workers' Control.* New York: Random House.

Hunt, J. G. 1971. "Leadership-Style Effects at Two Managerial Levels in a Simulated Organization." *Administrative Science Quarterly* 16 (December) , 476–485.

———, J. W. Hill, and J. M. Reaser. 1973. "Correlates of Leadership Behavior at Two Managerial Levels in a Mental Institution." *Journal of Applied Social Psychology* 3, 174–185.

Iman, S. 1972. "Fenlon Works: The Effects of Organizational Development." Unpublished Doctoral Dissertation. University of Michigan.

Industrial Relations Counselors. 1962. *Group Work Incentives: Experience with the Scanlon Plan.* New York: Industrial Relations Counselors.

Ivancevich, John M. 1972. "A Longitudinal Assessment of Management by Objectives." *Administrative Science Quarterly* 17 (March) , 126–138.

Jaques, Eliott. 1968. *Employee Participation and Managerial Authority.* London: Tavistock Publications.

Jenkins, David. 1974. *Job Power.* New York: Penguin Books.

"Job Satisfaction and Productivity." 1973. *Gallup Opinion Index.* April.

Johnson, R. T. and W. G. Ouchi. 1974. "Made in America (Under Japanese Management) ." *Harvard Business Review* (September–October) .

Kahn, Robert L. 1973. "The Work Module—A Tonic for Lunchpail Lassitude." *Psychology Today* 6 (February) , 35 ff.

———. 1973. "Organizational Development: A Review and Some Proposals." Unpublished, Ann Arbor, Michigan (May) .

———, and Daniel Katz. 1960. "Leadership Practices in Relation to Productivity and Morale." In Dorwin Cartwright and Alvin Zander, editors, *Group Dynamics: Research and Theory.* London: Tavistock Publications. Second edition, Evanston, Ill.: Row, Peterson.

Katz, Daniel and Basil S. Georgopoulos. 1971. "Organizations in a Changing World." *Journal of Applied Behavioral Science* 7 (May) , 342 ff.

Katz, Daniel and Robert L. Kahn. 1966. *The Social Psychology of Organizations.* New York: Wiley.

Kavanagh, Michael J. 1972. "Leadership Behavior as a Function of Subordinate Competence and Task Complexity." *Administrative Science Quarterly* 17, (December) , 591–600.

Kavcic, Bogdan, Veljko, Rus, and Arnold S. Tannenbaum. 1971. "Control, Participation, and Effectiveness in Four Yugoslav Industrial Organizations." *Administrative Science Quarterly* 16 (March) , 74–86.

Kennedy, Van D. 1954. "Grievance Negotiations." In A. Kornhauser, R. Dubin, and A. Ross, editors, *Industrial Conflict.* New York: McGraw-Hill.

Kerr, Clark. 1954. "Industrial Conflict and Its Mediation." *American Journal of Sociology* 60 (November) , 230–245.

———. 1964. *Labor and Management in Industrial Society.* New York: Doubleday.

———, John T. Dunlop, Frederick Harbison, and Charles A. Myers. 1964. *Industrialism and Industrial Man.* New York: Oxford.

Khandwalla, Pradip M. 1974. "Mass Output Orientation of Operations Technology and Organization Structure." *Administrative Science Quarterly* 19 (March) , 74–97.

Kohn, Melvin L. and Carmi Schooler. 1973. "Occupational Experience and Psychological Functioning: An Assessment of Reciprocal Effects." *American Sociological Review* 38 (February) , 97–118.

Korman, Abraham K. 1966. " 'Consideration,' 'Initiating Structure,' and Organizational Criteria—A Review." *Personnel Psychology* 19 (Winter) , 349–361.

Kornhauser, Arthur, and Otto M. Reid. 1965. *Mental Health of the Industrial Worker: A Detroit Study.* New York: Wiley.

Krulee, Gilbert K. 1955. "The Scanlon Plan: Co-operation through Participation." *The Journal of Business* 28 (April) , 100–113.

Kuriloff, Arthur H. 1963. "An Experiment in Management: Putting Theory Y to the Test." *Personnel* 40 (November–December) , 8–17.

Lammers, C. J. 1967. "Power and Participation in Decision-Making in Formal Organizations." *American Journal of Sociology* 73 (September) , 201–216.

Lawler, Edward E., III. 1966. "The Mythology of Management Compensation." *California Management Review* 9 (Fall) , 11–22.

———. 1969. "Job Design and Employee Motivation." *Personnel Psychology* 22 (Winter) , 426–435.

———. 1971. *Pay and Organizational Effectiveness: A Psychological View.* New York: McGraw-Hill.

Lawrence, Paul R. 1958. *The Changing of Organizational Behavior Patterns.* Boston: Harvard University, Graduate School of Business Administration.

———, and Jay W. Lorsch. 1967. *Organization and Environment: Managing Differentiation and Integration.* Boston: Harvard University, Graduate School of Business Administration, Division of Research.

———. 1969. *Developing Organizations: Diagnosis and Action.* Reading, Mass.: Addison-Wesley.

Leavitt, Harold J. 1972. *Managerial Psychology.* Third edition, Chicago: University of Chicago Press.

———. 1973. "Organizational Behavior, 1969." In Robert H. Doktor and Michael A. Moses, editors, *Managerial Insights: Analysis, Decisions, and Implementation.* Englewood Cliffs, N.J.: Prentice-Hall.

Lenk, Hans. 1964. "Konflikt and Leistung in Spitzensportmannschafter: Isozmetrische Strukturen von Wettkempfachtern in Ruden." *Soziale Welt* 15, 307–343.

Lesage, Pierre-Bernard. 1973. "Measuring Leadership Attitudes: A Construct Validation Study." Unpublished Doctoral Dissertation. University of Michigan.

Lesieur, Fredrick, editor. 1958. *The Scanlon Plan: A Frontier in Labor-Management Cooperation.* New York: Wiley.

Lewin, Kurt. 1946. "Action Research and Minority Problems." *Journal of Social Issues* 2, 34–46.

———. 1948. *Resolving Social Conflict, Selected Papers on Group Dynamics.* Gertrude W. Lewin, editor. New York: Harper.

———, Ronald Lippitt, and Robert K. White. 1939. "Patterns of Aggressive Behavior in Experimentally Created Social Climates." *Journal of Social Psychology* 10, 271–299.

Likert, Rensis. 1961. *New Patterns of Management.* New York: McGraw-Hill.

———. 1967. *The Human Organization: Its Management and Value.* New York: McGraw-Hill.

Lippitt, Ronald. 1951. *Training in Community Relations.* New York: Harper and Row.

List, Wilfred. 1973. "In Sweden the Byword is Cooperation." In G. Hunnius, G. D. Garson, and J. Case, editors, *Workers' Control.* New York: Random House.

Litwak, Eugene and H. J. Meyer. 1966. "A Balanced Theory of Coordination Between Bureaucratic Organizations and Community Primary Groups." *Administrative Science Quarterly* 11 (June) , 33–58.

Litwin, George H. and Robert A. Stringer. 1968. *Motivation and Organiza-*

tional Climate. Boston, Mass.: Harvard University, Graduate School of Business Administration.

Litzinger, William D. 1965. "Interpersonal Values and Leadership Attitudes of Branch Bank Managers." *Personnel Psychology* 18 (Summer), 193–198.

Livingston, J. Sterling. 1969. "Pygmalion in Management." *Harvard Business Review* 47 (July–August), 81.

Lowin, Aaron. 1968. "Participative Decision Making: A Model, Literature Critique, and Prescriptions for Research." *Organizational Behavior and Human Performance* 3 (February), 68–106.

———, W. J. Hrapchak, and M. J. Kavanagh. 1969. "Consideration and Initiating Structure: An Experimental Investigation of Leadership Traits." *Administrative Science Quarterly* 14 (June), 238–253.

Luce, Robert Duncan, and Howard Raiffa. 1957. *Games and Decisions*. New York: Wiley.

Luthans, Fred, and William E. Reif. 1974. "Job Enrichment: Long on Theory, Short on Practice." *Organizational Dynamics* 2 (Winter), 30–39.

Maier, Norman R. F. 1965. *Psychology in Industry*. Third edition, Boston: Houghton-Mifflin.

———. 1968. "The Subordinate's Role in the Delegation Process." *Personnel Psychology* 21 (Summer), 179–191.

———. 1970. "Male Versus Female Discussion Leaders." *Personnel Psychology* 23 (Winter), 455–461.

———, A. R. Solem, and A. A. Maier. 1964. *Supervisory and Executive Development: A Manual for Role Playing*. New York: Wiley.

———, and J. A. Thurber. 1969. "Problems in Delegation." *Personnel Psychology* 22 (Summer), 131–139.

Mann, Floyd C. 1961. "Studying and Creating Change." In W. G. Bennis, K. D. Benne, and R. Chin, *The Planning of Change*. New York: Holt, Rinehart, and Winston.

———. 1965. "Toward an Understanding of the Leadership Role in Formal Organization." In Robert Dubin, *et al., Leadership and Productivity*. San Francisco: Chandler.

Mansfield, Roger. 1973. "Bureaucracy and Centralization: An Examination of Organization Structure." *Administrative Science Quarterly* 18 (December), 477–488.

March, James G. and Herbert Simon. 1958. *Organizations*. New York: Wiley 477–488.

Margulies, N., and A. P. Raia. 1972. *Organization Development: Values, Process, and Technology*. New York: McGraw-Hill.

Marrow, Alfred J. 1969. *The Practical Theorist: The Life and Work of Kurt Lewin*. New York: Basic Books.

———. 1972. *The Failure of Success*. New York: Amacom.

———, David G. Bowers, and Stanley R. Seashore. 1967. *Management by Participation*. New York: Harpers.

Maslow, Abraham H. 1954. *Motivation and Personality*. New York: Harper.

———. 1965. *Eupsychian Management*. Homewood, Ill.: Dorsey.

———. 1970. *Motivation and Personality*. Revised edition, New York: Harper and Row.

Mayo, Elton. 1933. *The Human Problems of an Industrial Civilization*. New York: Macmillan.

———. 1947. *The Social Problems of an Industrial Civilization*. Boston: Harvard University, Graduate School of Business Administration.

McClelland, D. C. 1961. *The Achieving Society*. Princeton: Van Nostrand.

McGrath, Joseph E. 1964. "Toward a Theory or Method for Research on Organizations." In W. W. Cooper, H. J. Leavitt, and M. W. Shelly, II, editors, *New Perspectives in Organization Research*. New York: Wiley.

McGregor, Douglas. 1960. *The Human Side of Enterprise*. New York: McGraw-Hill.

———. 1967. *The Professional Manager*. New York: McGraw-Hill.

Mechanic, David. 1962. "Sources of Power of Lower Participants in Complex Organizations." *Administrative Science Quarterly* 7 (December), 349–364.

Meissner, Martin. 1971. "The Long Arm of the Job: A Study of Work and Leisure." *Industrial Relations* 10 (October), 239–260.

Melman, S. 1970–1971. "Managerial vs. Cooperative Decision Making in Israel." *Studies in Comparative International Development* 6.

Metcalf, Henry Clayton, and Lyndall Fownes Urwick. 1940. *Dynamic Administration: The Collected Papers of Mary Parker Follett.* New York: Harper.

Meyer, Herbert H. 1972. "The Effective Supervisor: Some Surprising Findings." In Alfred J. Marrow, editor, *The Failure of Success.* New York: Amacom.

Meyers, Fredrick. 1958. "Workers' Control of Industry in Europe." *Southwestern Social Science Quarterly*, 100–111.

Michaelsen, Larry K. 1972. "Leader Orientation, Leader Behavior, Group Effectiveness, and Situational Favorability: An Extension of the Contingency Model." Technical Report, Ann Arbor, Mich.: University of Michigan, Institute for Social Research.

Miles, Raymond E. 1964. "Conflicting Elements in Managerial Ideologies." *Industrial Relations* 4 (October), 77–91.

———. 1965. "Human Relations or Human Resources?" *Harvard Business Review* 63 (July–August), 148 ff.

———. 1968. "Leadership Attitudes Among Union Officials." *Industrial Relations* 8 (October), 108–117.

———. In press. *Theories of Management: Implications for Organizational Behavior and Development.* New York: McGraw-Hill.

———, and J. B. Ritchie. 1971. "Participative Management: Quality vs. Quantity." *California Management Review* 13 (Summer), 48–56.

Mire, Joseph. 1974. *European Trade Union Views of Worker Discontent.* Mimeographed.

Mohr, Lawrence B. 1971. "Organizational Technology and Organizational Structure." *Administrative Science Quarterly* 16 (December), 444–459.

Mooney, James. 1947. *Principles of Organization.* New York: Harper.

Morse, Nancy, and Everett Reimer. 1956. "The Experimental Change of a Major Organizational Variable." *Journal of Abnormal and Social Psychology* 52 (January), 120–129.

Mott, Paul E. 1972. *The Characteristics of Effective Organizations.* New York: Harper & Row.

Mulder, Mauk. 1971. "Power Equalization Through Participation?" *Administrative Science Quarterly* 16 (March), 31–38.

Myers, M. Scott. 1964. "Who Are Your Motivated Workers?" *Harvard Business Review* 42 (January), 73–88.

———. 1970. *Every Employee a Manager: More Meaningful Work Through Job Enrichment.* New York: McGraw-Hill.

Nealey, Stanley M., and Milton R. Blood. 1968. "Leadership Performance of Nursing Supervisors at Two Organizational Levels." *Journal of Applied Psychology* 52 (October), 414–422.

———, and Fred E. Fiedler. 1968. "Leadership Functions of Middle Managers." *Psychological Bulletin* 70 (November), 313–329.

———, and Terry W. Owen. 1970. "A Multitrait-Multimethod Analysis of Predictors and Criteria of Nursing Performance." *Organizational Behavioral and Human Performance* 5 (July), 348–365.

Northrup, Herbert, and Harvey A. Young. 1968. "The Causes of Industrial Peace Revisited." *Industrial and Labor Relations Review* 22 (October), 31–47.

Obradovic, Josip. 1970. "Participation and Work Attitudes in Yugoslavia." *Industrial Relations* 9 (February), 161–169.

———. In press. "Workers' Participation: Who Participates?" *Industrial Relations.*

Odiorne, George. 1962. "Managerial Narcissism—the Great Self-Development Binge." *Management of Personnel Quarterly* 1 (Spring) , 20–25.

Patchen, Martin. 1965. "Labor-Management Consultation at TVA: Its Impact on Employees." *Administrative Science Quarterly* 10 (September) , 149–174.

———. 1970. *Participation, Achievement, and Involvement on the Job.* Englewood Cliffs, N.J.: Prentice-Hall.

Pateman, C. 1970. *Participation and Democratic Theory.* London: Cambridge University Press.

Pelz, Donald C. 1952. "Influence: A Key to Effective Leadership in the First-Line Supervisor." *Personnel* 29 (November) , 209–217.

———, and Frank Andrews. 1966. *Scientists in Organizations.* New York: Wiley.

Perrow, Charles. 1965. "Hospitals: Technology, Structure and Goals." In James G. March, editor, *Handbook of Organizations.* Chicago: Rand McNally.

———. 1967. "A Framework for the Comparative Analysis of Organizations." *American Sociological Review* 32 (April) , 194–208.

———. 1970. *Organizational Analysis: A Sociological Perspective.* Belmont, Calif.: Wadsworth.

———. 1972. *Complex Organizations: A Critical Essay.* Glenview, Ill.: Scott, Foresman.

Peter, Laurence J. 1972. *The Peter Prescription.* New York: William Morrow.

Pfeffer, Jeffrey. 1972 (a) . "Size and Composition of Corporate Boards of Directors: The Organization and its Environment." *Administrative Science Quarterly* 17 (June) , 218–228.

———. 1972 (b) . "Merger as a Response to Organization Interdependence." *Administrative Science Quarterly* 17 (September) , 387–394.

———. 1973 (a) . "Size, Composition, and Function of Hospital Boards of Directors: A Study of Organization-Environment Linkages." *Administratvie Science Quarterly* 18 (September) , 349–364.

———, and Huseyin Leblebici. 1973 (b) . "Executive Recruitment and the Development of Interfirm Organizations." *Administrative Science Quarterly* 18 (December) , 449–461.

Pondy, Louis R. 1969. "Effects of Size, Complexity, and Ownership in Administrative Intensity." *Administrative Science Quarterly* 14 (March) , 47–60.

Porter, Lyman, and Edward E. Lawler, III. 1968. *Managerial Attitudes and Performance.* Homewood, Ill.: Irwin.

Pugh, D. S., D. J. Hickson, C. R. Hinings, and C. Turner. 1969. "The Context of Organization Structures." *Administrative Science Quarterly* 14 (March) , 91–114.

———, D. J. Hickson, and C. R. Hinings. 1969. "An Empirical Taxonomy of Work Organizations." *Administrative Science Quarterly* 14 (March) , 115–126.

Purcell, Theodore V., S.J. 1953. *The Worker Speaks His Mind on Company and Union.* Cambridge, Mass.: Harvard University Press.

Quinn, Robert P. 1973. "What Workers Want: General Descriptive Statistics and Demographic Correlates." In Robert P. Quinn and Thomas W. Mangione, editors, *The 1969–70 Survey of Working Conditions: Final Report to the Employment Standards Administration.* Ann Arbor: University of Michigan, Survey Research Center.

———, Robert L. Kahn, Joyce M. Tabor, and Laura K. Gordon. 1964. *The Chosen Few.* Ann Arbor: University of Michigan, Institute for Social Research.

Rapoport, Anatol. 1970. *Fights, Games and Debates.* Ann Arbor: University of Michigan Press.

Reedy, George E. 1971. "The Powers of the Presidency—Report on a Conference." *Centre Magazine* 4 (January/February) , 7–15.

Reeves, T. Kynaston, and J. Woodward. 1970. "The Study of Managerial

Control." In Joan Woodward, editor, *Industrial Organization: Behaviour and Control.* London: Oxford University Press.

Reilly, Anthony J. 1968. *The Effects of Different Leadership Styles on Group Performance: A Field Experiment.* Ames, Iowa: Iowa State University, Industrial Relations Center.

Rice, A. K. 1958. *Productivity and Social Organization: The Ahmedabad Experiment.* London: Tavistock Publications.

Ritchie, J. B. and Raymond E. Miles. 1970. "An Analysis of Quantity and Quality of Participation as Mediating Variables in the Participative Decision Making Process." *Personnel Psychology* 23 (Autumn), 347–359.

Roche, William J., and Neil MacKinnon. 1970. "Motivating People to Do Meaningful Work." *Harvard Business Review* 48 (May–June), 97–110.

Roethlisberger, F. J. 1951. "Training Supervisors in Human Relations." *Harvard Business Review* 29 (September), 47–53.

Rogers, Carl. 1961. *On Becoming a Person.* Boston: Houghton Mifflin.

Rosen, Ned A. 1970. "Open Systems Theory in an Organizational Sub-System: A Field Experiment." *Organizational Behavior and Human Performance* 5 (May), 245–265.

Rossel, Robert D. 1970. "Instrumental and Expressive Leadership in Complex Organizations." *Administrative Science Quarterly* 15 (September), 306–316.

———. 1971. "Required Labor Commitment, Organizational Adaptation, and Leadership Orientation." *Administrative Science Quarterly* 16 (September), 316–320.

Rowland, Kendrith M. and William E. Scott. 1968. "Psychological Attributes of Effective Leadership in a Formal Organization." *Personnel Psychology* 21 (Autumn), 365–377.

Ruh, R. 1972. "Research on the Scanlon Plan: A Brief Review of Previous Literature, a Model to Guide Future Research and Some Recent Data." Paper presented at the Nineteenth Annual Meeting of the Institute for Management Sciences. Houston, Texas (April).

———, R. Wallace and C. Frost. 1972. *Management Attitudes and the Scanlon Plan.* Midwest Scanlon Associates and the Michigan State University.

Rus, Veljko. 1970. "Influence Structure in Yugoslav Enterprise." *Industrial Relations* 9 (February), 148–160.

Rush, Harold M. F. 1969. *Behavioral Science Concepts and Management Application.* New York: The National Industrial Conference Board.

———. 1971. *Job Designs for Motivation: Experiments in Job Enlargement and Job Enrichment.* New York: The Conference Board.

———, and Phyllis S. McGrath. 1973. "Transactional Analysis Moves into Corporate Training." *The Conference Board Record* (July), 38–44.

Rushing, W. A. 1968. "Hardness of Material as Related to Division of Labor in Manufacturing Industries." *Administrative Science Quarterly* 13 (September), 229–245.

Sales, Stephen M. 1966. "Supervisory Style and Productivity: Review and Theory." *Personnel Psychology* 19 (Autumn), 275–286.

Sashkin, Marshall. 1972. "Leadership Style and Group Decision Effectiveness: Correlational and Behavioral Tests of Fiedler's Contingency Model." *Organizational Behavior and Human Performance* 8 (December), 347–372.

———, and Norman Maier. 1971. "Sex Effects in Delegation." *Personnel Psychology* 24 (Autumn), 471–476.

Sayles, Leonard. 1973. "Job Enrichment: Little That's New—and Right for the Wrong Reasons." *Proceedings of the Industrial Relations Research Association,* Madison, Wisconsin.

———, and George Strauss. 1953. *The Local Union: Its Place in the Industrial Plant.* New York: Harper and Brothers.

———, and Margaret K. Chandler. 1971. *Managing Large Systems.* New York: Harper and Row.

Schauer, H. 1973. "Critique of Co-determination." In G. Hunnius, G. D. Garson, and J. Case, editors, *Workers' Control.* New York: Random House.

Schein, E. H. 1969. *Process Consultation: Its Role in Organization Development*. Reading, Mass.: Addison-Wesley.

Schneider, B. and C. J. Bartlett. 1968. "Individual Differences and Organizational Climate." *Personnel Psychology* 21 (Autumn), 323–334.

Schrank, Robert. 1974. "Work in America: What Do Workers Really Want?" *Industrial Relations* 13 (May), 24–29.

Schregle, Johannes. 1970. "Workers' Participation in Management." *Industrial Relations* 9 (February), 117–122.

Schwab, Donald P., and Larry L. Cummings. 1970. "Theories of Performance and Satisfaction: A Review." *Industrial Relations* 9 (October), 408–430.

Scontrino, M. Peter. 1972. "The Effects of Fulfilling and Violating Group Members' Expectations About Leadership Style." *Organizational Behavior and Human Performance* 8 (August), 118–138.

Seashore, Stanley E., and David G. Bowers. 1963. *Changing the Structure and Functioning of an Organization*. Ann Arbor: University of Michigan, Institute for Social Research, Survey Research Center. Monograph. No. 33.

———. 1970. "Durability of Organizational Change." *American Psychologist* 25 (March), 227–233.

Selznick, Philip. 1949. *TVA and the Grass Roots*. Berkeley and Los Angeles: University of California Press.

Sexton, Patricia C., and Brendon Sexton. 1971. *Blue Collars and Hard Hats*. New York: Random House.

Shepard, Herbert A. 1960. "An Action Research Model." *An Action Research Program for Organization Improvement*. Ann Arbor: University of Michigan, The Foundation for Research on Human Behavior.

———. 1965. "Changing Interpersonal and Intergroup Relations in Organizations." In J. G. March, editor, *Handbook of Organizations*. Chicago: Rand-McNally.

Shepard, Jon M. 1970. "Functional Specialization, Alienation, and Job Satisfaction." *Industrial and Labor Relations Review* 23 (January), 207–219.

———. 1971. *Automation and Alienation: A Study of Factory Workers*. Cambridge, Mass.: MIT Press.

———. 1973. "Specialization, Autonomy, and Job Satisfaction." *Industrial Relations* 12 (October), 274–281.

Sheppard, Harold L. 1974. "Task Enrichment and Wage Levels as Elements in Workers' Attitudes." *Proceedings of the Industrial Relations Research Association*, Madison, Wisconsin.

———, and Neal Q. Herrick. 1972. *Where Have All the Robots Gone? Worker Dissatisfaction in the 70's*. New York: Free Press.

Sherif, Carolyn W., and Muzafer Sherif. 1953. *Groups in Harmony and Tension*. New York: Harper.

Shultz, George P. 1951. "Worker Participation on Production Problems: A Discussion of Experience with the 'Scanlon Plan'." *Personnel* 28 (November), 201–210.

Siassi, Iradj, Guido Crocetti, and Herz R. Spiro. 1974. "Loneliness and Dissatisfaction in a Blue Collar Population." *Archives of General Psychiatry* 30 (February), 261–265.

Simon, Herbert A. 1957 (a). *Administrative Behavior*. Second edition, New York: Macmillan.

———. 1957 (b). *Models of Man, Social and Rational*. New York: Wiley.

Slichter, Sumner. 1941. *Union Policies and Industrial Management*. Washington: The Brookings Institution.

Solomon, L. 1960. "The Influence of Some Types of Power Relationships and Some Strategies Upon the Development of Interpersonal Trust." *Journal of Abnormal Psychology* 61 (July), 223–230.

Stagner, Ross. 1957. "Union-Management Relations in Italy: Some Observations." *Current Economic Comment* (May).

Starbuck, William H. 1965. "Organizational Growth and Development." In

James G. March, editor, *Handbook of Organizations*. Chicago: Rand McNally.

Stern, Louis W. 1970. "Potential Conflict Management Mechanisms in Distribution Channels: An Interorganizational Analysis." Berkeley: University of California, Institute of Business and Economic Research, Working Paper in Marketing No. 60 (July).

Stinchcombe, Arthur L. 1959. "Bureaucratic and Craft Administration of Production." *Administrative Science Quarterly* 4 (September), 168–187.

Stogdill, R. M. 1948. "Personal Factors Associated with Leadership: A Survey of the Literature." *Journal of Psychology* 25 (January), 35–71.

———, and A. E. Coons, editors. 1957. *Leader Behavior: Its Description and Measurement*. Columbus, Ohio: Bureau of Business Research.

Strauss, George. 1955. "Group Dynamics and Intergroup Relations." In William F. Whyte, editor, *Money and Motivation*. New York: Harper and Row.

———. 1964. "Organization Man: Prospect for the Future." *California Management Review* 6 (Spring), 5–16.

———. 1970. "Organization Behavior and Personnel Relations." In Woodrow L. Ginsburg, *et al.*, *A Review of Industrial Relations Research*. Madison, Wisc.: Industrial Relations Research Association.

———. 1973. "Organization Development: Credits and Debits." *Organizational Dynamics* (Winter), 2–19.

———. 1974. "Workers' Attitudes and Adjustments." In Jerome W. Rosow, editor, *The Worker and the Job*. Englewood Cliffs, N.J.: Prentice-Hall.

———. In press. "Organization Development." In R. Dubin, editor, *Handbook of Work Organization in Society*. Chicago: Rand McNally.

———, and Eliezer Rosenstein. 1970. "Workers' Participation: A Critical View." *Industrial Relations* 9 (February), 197–214.

———, and Leonard R. Sayles. 1967. "The Scanlon Plan: Some Organizational Problems." *Human Organization* 16 (Fall), 15–22.

———. 1972. *Personnel*. Englewood Cliffs, N.J.: Prentice-Hall.

Sturmthal, Adolf. 1964. *Workers' Councils*. Cambridge, Mass.: Harvard University Press.

———. 1969. "Workers' Participation in Management: A Review of United States Experience." *International Institute for Labor Studies Bulletin* 6 (June), 149–186.

Survey Research Center, University of Michigan. 1971. *Survey of Working Conditions*. Washington, D.C.: U.S. Department of Labor.

Tagiuri, Renato, and George H. Litwin. 1968. *Organizational Climate*. Boston, Mass.: Harvard University, Graduate School of Business Administration.

Tannenbaum, Arnold. 1956. "Control Structure and Union Functions." *American Journal of Sociology* 61 (May), 127–140.

———. 1966. *Social Psychology of the Work Organization*. Belmont, Calif.: Brooks-Cole.

———. 1968. *Control in Organizations*. New York: McGraw-Hill.

———, and Floyd H. Allport. 1956. "Personality Structure and Group Structure: An Interpretive Study of Their Relationship Through an Event-Structure Hypothesis." *Journal of Abnormal and Social Psychology* 53 (November), 272–280.

———, and Robert L. Kahn. 1958. *Participation in Union Locals*. Evanston: Row, Peterson.

———, B. Kavcic, G. Wieser, M. Rosner, and M. Vianello. 1974. *Hierarchy in Organizations: An International Comparison*. San Francisco: Jossey-Bass.

Taylor, Frank Carter, Jr. 1971. "Associations Among Personal and Organizational Characteristics in Forty Branch Offices of a Securities Brokerage Firm." Unpublished Ph.D. thesis. University of Michigan.

Taylor, Frederick W. 1911. *Principles of Scientific Management*. New York: Harper.

Tead, Ordway, and Henry C. Metcalf. 1920. *Personnel Administration*. New York: McGraw-Hill.

Terkel, Studs. 1974. *Working*. New York: Random House.

Terreberry, Shirley. 1968. "The Evolution of Organizational Environments." *Administrative Science Quarterly* 12 (March), 590–613.

Terrien, Fred C. and D. C. Mills. 1955. "The Effects of Changing Size upon the Internal Structure of an Organization." *American Sociological Review* 20 (February), 11–13.

Thibaut, John W. and Henry W. Riecken. 1955. "Authoritarianism, Status and the Communication of Aggression." *Human Relations* 8 (May), 95–120.

Thompson, James D. 1967. *Organizations in Action*. New York: McGraw-Hill.

Thompson, Victor A. 1961. *Modern Organization*. New York: Knopf.

Thorsrud, E. and F. E. Emery. 1970. "Industrial Democracy in Norway." *Industrial Relations* 9 (February), 187–196.

Trist, E. L. and K. W. Bamforth. 1951. "Some Social and Psychological Consequences of the Longwall Method of Coal-Getting." *Human Relations* 4 (February), 3–38.

Turner, Arthur N. and Paul R. Lawrence. 1965. *Industrial Jobs and the Worker*. Boston, Mass.: Harvard University, Graduate School of Business Administration.

TVA and Tennessee Valley Trades and Labor Council. 1963. *General Agreement*. February 28.

Udy, Stanley H., Jr. 1962. "Administrative Rationality, Social Setting, and Organizational Development." *American Journal of Sociology* 68 (November), 299–308.

United Automobile Workers. 1973. "Summary of Agreement with Ford Motor Company." *Daily Labor Report*, November 5.

U.S. Bureau of the Census. 1971. *Annual Survey of Manufactures*.

Urwick, L. 1943. *The Elements of Administration*. New York: Harper.

Vroom, V. H. 1959. "Some Personality Determinants of the Effects of Participation." *Journal of Abnormal and Social Psychology* 59, 322–327.

———. 1960. *Some Personality Determinants of the Effects of Participation*. Englewood Cliffs, N.J.: Prentice-Hall.

———. 1964. *Work and Motivation*. New York: Wiley.

———. 1973. "A New Look at Managerial Decision Making." *Organizational Dynamics* 1 (Spring), 66–80.

———, and Floyd C. Mann. 1960. "Leader Authoritarianism and Employee Attitudes." *Personnel Psychology* 13 (Summer), 125–140.

———, and Philip W. Yetton. 1973. *Leadership and Decision-Making*. Pittsburgh: University of Pittsburgh Press.

Walker, Charles R., and Robert H. Guest. 1952. *The Man on the Assembly Line*. Cambridge, Mass.: Harvard University Press.

———. 1969. *Interpersonal Peacemaking: Confrontations and Third Party Consultation*. Reading, Mass.: Addison-Wesley.

Walton, Richard D. 1969. *Interpersonal Peacemaking: Confrontations and Third Party Consultation*. Reading, Mass.: Addison-Wesley.

———. 1970. "A Problem-Solving Workshop on Border Conflicts in Eastern Africa." *Journal of Applied Behavioral Science* 6 (October), 453–489.

———. 1972. "How to Counter Alienation in the Plant." *Harvard Business Review* 50 (November–December), 70–81.

———. 1974. "Innovative Restructuring of Work." In Jerome W. Rosow, editor, *The Worker and the Job*. Englewood Cliffs, N.J.: Prentice-Hall.

———, and Robert B. McKersie. 1965. *A Behavioral Theory of Labor Negotiations*. New York: McGraw-Hill.

Wanous, John P., and Edward E. Lawler. 1972. "Measurement and Meaning of Job Satisfaction." *Journal of Applied Psychology* 56 (April), 95–105.

Waters, Charles A. 1971. "The Scientific Data Based Approach to 'O.D.'" *Organizational Development, The State of the Art*. Ann Arbor: Foundation for Research on Human Behavior.

Weber, Max. 1947. *The Theory of Social and Economic Organization*. Translated by A. M. Henderson and Talcott Parsons. New York: Free Press.

Weick, Karl E. 1969. *The Social Psychology of Organizing*. Reading, Mass.: Addison-Wesley.

West German Trade Union Federation. 1973. In G. Hunnius, G. D. Garson, and J. Case, *Workers' Control*. New York: Random House.

Whisler, Thomas. 1970. *Information Technology and Organizational Change*. Belmont, Calif.: Wadsworth.

————, H. Meyer, B. H. Baum, and P. F. Sorensen, Jr. 1967. "Centralization of Organizational Control: An Empirical Study of its Meaning and Measurement." *Journal of Business* 40 (January), 10–26.

Westley, William A. and Margaret W. Westley. 1971. *The Emerging Worker*. Montreal: McGill-Queen's University Press.

Whyte, William F. 1948. *Human Relations in the Restaurant Industry*. New York: McGraw-Hill.

————. 1955. *Money and Motivation*. New York: Harper.

————. 1967. "Models for Building and Changing Organizations." *Human Organization* 26 (Spring), 22–31.

Whyte, William H. 1956. *The Organization Man*. New York: Simon and Schuster.

Wild, Ray, and R. Kempner. 1972. "Influence of Community and Plant Characteristics in Job Attitudes of Manual Workers." *Journal of Applied Psychology* 56 (April), 106–113.

Wilensky, Harold L. 1957. "Human Relations in the Workplace: An Appraisal of Some Recent Research." In C. M. Arensberg, *et al.*, editors, *Research in Industrial Human Relations*. New York: Harper and Brothers.

Wofford, J. C. 1971. "Managerial Behavior, Situational Factors, and Productivity and Morale." *Administrative Science Quarterly* 16 (March), 10–17.

Wood, Michael T., and Robert S. Sobel. 1970. "Effects of Similarity of Leadership Style at Two Levels of Management on the Job Satisfaction of the First Level Manager." *Personnel Psychology* 23 (Winter), 577–590.

Woodward, Joan. 1965. *Industrial Organization: Theory and Practice*. London: Oxford University Press.

————. 1966. "Management and Technology." *Problems of Progress in Industry–3*. London: Her Majesty's Stationery Office, 1958. Reprinted 1966.

————, editor. 1970. *Industrial Organization: Behaviour and Control*. London: Oxford University Press.

Work in America. 1973. Report of a Special Task Force to the Secretary of Health, Education, and Welfare. Cambridge, Mass.: MIT Press.

"The World of the Blue Collar Worker." 1972. *Dissent* 19 (Winter).

Yankelovich, Daniel. 1974. "The Meaning of Work." In Jerome W. Rosow, editor, *The Worker and the Job*. Englewood Cliffs, N.J.: Prentice-Hall.

Yukl, Gary. 1971. "Toward a Behavioral Theory of Leadership." *Organizational Behavior and Human Performance* 6 (July), 414–440.

Zand, Dale E. 1972. "Trust and Managerial Problem Solving." *Administrative Science Quarterly* 17 (June), 229–239.

Zupanov, J. 1973. "Two Patterns of Conflict Management in Industry." *Industrial Relations* 12 (May), 213–223.